Enchanting Powers

Harvard University
Center for the Study of World Religions

Religions of the World

Editor: Lawrence E. Sullivan

Cambridge, Massachusetts

Enchanting Powers

Music in the World's Religions

edited by

Lawrence E. Sullivan

Distributed by Harvard University Press
for the
Harvard University Center for the Study of World Religions

Library of Congress Cataloging-in-Publication Data

Enchanting powers : music in the world's religions / edited by Lawrence E. Sullivan.
    p.   cm. — (Religions of the world)
    Includes bibliographical references.
    Contents: Tantrism, rasa, and Javanese gamelan music / Judith Becker — World musics and world religions : whose world / Philip V. Bohlman — Music and historical consciousness among the Dagbamba of Ghana / John Chernoff — Historicism and the quest of D/divine music / Michael W. Harris — "Musicalizing" the Other : shamanistic approaches to ethnic-class competition among the upper Rio Negro / Jonathan D. Hill — Conceptualizations of music in Jewish mysticism / Moshe Idel — Music, myth, and medicine in the Choctaw Indian ballgame / Victoria Lindsay Levin — Islam and music : the legal and the spiritual dimensions / Seyyed Hossein Nasr — Music and the Confucian sacrificial ceremony / Rulan Chao Pian — Sounding the Word : music in the life of Islam / Regula Burckhardt Qureshi — Mythologies and realities in the study of Jewish music / Kay Kaufman Shelemay.
    ISBN 0-945454-09-0 (alk. paper).
    ISBN 0-945454-12-0 (pbk. : alk. paper)
    1. Music—Religious aspects. I. Sullivan, Lawrence Eugene, 1949– . II. Series: Religions of the world (Cambridge, Mass.)
ML2900.E56 1997
781.7—dc21   97-11171
                                                  CIP
                                                  MN

Acknowledgments

Grateful acknowledgment is made for permission to reprint the following:

Jonathan Hill, "Musicalizing the Other: Shamanistic Approaches to Ethnic-Class Competition along the Upper Rio Negro, in *Religiosidad y Resistencia Indígenas hacia el Fin del Milenio*. Quito, Ecuador: Ediciones Abya-Yala, 1994, pp. 105–128. Reprinted by permission of Ediciones Abya-Yala.

Kay Kaufman Shelemay, "Mythologies and Realities in the Study of Jewish Music," *The World of Music*, 1995, no. 1. Reprinted by permission of Florian Noetzel Verlag and Internationales Institut für Traditionelle Musik.

Pages 213–214: "Jump Dance Song," from *Choctaw Music and Dance* by James H. Howard and Victoria Lindsay Levine. Copyright © 1990 by the University of Oklahoma Press, Norman, Publishing Division of the University. Reprinted by permission of the University of Oklahoma Press.

Page 258: "Song for Welcoming the Spirits," from *Sonq Dynasty Musical Sources and Their Interpretation* by Rulan Chao Pian. Copyright © 1967 by the Harvard Yen-Ching Institute. Reprinted by permission of Harvard University Press.

Contents

Enchanting Powers: An Introduction

Lawrence E. Sullivan

> "Since music is the only language with the con-
> tradictory attributes of being at once intelligible and
> untranslatable, the musical creator is a being com-
> parable to the gods, and music itself the supreme
> mystery of the science of man."
> —Claude Lévi-Strauss (1970, 18)

Marsilio Ficino (1433–1499), the great humanist of Renaissance
Florence, contributed to the foundations of modern thought—and
of postmodern thought as well, especially through his influence on
Michel Foucault. Ficino attributed magical power to music and his
detailed analysis of the magic of music grounds his explanations
of the power of image, perception, and language, as these are
manifest in art, science, rhetoric, and social psychology (Ficino
1959b; Field 1988).* Though his notions defy brief summary, a few
examples suggest how the understanding of aural reality, especially
through analysis of religious music, can serve as the ground for
knowledge of and action within the wider world, whether social,
material, or spiritual.

Ficino works within the framing notion of an ensouled world,
an idea he develops under the influence of the third-century

* I am grateful to the Villa I Tatti Center for Renaissance Studies in Florence,
Italy, and particularly to its director Walter Kaiser, for the invitation to spend the
1996–1997 scholastic year researching the impact of world religions on Renaissance thought, especially its esoteric knowledge and occult sciences.

Neoplatonic thinker Plotinus (whose works Ficino translated from Greek into Latin). Ficino's extended treatment of musical magic comprises the final section of *De vita coelitus comparanda* ("On Obtaining Life from the Heavens"), which was a medical commentary inspired by Plotinus's *Enneads* (Copenhaver 1986).

In his stimulating book *Music in Renaissance Magic* Gary Tomlinson argues, as did the historian of religions Ioan P. Couliano (Couliano 1987), that Ficino also draws inspiration from the ninth-century Arabic work *De radiis* ("On Rays") by the medieval Islamic philosopher al-Kindi (al-Kindi 1975). According to this view, all realities emit vibrating rays which together compose the harmonious chorus of the universe. The well-tempered human spirit (which for Ficino mediates between the body and soul) recognizes that each sonic emission is attuned to other resonances which reverberate in accord with the first sound because they resemble it in some measure. "Often one string even trembles at the vibration of another, as if it felt [the other string] by virtue of their concord: and this [happens] above all because they are tuned in the same consonance" (Plotinus, *De rebus philosophicis,* fol. 222r-v; translated from Ficino's Latin edition by Tomlinson 1993, 86). These carry-on echoes, in their turn, evoke continuing syntonies which reverberate in shifting patterns throughout the entire cosmos. "And if the motion is conveyed from one lyre to another, this also must be thought to arise from a certain mutually felt harmony: and therefore in the universe there is a single harmony, however much it arises from opposites" (ibid).

Insofar as Ficino's view resonates with al-Kindi's, they hold that a universal harmony of the whole in its plenitude lends primary force to any expressed reality. Universal harmony infuses into each particular ray an operative force far greater in magnitude than the single ray's own small voice (Couliano 1987). Even the qualities of words spoken by individual human beings, for instance (together with the cognitive, conceptual, and social consequences they provoke), derive ultimately from the interlinked descants and multivocal harmonies from which all sounds, spoken and otherwise, arise in the first place. (Here we find ourselves near the landscape reconnoitered by Jacques Derrida and Michel Foucault and scored by *traces* and *paroles étoufées*—the infinity of unsounded sounds and suppressed voices which inevitably compose the background silence lurking beneath the text of any inscribed word and lending it power.) Among the fundamental qualities of spoken words that arise from the background of celestial harmonies of the universe described by al-Kindi and Ficino are their effect, movement, force, and meaning. The meaning of words and images—as they convey ideas and mobilize society—is musically determined (Tomlinson 1993, 121).

Ficino was a medical physician, as was his father, and thus familiar with the advances in the pharmacopeia of his day. Nonetheless, he remained convinced that music was more effective than medicinal compounds in ameliorating certain conditions of the body, because music better channeled celestial benefits. Though music and medicines both formed compounds of elements drawn from different realms of the physical and spiritual world, musical compositions were the more fluid and more flexible and, therefore, better mimed the celestial qualities essential to optimal health.

Humans, who are the musical beings par excellence, play a unique role in this world of resemblances, since they participate in material reality through their bodily life but also in immaterial reality through the life of the imagination. Human fantasy allows the human spirit to conjure within itself images that resemble any and all forms of reality—material, spiritual, or even divine. Thus the human spirit is a microcosm of all that exists in the cosmos; the spirit is the part which magically contains the whole. Since the human being is created in the image of God, the human imagination, which is a faculty of the spirit, possesses *the* resemblance of primary importance in the cosmos.

Music is the most malleable and most profound expression of this human imaginal power to reflect all realities in the phantasms it generates. Through musical phantasms human beings give voice to universal harmony, by performing music that resembles the sound of the celestial spheres. Humans even imitate the sound of the divine being (as heard, for example, in the syllables of the hidden, true name of god). In *De divino furore*, Ficino analyzes frenzied song, performed during a state of prophetic furor. Such musical frenzy symptomatizes the condition of soul loss or of possession of the soul by another being. The frenzied song of the prophet is a paradigmatic imitation on earth of the heavenly being who possesses the soul or whom the soul confronts during its ecstatic wandering. Thus, frenzied song draws its power "from its place in the similitudes linking heaven and earth" (Tomlinson 1993, 196). Specifically, magical music allows humans to close, at various points and at will, the circle of similitude which constitutes the universe: "the world order of harmonious resemblance made possible the human imitation of superlunar musics; this song took its power from a play of externalized phantasms; and these were a by-product of a cognition driven by cosmic resemblances" (Tomlinson 1993, 196).

In a world pervaded by spirits and a soul of its own, spirits are modulated and moderated through liturgy, the disciplined arts (including prayer as well as pictorial and musical practice), and other ergetic practices (Werner 1984, 7–8 et passim). Magical control is gained through practical knowledge of the images (sonic, linguistic, visual) encountered during soul loss and soul possession. These psychological states (that is, conditions in which the spirit is transmogrified) offer unusual entry points into the networks of spiritual sympathies and resemblances that bind one reality to another and all realities to all others. In their severe forms, soul loss and soul possession, as well as the short circuits they trigger in the systems of resemblances which radiate throughout the universe, are concerns of medicine and mysticism, and they mobilize care of the soul as well as the body.

In Ficino's view, music is a key both for medics and mystics who deal with conditions of frenzy and prophetic furor (Godwin 1995, 17–19 passim), as well as other alterior states. In states of furor, the rational but imaginative human spirit evokes within itself resemblances convoked from three distinguishable systems resonating on at least three separate levels of cosmic existence: the first system is one of resonances evoked by providence (which calls into being the chain of reverberating minds); the second system is evoked by fate (calling forth the chain of associated *idola*); and the third system is evoked by nature (thus setting into action the chain of irrational souls) (Tomlinson 1993, 196). Music makes of the human spirit a master-link in these and the myriad other chains of resemblances and systems of correspondences which compose the universe. Music magically modulates the spirit as well as the world that resounds with it. Music is the most effective sign of the human spirit and its transformative capacities.

Ficino's view of the fundamental importance of sound, especially music, to the functioning of the world and human knowledge of it is unusually comprehensive, but it is by no means unique. From ancient times, thinkers and practitioners alike have employed music to ground their understanding of the universe and the role of humans in it. Socrates invokes music as a primary model for justice and "the mean." For him, as Plato gives him voice in *The Republic*, the musical scale is where moderation reigns in a demonstrable way and, therefore, the musical scales model the virtues—especially distributive justice—which allow all people to "sing the same chant together" (*Republic* 331e–432a). In Book III of his *Elements of Harmony*, Ptolemy organizes his zodiacal calendar of time as well as his influential physics of space according to the tones of two-octave musical scales (Neugebauer 1969; Düring 1934). In *The Music of the Spheres: Music, Science and the Natural Order of the Universe*, Jamie James traces the development and influence of important systems of thought and practice built on musical founda-tions: from Pythagoras and classical expressions in Plato's *Republic* and its Myth of Er as well as Cicero's reprise of Plato in *De Republica* and its recounting of "the Dream of Scipio," to Johannes Kepler's elegant summa of modern mathematics, *The Harmony of the Universe* (James 1993). Kepler measured with accuracy the subtleties of planetary motion, comparing the differences in speed of each planet at its closest point to the sun, when planets move most swiftly, with their movement at slowest speed farthest away from the sun. From the ratio of those two velocities, he notated musical intervals. "Mars, for example, covered a perfect fifth, from C to G, the ratio 3:2, while Saturn sounded out a perfect third. All the planets could produce glorious glissandos—slides up or down—as they intoned their way around their orbits, until each planet produced its own song" (Levenson 1994, 112). Kepler's mathematically fruitful ecstasies were due to the conviction that in the music of the spheres he had perceived directly the deepest patterns of creation: "The movements of the heavens are nothing except a certain ever-lasting polyphony" (Kepler 1955, 98). Kepler's religious rapture at his discovery was a reflective image of the very delight that God the Workman had taken in His own creative works (Levenson 1994, 112).

Sir Isaac Newton, genius of enlightenment physics and mathematics, remained dedicated throughout his life to the fundamental musico-theological proposition that (in his own words):

> The soul of the world, which propels into movement this body of the universe visible to us, being constructed of ratios which created from themselves a musical concord, must of necessity produce musical sounds from the movement which it provides by its proper impulse, having found the origin of them in the craftsmanship of its own composition. (James 1993, 167; also Levenson 1994, 112–15)

More recently, music has become the main analytic inspiration and organizational model for Claude Lévi-Strauss's four-volume *Mythologiques: An Introduction to a Science of Mythology* which examines, in his view, the deepest structural operations of the human mind, the science of the concrete. In the "Finale" section of the last volume, Lévi-Strauss himself reckons the work to be the most significant contribution toward the understanding of mythology since Plotinus, his musical and mythical muse. Lévi-Strauss also acknowledges that he derives inspiration from Arnold Schoenberg's all-encompassing mystico-mathematical theories of music. But Schoenberg, unlike Lévi-Strauss, composed his thoughts and his music within a strongly held, devout religiosity. A musical work was, at base, a religious work evoking a trained listener's contemplation and a moral entity of the first order, calling forth a new and comprehensive response that is at once intellectual, emotional, and aesthetic (Cook 1990, 180ff.; Ridley 1995, 4). In the text of

Schoenberg's unfinished sacred oratorio *Die Jakobsleiter* ("Jacob's Ladder"), for example, the angel Gabriel explicitly replays the great theme of musical consonance between creator and creature when he introduces and describes the character called "The Chosen One":

> he who is a likeness. . .endowed with true splendor. . .who resembles the One far higher being, just as the distant overtone resembles the fundamental tone, whilst others, deeper, themselves nearly fundamentals, are farther removed from him, as a glittering rock crystal is further from a diamond than is pure carbon! (James 1993, 220)

From the fundamental tone radiates the great chain of beings, related as tones and overtones that resemble it and them to greater and lesser degrees. In Schoenberg's view, the outwardly perceived acoustical qualities were no more than by-products of a truly creative act—in the fundamental and religious sense of the word—and which, by definition therefore, followed its own inner principle (Schoenberg 1984, 121).

The desire to hold music fundamental to the creation of the universe and the human being's vocation in it is not only a theorizing impulse of western culture. Guy L. Beck has evaluated a spectrum of Hindu sectarian developments. In his *Sonic Theology: Hinduism and Sacred Sound* he finds common to them all a basic commitment to configurations of sacred sound: Śaiva-Āgamas, Śaiva-Siddhānta, Kashmiri Śaivism, Śākta-Tantra, the Pāñcarātra texts, and the major Vaiṣṇava Sampradāyas. In these and other traditions of South Asia, Beck discloses the central role of sonic cosmologies and meditations, of mystical analyses of internal language, and of acoustical embodiments of divine beings. According to Beck, even Hindus whose traditions had distinct and irreconcilable theological aims agree that sonority inaugurates and sustains the soteriological quest toward the desired god, goddess, or condition. Sound is, at its base, sacred in origin; and sacrality, in its root expression, is sonorous. That is why "the soteriological modus operandi for the Hindu aspiring for liberation or association with a chosen deity involves a sonic act informed by a sonic theology" (Beck 1993, 213).

Non-western cultures without longstanding written traditions of scripture also reckon music to be the primordial reality that modulates other cosmic and cultural manifestations. Steven Feld, in a much praised book entitled *Sound and Sentiment,* argues that sound constitutes the very cultural system, in all its myriad expressions, of the Kaluli people of Papua New Guinea. And Feld takes pains—he even weeps—to show us that this is the way the Kaluli hear reality; that is, through music and other fundamental sonic performances such as lamentation. A quite different but equally comprehensive musical basis for reality is put forward by the Kalapalo people of the Upper Xingu Basin in the southern reaches of the Brazilian Amazon. In *A Musical View of the Universe,* Ellen Basso describes how Kalapalo religious experiences are the outcome of complex spectacles (dramatic presentations of history, social existence, poetry, arts, and fantasy) whose finely tuned symbolisms and psychodynamics are orchestrated, above all, through ritual music. Through sonic symbolism, distinctive consciousnesses and dispositions to act are brought into being. Indeed, Kalapalo ritual music, by definition, communicates between insurmountably separated categories and states of being. "Through sound cosmic entities are rendered into being" and through music, then, the Kalapalo succeed in realizing a single universe with profound moral and emotional resonances effected by the motion of sound through space (Basso 1985, 311).

The propensity of musical ideas to ground entire cosmologies and systems of thought, though long recognized, is not admired by all scholars today. Richard Leppert, who emphasizes the importance of a music's specific materiality, history, and gendered expression, recognizes music's apparently totalizing capacity—an omnidimensionality perhaps related to its religious resonance—but is suspicious and critical of it. All art may "aspire to the condition of music" (Leppert 1994, 233) precisely because of music's manifest comprehensiveness, in every sense of the word. By way of example, Leppert opines that "music is visually extravagant" (ibid., 101); "music is time that draws attention to itself (ibid., 195); and "music is a metaphor of self and being in history" (ibid., 230). But music's ability to point to all things and, in that very gesture, distract the hearer and thus escape being called into question, may be the outcome of a spell it casts on listeners or a false consciousness that it conjures in order to distract from its true intentions and lull into silence. "The totality music sometimes encodes," for Leppert, "is an otherwise unrealized aspiration—not in art but in life" (Leppert 1994, 233).

The construction of a full-fledged magical theory of music like Ficino's or a comprehensive musical cosmology like Kepler's was never the purpose of this book nor of any one of its essays. Indeed, some of the contributors share Leppert's concern and appreciate this present moment when the scholarly world is deliberately resisting grand theory or is leaving it to physicists. They discourage over-arching interpretations of music or religion in favor of carefully delineated contexts of meaning. Others, aware of the conflict of interpretations inherent between a narrative history of the particular, on the one side, and an analytic disclosure of perduring general structure (Treitler 1989; Allen 1978), on the other side, offer constructive solutions analogous to ones offered by Clifford Geertz and Marshall Sahlins for integrating history into structural anthropology: find the structures in history and, conversely, find the history embedded in religious and musical structures that have been transformed even in the course of their reproduction through time.

Though presentation of a global musical worldview is not the goal, nevertheless a number of contributors, drawn by the strong conviction and discourse of the religious communities themselves, do ascribe an enchanting power to religious music—a power to attract all kinds of non-musical realities. In closely argued case histories, they carefully analyze the power of music's affinity—its mimetic capacity to attune itself to other realities or provoke other realities into resonating in tune with it. Religious music adapts its sacrality and redemptive power to new cultural expressions encountered through colonialism, immigration or market forces (such as advertising or distribution systems). In this way, each contributor discloses important correspondences between religious music and other fundamental realities in the cultural world of the performers, including: patterns of history or social organization or emotion; conditions of the soul; powers of the state; histories of material production; structures of law; motivations that vitalize new generations; manifestations of ethnicity and class; models of cultural memory; and even local conflicts and forms of disenfranchisement provoked by the politics of globalism itself (as evident in global economies of music recording and distribution as well as in universalizing forms of analysis). These elements and more are found embedded in religious musics and transported within their performed expressions. The summary result of the volume is an enlarged appreciation of the amazing range of realities that religious music draws within the social compass and orchestrates on the cultural stage in order to provoke contemplation or critical reflection.

It is hoped that this volume will make common cause with excellent new works in the comparative and interdisciplinary study of musical cultures worldwide (see Nettl and Bohlman 1991 for an appraisal by leading figures in the field). More to the point, we hope that this collection of essays will stimulate the incipient interest in the nature, meaning, and function of religious music in the traditions of communities throughout the world (e.g., Spencer 1994). For it is clear that the religious character of the music is a key element accounting for its distinctive role in the processes of reflection, transmission, and change that constitute human culture. As evident in this volume, we cannot deny that knowledge of "the other's" religious music has provoked profound reorientations in entire civilizations over the course of time because of the complex of ideas, sensations, and associations music carries with it. To hold in one's hand a volume replete with a number of such traditions of sacred music, then, carries with it both serious responsibilities and great promise.

Enchanting Powers is the fruit of a year of special research on music of the religions of the world at the Harvard University Center for the Study of World Religions, an international center fostering multidisciplinary research and education. Many of the articles were first presented in the form of lectures at the Harvard Center during the year of special study. Thanks go to all contributors, especially Philip V. Bohlman of the University of Chicago and Kay Kaufman Shelemay of Harvard University, whose advice helped shape the original plans for the research and lecture series as well as the volume. I also wish to thank fellows, faculty, and staff at the Harvard University Center for the Study of World Religions for their advice and assistance, especially Thomas L. Bryson and Narges Moshiri who coordinated the lecture series. The Center is fortunate to have as its publications editor Kit Dodgson, who admirably advanced the production of this book at every stage, from editorial preparation of manuscripts to the final publication. Her professionalism and courtesy set a tone that well benefits both contributors and readers.

Bibliography Cited

Allen, Douglas
 1978 *Structure and Creativity in Religion: Hermeneutics in Mircea Eliade's Phenomenology and New Directions.* Religion and Reason, 14. The Hague: Mouton.

Basso, Ellen B.
 1985 *A Musical View of the Universe: Kalapalo Myth and Ritual Performances.* Philadelphia: University of Pennsylvania Press.

Beck, Guy L.
 1993 *Sonic Theology: Hinduism and Sacred Sound.* Columbia: University of South Carolina Press.

Bloom, Allan, trans.
 1968 *The Republic of Plato.* New York: Basic Books.

Cook, Nicholas
 1990 *Music, Imagination, and Culture.* Oxford and New York: Oxford University Press.

Copenhaver, Brian P.
 1986 "Renaissance Magic and Neoplatonic Philosophy: 'Ennead' 4.3-5 in Ficino's 'De vita coelitus comparanda.'" In Gian Carlo Garfagnini, *Marsilio Ficino e il ritorno di Platone: Studi e documenti,* 2:351–69. Florence: L. S. Olschki.

Couliano, Ioan P.
 1987 *Eros and Magic in the Renaissance.* Trans. Margaret Cook. Chicago: University of Chicago Press.

Düring, Ingemar
 1934 "Ptolemaios und Porphyrios über die Musik." *Goteborgs Hogskolas Aarsskrift* 1:122–28.

Feld, Steven
 1982 *Sound and Sentiment: Birds, Weeping, Poetics, and Song in Kaluli Expression.* Publications of the American Folklore Society, n.s., 5. Philadelphia: University of Pennsylvania Press.

Field, Arthur
 1988 *The Origins of the Platonic Academy of Florence.* Princeton: Princeton University Press.

Ficino, Marsilio
    1959a   *De divino furore.* In *Opera omnia*, ed. Mario Sancipriano, 1:612–15. Turin: Bottega d'Erasmo.
    1959b   *Opera omnia.* Ed. Mario Sancipriano. 2 vols. Turin: Bottega d'Erasmo.
    1978a   *De vita coelitus comparanda.* See Book 3 of *De vita libri tres,* ed. Martin Plessner and Felix Klein-Franke. Hildesheim and New York: G. Olms Verlag.
    1978b   *De vita libri tres.* Ed. Martin Plessner and Felix Klein-Franke. Hildesheim and New York: G. Olms Verlag. Reprint of 1498 edition.

Garfagnini, Gian Carlo
    1986   *Marsilio Ficino e il ritorno di Platone: Studi e documenti.* 2 vols. Florence: L. S. Olschki.

Godwin, Joscelyn
    1995   *Harmonies of Heaven and Earth: Mysticism in Music from Antiquity to the Avant-Garde.* Rochester, Vt.: Inner Traditions International.

James, Jamie
    1993   *The Music of the Spheres: Music, Science and the Natural Order of the Universe.* New York: Grove Press.

Kepler, Johannes
    1955   *The Harmonies of the World.* Great Books of the Western World, 16. Chicago: Encyclopedia Brittanica.

al-Kindi
    1975   *De radiis.* Ed. M.-T. d'Alverny and F. Hudry. In *Archives d'histoire doctrinale et littéraire du moyen age*, pp. 139–260. Paris.

Leppert, Richard
    1993   *The Sight of Sound: Music, Representation, and the History of the Body.* Berkeley: University of California Press.

Levenson, Thomas
    1994   *Measure for Measure: A Musical History of Science.* New York: Simon & Schuster.

Lévi-Strauss, Claude
    1970   *The Raw and the Cooked. Introduction to a Science of Mythology*, vol. 1. Trans. John and Doreen Weightman. New York: Harper and Row.

Neugebauer, Otto
    1969   *The Exact Sciences in Antiquity*. 2nd ed. New York: Dover Publications.

Nettl, Bruno and Philip V. Bohlman, eds.
    1991   *Comparative Musicology and Anthropology of Music: Essays on the History of Ethnomusicology*. Chicago Studies in Ethnomusicology. Chicago: University of Chicago Press.

Plotinus
    1966-88   *Enneads*. Ed. and trans. A. H. Armstrong. 7 vols. Loeb Classical Library. Cambridge, Mass.: Harvard University Press.

Ridley, Aaron
    1995   *Music, Value and the Passions*. Ithaca, N.Y.: Cornell University Press.

Schoenberg, Arnold
    1984   *Style and Idea: Selected Writings of Arnold Schoenberg*. Ed. Leonard Stein and trans. Leo Black. Berkeley: University of California Press.

Spencer, Jon Michael, ed.
    1994   *Theomusicology. A Special Issue of Black Sacred Music: A Journal of Theomusicology*, 8, no. 1 (spring). Durham: Duke University Press.

Tomlinson, Gary
    1993   *Music in Renaissance Magic: Toward a Historiography of Others*. Chicago: University of Chicago Press.

Treitler, Leo
    1989   *Music and the Historical Imagination*. Cambridge, Mass.: Harvard University Press.

Werner, Eric
    1984   *The Sacred Bridge: The Interdependence of Liturgy and Music in Synagogue and Church during the First Millennium*, vol. 2. New York: Columbia University Press.

Tantrism, *Rasa*, and Javanese Gamelan Music

Judith Becker

This is the teaching on instrumental music for the gamelan, called the "Sacred Teaching on Resonant Sound," handed down from Bhagawan Narada to the great kings of old in the Middle World. This teaching brings peace and prosperity to the kingdom of our lord king. In what follows we will speak of the scales. . .of the instruments. . .of things that cause sound through [the action of] air, and [those that depend on] the amplifying power of metal.
    —*Aji Gurnita*, ca. 19th century, Bali, Indonesia

Music plays a constitutive role in the religious practices of many peoples, as a marker of liturgical moments, as an adhesive in producing psychological and physical unity in a congregation, and as a component in states of religious ecstasy. For the most part, however, the role of music in religious practices is not scripturally defined. Its function comes about through age-old custom and is part of "common," unreflective understandings. In medieval Java, and in those institutions such as Javanese court circles where old practices are still, if minimally, maintained, Tantric beliefs about the relation of music to spiritual development are still discernable. Listening to certain kinds of music was thought to be a stepping-stone toward the ultimate goal of enlightenment. Through a state of relaxed yet focused listening, a piece of music or a statue or a mandala drawing could become a *yantra*, a vehicle for the descent of a personal deity. Thus music, or at least certain kinds of music, could be a meditative aid. This belief may strike modern readers as suspiciously akin to some New Age doctrines. The differences lie in the fact that Tantric meditative practices were never assumed to be easily accessible. Only years of study with a knowledgable spiritual guide could lead one to the stage of meditational visualization of a deity through music.

It is the power of artistic performance as performance, as music, and as dance that makes it such a potent vehicle for other meanings. Inert images or silent texts are also multivocalic, speaking to us on several levels of meaning simultaneously; but performances including music and dance affect us not only visually and mentally but kinesthetically as well and thus are widely used as vehicles for transformation. Within certain religious communities in India and in medieval Java, what we call "aesthetics," or art appreciation, was about transformation.

In medieval India, Tantric Śaivite theorists developed an aesthetic theory centered on the concept of *rasa*—a theory that was known at least in part, and perhaps in its entirety, in Java. As in India, the Tantric theory of *rasa* assumed an independent existence and became an aesthetic theory incorporated into the general cultural milieux, no longer specifically identified with Tantrism.

Java's Tantric past has been all but forgotten in contemporary Indonesia. The conversion of Java to Islam, the subsequent era of colonialism, the emergence of nationalism and ultimate independence have obscured the legacy of Tantric Buddhism and Tantric Śaivism (Śiva worship) in Javanese religious practices. Nevertheless, Tantric aesthetic tenets can still be found in the practice of and the writings about the performing arts. In dance and in music the idea that aesthetic appreciation can lead to enlightenment, that the arts can be vehicles for meditation, and that music can entrain the spirit still prevails. Especially in Central Javanese court circles, medieval Indian ideas of aesthetic spirituality can still be discerned. In the late medieval period in Java, as Islam gradually rose to ascendency, Tantric beliefs concerning the arts assimilated with similar Sufi doctrines. The Javanese interpretation of Indian *rasa* theory produced a synthesis of beliefs associated with Sufi Islam and beliefs of Tantric Buddhism and Śaivism.

Essential Tantric and Sufi doctrines concerning meditative practices and music often overlap, and both provide a satisfactory, comprehensive explanatory mechanism for a range of Javanese mystical writings. The three texts on gamelan discussed in this article indicate the specific religious content of Central Javanese court music. A performance of a gamelan piece was meant to be polysemic, to be understood as music, as entertainment, as a religious metaphor, and (for the spiritually prepared) as a vessel (*yantra*) into which a personal deity is mentally projected.

Javanese musicians use the Sanskrit term *rasa* to cover a host of meanings, feelings, intentions, and ideas which can be communicated by a *gendhing* or a dance performance, a song, or a poem. One of the strongest undercurrents of meaning of the term *rasa* is a religious sense, a feeling of unity with the world beyond oneself, a transcendental experience induced by an artistic event. From the invoking of indigenous deities in the many trance performances of Java to the stories of Indic gods in the *wayang kulit* shadow-puppet theater to the quiet religiosity of the playing of a court gamelan, the spiritual dimension of artistic performance is consistently emphasized.

However, there is a difference in the degree of self-consciousness, of awareness of the spiritual meanings of the different genres, not only between participants within one genre but across genres as well. For trance performances and for shadow-puppet theater (*wayang kulit*) the content of the religiosity (i.e., Who are the deities? Why are they invoked? What is the hoped-for consequence?) is often explicit and well understood by both the performers and the audience. We know why such activities are sacred; we can understand why they are hedged with taboos, why the practitioners must risk coming into contact with otherworldly beings; we know the mythic sources of the extraordinary power of these performances.

A gamelan performance at court, however, while partaking of

much the same spiritual aura, seems by contrast to be a religiosity devoid of content. Many Javanese musicians and members of the audience are likely to be somewhat inarticulate about the spiritual meanings of the performance, making what we interpret as "mystical" replies to inquiries.

Although Islamic terminology is often found in gamelan stories today, and Islamic doctrines, particularly Sufi doctrines, have become an important part of contemporary aesthetic dialogue, the influence of Islam alone cannot account for the religious ethos of Javanese court arts. In the continuing dialogue and interpenetration between Islam and Javanese performance traditions, many pre-Islamic genres in Java have been reinterpreted and incorporated into the realm of Javanese Islamic music. Genres with long histories—such as *wayang Menak*, the Islamic variant of the shadow-puppet genre; the court gamelan *sekati* performances played in honor of Muhammad's birthday; the court *bedhaya* dance legitimizing the first Islamic sultan; and the *majapat* song tradition—have become associated with Islamic stories and Islamic texts and are justly designated as Islamic musical expressions. They carry overt Islamic religious messages in their texts even though their ethos of restraint and control is not characteristic of Islamic music in the Near East and India. Typically, musical genres used in the service of the Islamic faith both inside and outside Indonesia have a certain rhythmic prominence and intensity which drives the believer to states of ecstacy. The practice *dhikr,* with its fast rhythms on the *rebana* (frame drum) and highly repetitive and strongly articulated texts, is more representative of many genres of Muslim music. The ethos of the ecstatic music of the Sufis (for example, the *qawwālī* music of Pakistan) is diametrically opposed to the serenity of mood and subdued emotionality of a palace gamelan performance. Also, doctrinally acceptable religious music of Islam is necessarily subordinated to a religious text; music is a vehicle for sacred words. The text is the primary instrument of ecstasy; music is relegated to a supporting role.

A *gendhing* (gamelan piece) need not have any text at all. The atmosphere of a religious offering continues to imbue court performances, with their peculiar ethos of subdued emotionality, restraint, and control. The religiosity of these performances within an Islamic context seems strangely contentless. However, the Javanese texts on gamelan discussed and framed in this article indicate that court music has a quite specific religious content. The aesthetic attitude of contemporary Javanese gamelan musicians has been a long time in the making. The past still lives on in the present, in the cultural memories and attitudes of musicians and in their stories about their artistic traditions.

Tantrism, as a religious ideology, entered Java as an integrated element of Śaivism and Buddhism. Over time, and particularly after the ascent of Islam in the sixteenth century, Tantric beliefs ceased to be identifiable as a distinct ideology and blended into the general stock of Javanese cultural beliefs and practices. Therefore, it is not surprising that the word Tantrism is not used in Java today to identify certain patterns of belief with clear Tantric historical precedents.

Among Indian Tantric philosophers, Buddhist and Śaivite, the aesthetic experience was linked to the pursuit of enlightenment. The best-known Indian philosopher who wrote extensively on this theory of aesthetics was Abhinavagupta, a Tantric Śaivite who lived in Kashmir, India, in the tenth century. Abhinavagupta wrote extensively, incorporating works of earlier theorists into his own works, clarifying and systematizing aesthetic terminology. After his death his influence continued in the writings not only of his students but in the incorporation of his ideas into the writings and teachings of philosophers from other schools as well (Masson and Patwardhan 1977, 290). Whether directly from the writings of Abhinavagupta or indirectly from later writers, the theory of aesthetics which promoted artistic means as a path to enlightenment was well known in Indonesia in medieval times (Hooykaas 1958, 28; Robson 1979, 304; Sears 1986, 47–53).

The English term "aesthetics" has come to mean the study of the basis of evaluating objects designated as "artistic" that have been isolated from their cultural context (Sparshott 1983, 3). This was not its original Greek meaning (*aesthētikos,* "of sense perception"), nor is it the meaning of comparable terms used in India and Indonesia. The idea of aesthetic appreciation in Tantric teachings has to do with a special kind of perception, of paying full attention to whatever is before one at the moment. One is taught constantly to strive to be in the present, not mentally reliving the past nor rehearsing the future, to be mindful of every moment and to see, hear, taste, smell, and touch without preconceptions, without the intervening overlay of the memory of all one's past sensory experiences. To see things as they are, to hear music as it is, without precognition or judgment, is to perceive aesthetically. The Tantrics of medieval India linked the study of perception and cognition with aesthetics. This preparation for spiritual development in Buddhist doctrines is called "mindfulness" and involves not only the perception of events and objects we would call artistic but relates as well to ordinary, everyday action. To be "mindful," to be totally within the present, means to give full attention to lifting a glass of water or to walking across a room.

Our understanding of aesthetics as relating to quality and to standards of performance, however, is not entirely irrelevant in discussing Tantrism and music. In India and in Indonesia, religious objects, dances, musical instruments, and musical performances were produced according to a strict canon. Each fine detail of execution was done according to tradition. The "correct" way was the beautiful way, and the methodology for perfect execution was handed down from generation to generation. Quality craftsmanship has always been highly valued and inferior products or performances are routinely rejected. The aesthetic dimension (in our sense of evaluation) of statues, musical performances, or dances relates to standards of compositional technique and execution. Javanese dancers, musicians, and critics can and do talk endlessly about technique, about execution, about the degree of polish of a performance, and they do so with an extensive technical vocabulary. In Java and in neighboring Bali it is a given that performances, especially ritual performances, will be of as high quality as possible given the skill and experience of the performers and the monetary resources of the sponsors. Buddhist scriptures advise that only the best of urban music or courtly music should be used in rituals. "Best," of course, relates to the consensus of opinion of the elites of the society in question. In Tibet, Tantric Buddhists borrowed the instrumental ensembles of the Muslim courts of North India as the basis of their ritual music. In Java and Bali, the gamelan ensembles of the courts became the vehicles for the creation of a Tantric religious atmosphere. In each case, only the best was good enough.

However, it is not the evaluative system of Javanese music that is intended by the term "aesthetics" in this study. Refinement of perception, according to Tantric philosophy, can lead to a refinement of cognition and a dissolution of the boundaries between oneself and the thing perceived. Aesthetics as clarified perception becomes a cornerstone of spiritual practice and an important source of meaning in a gamelan performance.

Teachings concerning the five senses (*pancèndriya*), and the meditative process of understanding the way in which consciousness shapes and colors the input from the senses, are found in Old Javanese Tantric literature, both Śaivite and Buddhist. Early Buddhists in India developed a theory of consciousness which remains a cornerstone of Tantric Buddhist ideology. An important goal of meditation is to develop sophisticated awareness and understanding of the act of perception and its relation to the arising of consciousness. According to Buddhist theories of perception, consciousness is not a passive receiver of messages transmitted through the sense organs, but takes an active, even dominant, role in the mental construction of what is seen, heard, smelled, tasted, or touched. The sense organs are referred to as *endriya* or *indriya*; thus the five sense organs are called *pancadriya* or *pancèndriya* (*panca,* "five"). The object of the sense of sight, e.g., a tree, plus the organ of sight (the eyes) are called *āyatana*s, or "entrances" for consciousness. Consciousness then takes over from the *āyatana*s and adds memory, will, desire, hope—all the emotional aspects, also called *rasa*s, that are an integral part of all cognition. What we see, hear, smell, taste, or touch is only minimally determined by the *āyatana*s, the sense objects plus the sense organs (Stcherbatsky 1974, 7–10). The diagram below illustrates the relationship between what is seen, heard, etc. (field or object), the organ which sees, hears, etc. (sense organ), and the arising consciousness (awareness).

INTERNAL		EXTERNAL
AWARENESS	SENSE	FIELD OR OBJECT
1. eye perception (*rasa*)	sight	forms
2. ear perception (*rasa*)	hearing	sounds
3. nose perception (*rasa*)	smell	smells
4. mouth perception (*rasa*)	taste	tastes (also called *rasa*)
5. body perception (*rasa*)	touch	tangibles
6. mental perception (*rasa*)	mind	mental events (dreams and memories)

(Adapted from Beyer 1978, 96)

As described in Buddhist scriptures, two more kinds of awareness or consciousness exist beyond the five sense perceptions and the sixth, mental perception. The seventh consciousness is that pervaded by the sense of "I," the ego, which appears to "lie behind and appraise the processes of mental perception" (Beyer 1978, 95). The eighth kind of consciousness is "underlying awareness," the storehouse of consciousness, the karmic continuum, which manages and maintains mental activity at all other levels.

One of the aims of meditation is to come to an intuitive, experiential understanding (not an intellectual one) of the process of cognition, of the levels of consciousness. Based upon this understanding, the practitioner hopes to free perceptions from the disturbance of the emotions, from all the unnecessary and imaginary projections coming from the different levels of consciousness. This ancient Buddhist concept is reflected in the description of a doctrine of the Javanese mystical sect, Sumarah:

The general understanding is that normal consciousness is dominated by an attention which is focused in thoughts, filled with
attachment to the data received through the senses, and directed,
for the most part subconsciously, by desires and emotions. . . .
Beyond the senses and thoughts there lies a cleaning of internalized
subconscious blockages, so that gradually perception is less filtered
through subjective structures. As a person becomes open, as even

inner blocks are released, he or she becomes increasingly conscious of precisely what information enters the sphere of awareness—it becomes possible to distinguish "inner noise" from messages received. (Stange 1984, 121)

The understanding, and definition, of the term *rasa* as relating to perception, to awareness, and to the rise of consciousness among contemporary Javanese mystical sects is one of the most striking examples of the sustaining power of Tantric interpretations.

> Rasa is at once the key to individual entry into Sumarah meditation. . . . In Indonesia the word "rasa" means "feeling," both in the physical and emotional sense; in the more spiritually resonant Javanese it also means "intuitive feeling." Rasa is at once the substance, vibration, or quality of what is apprehended and the tool or organ which apprehends it. (Stange 1984, 119)

In Indian scriptures, in Old Javanese literature,[1] and in Javanese *kebatinan* sects, the function of perception (*rasa*) is located in the heart, "the tool or organ which apprehends it." Throughout Old Javanese literature, the heart, *cakra*, is the preferred seat of the visualized deity with which the spiritual practitioner is identified.[2] In the following quote from the opening invocation (*manggala*) of the Śaivite poem *Wrttasañcaya* (fifteenth century C.E.), she who is "enthroned on the lotus in the depths of my heart" is the goddess of speech Wāgīswarī, also known as Sarasvatī.

Wrttasañcaya:
> Goddess of speech, look down on me, thy servant, who worships thee without interruption, consort of the Creator (Brahmā). My mind

---

[1] The term "Old Javanese" refers to the literary language of medieval Java (i.e., eighth–sixteenth centuries C.E.) in which religious scholars and poets wrote thousands of manuscripts on religion, history, and statecraft and into which Sanskrit scriptures and epics were translated or rewritten (Pigeaud 1967–70, vols. 1–3).

[2] *Cakra*s, or *padma*s as they were often called in Old Javanese literature, are centers of psychic energy located at specific points along the spinal chord.

is concentrated on thee, enthroned on the lotus in the depths of my heart, and praises thee continuously, that thou mayest grant me the favour of being free from sorrow, suffering and adversities. May I by thy blessing obtain knowledge and all other human accomplishments, without meeting any obstacles. (Zoetmulder 1974, 105)[3]

The symbol of the heart in Tantric writings is meant to be understood as multivocalic, as resonant on several levels. All key terms in Tantric scriptures are to be read as subsuming at least three levels of meaning: the conventional meaning (*abhidhā*), the secondary meaning (*lakṣanā*), and the suggested meaning or resonance (*vyañjanā*) (Muller-Ortega 1989, 12). The heart, a key term, means the physical organ and, as a secondary meaning, refers to the *cakra* at the position of the heart. Beyond those meanings, the heart can be a metonym for the experience of unity with all creation, called *rasa sejati* or *rasa murni*. Describing the meanings of the heart in the writings of the tenth-century North Indian Tantric philosopher Abhinavagupta, Muller-Ortega explains:

> The Heart here finally becomes quite simply a metaphor for consciousness. . . . Abhinavagupta's usage of the term Heart seems to be directed toward the cakra. The elevation of the symbol to its final height, however, occurs only when the Heart is no longer used to refer to the cakra, but rather, by synecdoche, comes to be a term applied to the Ultimate itself. (Muller-Ortega 1989, 64, 77)

In mystical Sufism, the heart (*qolbu*) is likewise the place where the union of worshipper and Allah takes place. The language of Islamic mysticism in which the worshipper feels communion with Allah in his/her heart may approximate the language of the Tantric practitioner who visualizes his/her personal deity, or *istadewata*, at

---

[3] *Wṛttasañcaya, manggala*

"Sang hyang Wāgīśwarī ndah lihati satata bhaktingkw i jöng dhātṛdewī pinrih ring citta munggw ing sarasija ri dalem twas lanenastawangku nityāweha ng warānugraha kaluputa ring duhkha sangsāra wighna lawan tāstu wruheng śāstra sakalaguṇa ning janma tapwan haneweh." (Zoetmulder 1974, 483).

the heart *cakra*. The Javanese description given below of the highest Islamic spiritual state, *sujud*, begins in duality with a separation between man and God, or between servant and Lord. But when it concludes with "there is no one who exercises sudjud and no one who receives it," the distinctions between the two traditions, Sufism and Tantrism, disappear.

> For him who has been given this grace there is suddenly a feeling that his *sudjud* [communion with God] is removed from within the chest in the inwardness (*sanubari*) into the anatomical heart (*djantung*), wherein the *Qolbu* is situated. The feeling of *sudjud* will be felt only for a short time, then it disappears, nothing will be felt any more.
>
> The reason why the feeling [rasa] disappears is explained as follows: Both the servant and the Lord have already become one, therefore automatically there is no one who exercises *sudjud* and no one who receives it. (Hadiwijono 1967, 160)

In Tantric thought and in the teachings of Javanese mystical sects, religious knowledge is to be gained through the careful and systematic development of one's spiritual faculties through meditation. The spiritual quest is individual and not congregational, meditative and not devotional, body-centered, inward, and immanent, not transcendent. To understand the macrocosmos, one begins with the body.

> Feeling [*rasa*] in its turn may in the first instance mean awareness of physical sensation within the body, but that gross-level rasa becomes progressively more subtle—it shades through inner physical sensation into awareness of the emotions and ultimately into *rasa sejati*, the absolute or true feeling which is itself mystical awareness of the fundamental vibration or energy within all life. (Stange 1984, 119)

At the simplest level, *rasa* means "taste," "flavor"; *rasa* also means emotions such as joy, sadness, etc.; *rasa* may mean the act of perception, or the meta-act of perceiving perception, a kind of complete cognition which includes elements both mental and emotional; and finally, *rasa* can refer to the refined sensation of the spiritually advanced practitioner, the feeling of unity with all creation. The different meanings of the term *rasa* in Javanese mystical writings are similar to the different meanings found in texts on Indian aesthetic theory. Sometimes the term *rasa* is partially disambiguated in Javanese as the distinction is made between ordinary feeling, sensation, or perception (*rasa*) and the extra-ordinary, internal, and refined cognition, *rasa sejati* or *rasa murni*. In Indian aesthetic writings, *rasa* was used in all these different ways (Masson and Patwardhan 1977, 286, n. 5).

"Wèdha Pradangga Kawedhar" (Knowledge of gamelan revealed), by B. Y. H. Sastrapustaka

Early in 1979, a manuscript entitled "Knowledge of Gamelan Revealed" was given me by its author, the late B. Y. H. Sastrapustaka, a well-known court musician from the Central Javanese city of Yogyakarta.[4] Included in the manuscript is an interpretation of the names of the keys of the gamelan instruments. The exegesis of the names of the keys (relating them to points in the head and trunk of the body, to the five senses, and to the six *rasa*s) restated similar themes I had either read or been told about relating Javanese gamelan performance to spiritual practices. The continuum of meaning of the term *rasa*, from "taste" in a literal sense, to perception of "taste" and to all sensory perception, to consciousness of the processes of perception, and, ultimately, to a state of spiritual enlightenment, makes the following passage from

---

[4] "Knowledge of Gamelan Revealed," translated by R. Anderson Sutton in volume 1 of the three-volume set, *Karawitan: Source Readings in Javanese Gamelan and Vocal Music*, edited by J. Becker and A. H. Feinstein. The body of this manuscript is discussed and analyzed in my book *Gamelan Stories: Tantrism, Islam, and Aesthetics in Central Java* (1993). A version of "Knowledge of Gamelan Revealed" that the author gave me in 1986 contains a passage on the spiritual/aesthetic aspect of studying gamelan performance and listening to gamelan *gendhing* omitted in the published 1984 version. This article focuses on that important passage in which the author discusses *rasa*.

Sastrapustaka's text particularly difficult to translate. Also, there is an inevitable awkwardness in English, where the use of multiple meanings of the same term in a single passage is not acceptable. A further complication arises because in Javanese the noun *rasa* in all its meanings is also made into a verb, i.e., "to rasa." In spite of these inherent difficulties, and the problem that there are no concepts in English exactly commensurate with those expressed here, the passage is still, even in translation, revealing.

> The tones of the five keys discussed earlier, when they are laid out, when they are arranged, when they are composed according to established criteria, then they become vessels whose contents are many forms of *gendhing*.[5] At the same time, the tones of the five bronze keys (form, way, life, attraction, and feeling) become images/ representations of the meaning of the sound of the gamelan that have three different arrangements, or three different characters: *pathet enem, pathet sanga,* and *pathet manyura* [musical modes].
>
> The sound reverberations of the gamelan that have the three different characters mentioned above, the coming into existence of *gendhing* of a particular nature, can then be experienced as beautiful and pleasurable as they unfold the power of *rasa*: joy, happiness, pain, tension, nobility, sadness, meditation (*semedi*), exaltation, sympathy, high energy, sexual love (*asmara*), displeasure, yearning, and excitement.
>
> As already stated earlier, the tones of the gamelan keys *barang* [1], *gulu* [2], and *dhadha* [3] symbolize the human body [the three upper *cakra*s]. The tone *lima* [5] symbolizes and means desire/ attraction (*sengsem*), that is, attraction to, or desire for all goodness and beauty whose source comes from the five senses. As for tone *enem* [6], as said above, it symbolizes and means *rasa*.

[5] The five keys of the *slendro* gamelan are laid out as follows:

barang/

panunggul	gulu	dhadha	lima	enem
(1)	(2)	(3)	(5)	(6)

The sources for these are two: the "five" is the five senses, and also from being felt (verbal form of *rasa*). To make it complete is "six," whose source is within the heart (*manah*), indeed, that which we call *rasa sejati*, activities and actions for the purpose of feeling, to *rasa*.

Whatever is it that is experienced, that is "*rasa-ed*" by the above-mentioned *rasa sejati* that is inside the heart?

Remember: every person has *rasa*, that is, *rasa* for the purpose of experiencing feelings. That which is experienced by the afore-mentioned *rasa sejati* takes the form of joy, cheerfulness, happiness, sorrow, grief, etc.

This completes the explanation of the meaning of the names of the bronze keys of the gamelan, that is *barang* [thing], *gulu* [neck], *dhadha* [chest], *lima* [five], *enem* [six] (form, path, life, attraction, feeling); taking the form of, the appearance of, a complete human figure, physical, spiritual, and *rasa*.

It is now very clear that in studying and striving to cultivate the artistic skills of gamelan playing, the aim and intention is not the cultivation of physical skills alone. The aim of study is none other than the studying and striving to cultivate one's own self in order that one be inclined towards nobility of spirit, the ethical essence of the *rasa* of beauty which is secreted within one's spiritual and physical self, accompanied by sharpness of consciousness, refinement of *rasa* and strength of purpose. (Sastrapustaka 1986, 9–10, translated by N. Florida and J. Becker)[6]

---

[6] *Wèdha Pradangga Kawedhar: Sastra Sinandi Ingkang Piningid Dumunung ing Wilahaning Gangsa*

. . .Larasing gangsa gangsal warni wau, manawi dipun racik, lan dipun rakit, katata miturut wewaton ingkang sampun katemtokaken, lajeng dados wadhah ingkang isi mawarni-warni wujuding gendhing. Wondene laras wilahaning gangsa: *barang, gulu, dhadha, lima, enem*: (*wujud, dalan, urip, sengsem, rasa*), boten sanes inggih dados gegambaran kawedharing suwantenipun gangsa ingkang gumelaripun asipat tigang warni: "*Pathet enem, Pathet sanga, Pathet manyura.*"

Kumandhanging suwantenipun gangsa ingkang sampun gadhah sipat tigang warni wau, dumadosing gendhing tuwuh watakipun (karakter) lan tumunten saged dipun raosaken kaendahan sarta kanikmatanipun, saha

The use of the terms *rasa* and *rasa sejati* in Sastrapustaka's text
and within the Javanese Sumarah movement conforms to the
definition of *rasa* as discussed in the writings of medieval Kashmiri
Śaivite philosophers. The Sanskrit terms translated as "the aesthetic
experience," e.g., *rasanā, camatkāra, āsvāda,* are all synonyms for
a consciousness which is without obstacles, i.e., without emotional

---

ambabar dayaning raos: *gambira, bingah, susah, sumedhot, luhur, wingit,
semedi, agung, trenyuh, sigrak, asmara, renyah, sereng, greget.*

Sampun kasebut ing ngajeng, bilih laras wilahaning gangsa punika, ing
bageyan: *barang, gulu, dhadha,* mujudaken pasemon gegambaraning
badanipun manungsa, Laras: lima: mujudaken pasemon lan pikajeng:
sengsem: inggih sengsem dhateng sawarnining: kasaenan lan kaendahan
sumberipun saking: Pancandriya. Dene laras: enem: sampun kasebut ing
ngajeng, mengku pasemon lan pikajeng *rasa.*

Sumberipun wonten kalih: ingkang gangsal ugi saking: Pancandriya, lan
kanthi dipun raos-raosaken. Jangkepipun enem, sumberipun wonten
salebeting manah, inggih ingkang dipun wastani: *rasa sejati,* tumandang
lan tumindakipun kangge ngraos-ngraosaken.

Punapa ingkang dipun raos-raosaken *rasa sejati* ingkang wonten
salebeting manah punika?

PENGET: Tiyang punika gadhah raos, inggih raos punika ingkang
minangka kangge ngraosaken. Dene ingkang dipun raosaken *rasa sejati*
wau, awujud: suka, gambira, bingah, susah, sedhih lss.

Sampun jangkep anggenipun nlusuri bab: kawedharing wilahan gangsa
gangsal laras wau sampun saged udhar, inggih punika: *barang, gulu,
dhadha, lima, enem: (wujud, dalan, urip, sengsem, rasa),* ingkang lajeng
gumantha awujud blegering manungsa, jangkep, sajiwa-raga, lan raosipun.

Sapunika lajeng cetha sanget, bilih sinau, ngudi olah kagunan karawitan
punika, maksud lan tujuwanipun, boten sanes inggih nyinau lan ngolah
badanipun piyambak, ingkang supados tumiyung dhateng kautaman,
kasusilan raos kaendahan ingkang piningid wonten ing jiwa-raganipun,
kinanthen: landhep, lantiping cipta saha alusing raos tuwin kiyating
karsa. . . . (Sastrapustaka 1986, 9–10)

In addition to the passages quoted above, Sastrapustaka's essay includes a
section presenting an exegesis of the meanings of the names of the keys of the
gamelan; a section on *wayang kulit*; a linguistic discussion concerning the
correctness of the usage of *enem,* "six," versus *nem*; an explanation of the
character of each *pathet*; and an etymological, historical, submorphemic, and
syntactic analysis of the word *pathet.*

interference (Masson and Patwardhan 1969, 46). By losing one's strong sense of self in absorption in a play, in a painting, in a dance, in a poem, or in a musical performance while simultaneously recognizing emotions of love, compassion, pity, disgust, etc. (whatever emotion is evoked by the artistic event), one learns to understand one's emotional reaction to the event. It becomes possible to observe one's own emotional reactions without simultaneously experiencing in "real" life the event which triggered the emotion. In both contemporary Javanese mystical sects and in the works of Abhinavagupta, the process of refined cognition (one sense of the term *rasa sejati*) is described as the mind watching the mind. According to Abhinavagupta,

> Rasa is. . .simply and solely a mental state which is the matter of cognition on the part of a perception without obstacles and consisting in a relish. (Gnoli 1968, 62)

Similarly, as understood within Javanese mystical sects:

> *Rasa* is the experiential context of human life. . . . *Rasa murni* ["pure *rasa*," a synonym for *rasa sejati*] is the "feeling of feeling" and as such does not constitute any particular affective response. (Howe 1980, 72)

One learns to distinguish pure perception from one's normally muddied reactions to stimuli received by the brain, through the senses, from the world outside. Transcending the emotions, the practitioner experiences a feeling of unity with the thing perceived, a dissolving of the sense of self and other. Experiencing *rasa/ rasa sejati/ rasa murni* results in a special kind of contentment, or joy, or delight that in India is equated with the highest form of knowledge, *prajña*, sometimes translated as "aesthetic appreciation." A twentieth-century Western writer on Tantric Buddhist aesthetics, Herbert Guenther, expands on the same topic.

> This continuous delight is an inalienable component of aesthetic perception. . .the more a person is able to appreciate what there is the more he feels contented, and the more contented he feels, the

more he will be able to appreciate. There is in such an experience both depth and brightness, which contrasts sharply with the ordinary shallowness and dullness of our perception. . . . But although we may speak of depth and brightness in aesthetic perception and aesthetic experience, they are not two, but inseparably together, and this togetherness (*sahaja, yuganaddha*) is the fundamental "original and pristine awareness" which we lose when we perform abstracting acts by attending to parts of things, by seeing the object not so much *per se* but as an instance in a larger category, in brief, by conceptualizing and indulging in the fictions of our own making about what there is. (Guenther 1976, 17)

Related beliefs are expressed in Sastrapustaka's text where the goal is to learn to perceive all sensory inputs and emotions as *rasa sejati*. Training in what we would call "the arts" is at the same time spiritual training. Connoisseurship is *not* the aim; value judgments block *rasa sejati*. Seeing "the thing as it is," hearing "the thing as it is," without the overlay of feelings, memories, associations, or desires is the strived-for goal. One's perceptions should become "god-like."

In the writings of Abhinavagupta, the aesthetic experience and the mystic experience of union with the deity are said to be similar and derived from the same source but are not identical. The aesthetic experience is a kind of steppingstone, a preliminary apprenticeship to the ultimate mystic experience. In both, one dissolves the force of space and time, dissolves one's bonds to history, and enters a timeless world where there is no "I" and no "other." Just as mystical union dissolves oneself into the deity, aesthetic union dissolves oneself into the object of contemplation, the dance, the poem, or the music. As taught by Abhinavagupta, the differences between mystic union and aesthetic experience remain important, a distinction also found in Javanese sources. In the aesthetic experience, one retains a trace, a lingering of the emotion derived from that projected by the artistic object.

Mystical experience involves the annihilation of every pair of opposites; everything is reabsorbed in its dissolving fire. . . . The limited "I" is completely absorbed into Śiva or Bhairava, the adored object; everything vanishes from the field of consciousness. Aesthetic experience, on the other hand, requires the presence of the latent traces of delight, etc., ...

". . .Aesthetic enjoyment consists in the tasting of one's own consciousness; this tasting is endowed with extreme pleasantness (beauty), which it obtains from a contact with the various latent traces of pleasure, pain, etc. . . ." (Abhinavagupta, in Gnoli 1968, 82–83, n. 4)

Another distinction made by Abhinavagupta between mystic union and the aesthetic experience is the lack of any attempt at control or of any willfulness in the aesthetic experience.

". . .It [aesthetic enjoyment] differs both from ordinary perception, which is full of obstacles (pragmatic requirements, etc.), and from the perception of the yogins, which is not free from harshness". . . . It is particularly suitable to people endowed with a "gentle mind." (Abhinavagupta, in Gnoli 1968, 83–84, n. 4).

The same distinction was made in medieval Java. Learning to experience refined perception, especially related to music and poetry, was a sign of progress on the path to the ultimate mystic experience, unity with a deity.

By creating a poem or relishing it after it is complete, one may be transported into the ecstatic rapture of *langö,* the aesthetic experience, and in the receding of one's consciousness accompanying this one is able to sense the approach of that mystical union with the divinity in which all consciousness of the self vanishes. (Zoetmulder 1974, 184)

In the opening invocation, the *manggala,* of many Old Javanese Śaivite manuscripts, the author states that the purpose of producing a work of beautiful literature is to attain union with an internally visualized, meditative deity. The poet dedicates the poem to his own personal deity, his *iṣṭadewata,* in the hope that, through a kind of aesthetic rapture, he may go beyond this state and attain union with the chosen deity, or, if a Buddhist, that he may realize his own divinity. The following *manggala* is from the fifteenth-century Śaivite text *Śiwarātrikalpa*:

> It is in His immaterial form that He, the god of gods [Śiva], is kept concealed in the innermost depth of the soul by him who has reached maturity in the search for beauty. In material form he is everlastingly enthroned in the midst of the heart-lotus. One who has attained this stage practises meditation (*dhyāna*), sings songs of praise (*stuti*), recites the "peak-formula" (*kūṭa mantra*), murmurs prayers (*japa*) and performs mystic gestures (*mudra*). My heart has but one desire: to be granted the favour of not failing in the conquest of beauty. (Zoetmulder 1974, 176)[7]

In the *manggala* of the *Śiwarātrikalpa*, the word translated as "beauty" is *langö*. Another translation is "aesthetic experience." Derivatives of the term include *kalangwan/ kalangon*, "the fine arts," or, as an adjective, "overcome by feelings of longing," i.e., *kesengsem*, "overcome by attraction/ enchanted." In medieval Java, as in India, the aesthetic experience was one of the paths for obliterating duality, of experiencing *adwaya*, the union of self and non-self.

> Among these terms the words *langö, lengeng, lengleng* and their derivatives take pride of place. What they convey is a feeling that is perhaps best rendered by "rapture." It is a kind of swooning sensation, in which the subject is completely absorbed by and becomes lost in its object, the appeal of which is so overwhelming

---

[7] *Śiwarātrikalpa, manggala,* canto 1
stanza 1:
Sang hyang ning hyang amūrti niṣkala sirāti-kinenep ing akabwatan langö
sthūlaākāra sira pratiṣṭhita haneng hṛdayakamalamadhya nityaśa
dhyāna mwang stuti kūtamantra japa mudra linekasaken ing samangkana
nghing pinrih-prih i citta ni nghulun anugrahana tulusa digjayeng langö.
(Zoetmulder 1974, 483)

that everything else sinks into nothingness and oblivion. All intellectual activity ceases; the perception of the object itself becomes vague, and in an experience of oneness that blurs the distinction between subject and object, consciousness of the self vanishes too. . . .

Objectively *langö* is the quality by which an object appears to the aesthetic sense. It does so not by the clarity and immediacy of its beauty, but, on the contrary, because it seems distant, half-hidden and apparently inaccessible; because it is suggestive, but does not reveal itself fully; because it allures, hinting at as yet unrevealed riches, so that the seeker after beauty is consumed by longing and the desire to reach it.

Thus by reason of its ambivalence the word *langö* can mean the aesthetic experience as well as beauty itself. (Zoetmulder 1974, 172–73)

The "quality by which an object appears to the aesthetic sense" described in Old Javanese literature as seemingly "distant," "half-hidden," and "suggestive" is also found in the writings of Indian aesthetic philosophers. The hint of a vague nostalgia, sweet yet melancholic, on reading a poem or hearing a piece of music was believed to be a result of indistinct memories of a former life. Abhinavagupta, writing in the tenth century C.E., was well acquainted with the works of the dramatist Kālidāsa, who lived and wrote in northern India in the fourth century C.E. Kālidāsa himself expresses this kind of perception as:

Seeing moving sights, and hearing soft sounds, even a man who is happy is filled with strange longings. Surely it is because he vaguely remembers, though he is not fully conscious, affections formed in an earlier life that are fixed inside him through the latent impressions they leave behind. (from *Śākuntala* by Kālidāsa as quoted in Masson and Patwardhan 1969, 57)

One of several Javanese expressions relating distantly heard gamelan music with a particularly touching beauty is *ing kadohan gamelane ngangkang cat ceta cat ilang,* "the gamelan wafts in the distance, now clear, now faint" (Kartomi 1981, 16). The Indian metaphysical equation of music heard indistinctly and the latent memories of a former life may be related to the value placed by the Sumatran Mandailing peoples on hearing music from a distance, *onak nidige siandao,* "lovely when heard from afar." As described by Kartomi, the Mandailing consider faintly heard music to be especially powerful and beautiful.

> When heard in the distance, music produces a pleasant, meditative, wafting (*sayup*) effect which inexorably entices the listener—whether human or spiritual—to move from the periphery of the sound to its centre, namely, the place where the music is being played. A listener close to the source of musical sound hears all the details, but on hearing it from a distance, all the details merge into a serene, unified whole. Like the experience of meditation, listening gives one an inner strength, and this strength may be accumulated in ever greater quantities as one listens. (Kartomi 1981, 14)

Larasing Gendhing, by Socrachman

Another twentieth-century document from Yogyakarta which also relates listening to gamelan music to spiritual practice both invokes some of the same imagery as does "Knowledge of Gamelan Revealed" and introduces distinctly Islamic ideas and terminology.[8] Soerachman was not himself a practicing musician, but, like other high-born Central Javanese, he had a keen appreciation of gamelan music and used stories of the *wayang kulit* and its characters as templates for the interpretation of contemporary persons and events. Among the ascetic mystical practices he reportedly carried out were forty-day fasts, forty days without sleep, and sitting at night in the

---

[8] The text was given to Aline Scott-Maxwell by her teacher, Soerachman, in the late 1970s.

confluence of two rivers. Though deeply committed to spiritual practice, Soerachman followed no formalized religious organization.[9] Below is the entire text of Soerachman's short document on the relation of gamelan music and meditation.

Larasing Gendhing: "The fitting together of Javanese melodies and musical instruments"[10]

In former times, the times of the Javanese kings, when making supplication to the Lord Most Powerful (*Gusti Ingkang Maha Kawasa/ Tuhan Jang Maha Esa*), that was the time for focusing ideas-feelings (thoughts/ the five senses) to become one essence with the sound of the gamelan whose tuning/ tones fit together with one's wish that the sound surge until it touches the heart. The method is as follows:

1. Begin by sitting while listening to *gendhing Kinanthi Teplek*.
kinanthi = with
teplek = sit up straight
2. Begin to focus the mind and senses while listening to *gendhing Laras Driya*.
laras = to gather, collect ["to tune"]
driya = senses, thoughts
3. If meditation attains divine inspiration (*sasmita/ ilham*), then listen to *gendhing Asmara[n]Dana*.
asmara = *samar* (dim, vague, indistinct) [*asmara* = 'love, passion']
dana = gift from the Lord

---

[9] "I remember asking them once whether Pak Rachman (Soerachman) was also a member of Sumarah, the reply being that he did not feel it was necessary." (Scott-Maxwell 1989, pers. comm.)

[10] The translation of the title is the English translation of the Indonesian as given to Aline Scott-Maxwell by Soerachman. The biographical information about Soerachman was communicated to me by Aline Scott-Maxwell.

4. When meditation is to finish, then 'make oneself one with' *gendhing Kinanthi Sandung.*[11]

 kinanthi = with

 sandung = 'trip over', 'stumble' [?]

[11] I could not locate notation for *Kinanthi Teplek.* Since there are several different *Asmarandana*s, I have included two. Javanese Kepatihan notation for Ketawang *Laras Driya,* Ladrang *Asmarandana Kenja Tinembe,* Ladrang *Asmarandana Bawaraga,* and Ketawang *Kinanthi Sandung* are given below:

Ketawang Laras Driya, pelog pathet lima

```
                                                      N
A   . 2 . 1     . 2 . 6     . 2 . 1     . 6 . 5
    . 2 . 1     . 2 . 6     . 2 . 1     . 6 . (5)
    2 2 . 3     5 6 3 5     6 6 2 1     2 6 3 5
    2 4 5 4     2 1 2 6     2 3 2 1     6 5 3 (5)
                  Lik:      5 5 . 6     1 . 2 (1)
B   . 1 1 .     6 6 1 2     5 3 2 1     6 5 3 5
    1 1 . .     3 2 1 6     5 1 5 4     6 5 4 (2)
    . . 2 3     5 6 3 5     6 6 2 1     2 6 3 5
    2 6 1 2     5 6 2 1     5 6 5 2     1 6 3 (5)
```

Ladrang *Asmarandana Kenja Tinembe,* slendro pathet sanga

```
                      N
Irama 1: 2 1 2 6     2 1 6 5
         6 1 5 6     2 1 6 5
         6 1 5 6     2 1 6 5

                                                        N
Irama 2: 2 2 3 5     2 1 2 6     2 3 2 1     6 5 3 5
         . 5 6 1     5 3 5 6     2 3 2 1     6 5 3 5
         . 5 6 1     5 3 5 6     2 3 2 1     6 5 3 5
         2 3 5 3     2 1 2 1     3 5 3 2     1 6 3 5
```

Ladrang *Asmarandana Bawaraga,* slendro pathet sanga

```
                                                        N
Irama 3: 1 2 1 6     2 1 6 5     1 2 1 6     3 1 3 2
         5 6 2 1     3 2 1 6     3 5 2 1     3 2 1 6
         1 5 2 1     3 2 1 6     3 5 2 1     2 6 3 5
         3 2 3 2     1 2 1 6     3 5 2 1     2 6 3 (5)
```

Thus it is clear, if one meditates (*semedhi*)/ purifies ideas-feelings, begins by sitting with a straight back, then focuses the mind and the senses, then, without willing it to be so, one receives the divine gift from the Lord Most Powerful. This is the explanation about the situation of Gamelan and *Gendhing* which corresponds to the Science of Man's Perfection (*Ilmu Kasampurnan*).[12]

Sufi Islam and "The Science of Man's Perfection"

Sastrapustaka's text contains few terms relating to Islam. His exegesis relies upon pre-Islamic Indic theories of the *cakra*s, of the five senses and the six *rasa*s. More usually, contemporary mystical treatises include a large measure of Sufi terminology and Sufi constructions of reality. Soerachman's short text is illustrative.

When Soerachman writes of the "Science of Man's Perfection" (*Ilmu Kasampurnan*) he refers to a mystical Sufi doctrine that teaches the way in which the devotee may become one with Allah. This spiritual practice consists of seven stages, of which the last is the stage of the "perfect man" (*âlam al insân al kâmil*). The "perfect

---

Ketawang *Kinanthi Sandung*, slendro pathet manyura

```
                        N
      6  1  5  6      1  2  1   6
      3  2  6  5      1  6  5  (3)
      5  2  5  3      6  1  6   5
      2  3  5  3      2  1  6  (5)
      2  3  1  2      3  5  3   2
      6  1  2  3      6  5  3  (2)
```

[12] *Larasing Gendhing*:

Pada djaman dahulu kala (kuna) para Radja di Tanah Djawa, apabila mempunjai permohonan kepada *Pangerannya* (GUSTI INGKANG MAHA KAWASA, TUHAN JANG MAHA ESA), ialah sewaktu mengheningkan *tjipta-rasa* (angen-angen/ pantja driya) itu bersamaan dengan bunyinya *gamelan* yang *larasnya* tjotjok dengan kehendak/ keinginannya yang suaranya mengalun sampai mendjadikan tersentuhnya hatinya. Terangnya sebagai dibawah ini.

man" is a person of highly advanced spiritual practice who has realized his essential oneness with the divine being in whose likeness he is made (Hadiwijono 1967, 72). Attaining unity with the divine, the ultimate aim of Sufi mystical practice, is known as *fanâ*, "passing away," or liberation. According to orthodox Sufi practice, *fanâ* is described as follows:

It is moral transformation of the soul through the extinction of all its passions and desires. It is also a mental abstraction or passing away of the mind from all objects of perceptions, thoughts, actions and feelings through its concentration upon the thought of God. Here the thought of God signifies contemplation of the divine

---

1. Mulai duduk itu bersama-sama diperdengarkan bunyinya gamelan dengan *gending "Kinanthi Teplek."*

    Kinanthi = klawan/ sarana

    Teplek = mantap/ duduk tegak

2. Mulai mengheningkan tjipta rasa, diperdengarkan *gendhing "Laras Driya."*

    Laras = djudjur, kumpul

    Nglaras = ngumpulake

    Driya = angen-angen/ pikiran/ kekarepan

3. Apabila *semedinya* sudah memperoleh "sasmita/ ilham," lalu diperdengarkan

    gendhing "Asmara Dana."

    Asmara = samar/ ora kinira-kira

    Dana = anugerah, pemberian oleh Tuhan

4. Apabila semedinya akan selesai, lalu bersamaan dengan *gendhing "Kinanthi Sandung."*

    Kinanthi = klawan/ sarana

    Sandung = kesandung/ kesimpar

Djadi terangnya, kalau orang semedhi/ mengheningkan tjipta-rasa, itu dimulai dengan duduk tegak lurus, kemudian mengumpulkan angen-angennya, disitu lalu tidak terkira-kira memperoleh lamat/wisik/dawuhing Pengeran, utawa tanda akan menerima anugerahnya Tuhan Yang Maha Esa. dengan tidak terkira-kira (samar). Beginilah keterangan bab keadaannya Gamelan dan Gending, yang tjotjok dengan Ilmu Kasampurnan. (Soerachman, ca. 1980)

attributes. And finally it is the cessation of all conscious thoughts. The highest stage of *fanâ* is reached when even the consciousness of having attained *fanâ* disappears. This is what the Sufis call "the passing away of passing away (*fanâ al fanâ*)." (Nicholson 1914, 60)

An integral part of orthodox Sufi mysticism, the doctrine of the "perfect man" is put forward in the writings of the fifteenth-century Sufi mystic from Baghdad, Abd al-Karim al Jili, in a work entitled *al-Insân al-Kâmil fi ma-rifat al-Awākhir wa' l-Awā'il,* "The man perfect in knowledge of the last and first things." A copy of this work in Arabic with an interlinear translation in Javanese has been found in the town of Banten, on the northwest coast of Java. Also, citations from this work abound in the collection of student notebooks (*primbon*) gathered together by the Dutch scholar Snouk Hurgronje (Drewes 1967, 299). The same work is again mentioned in the nineteenth-century text from Surakarta, the *Serat Cenṭini* (Soebardi 1971, 340).

The theological distinction between "union with the deity" and "becoming the deity" is a fine one, fraught with perils in contemporary Islamic societies. To lean toward "becoming the deity" is to flirt with heresy, a state that is increasingly intolerable to orthodox Muslims. In sixteenth-century Java, Islamic teachers were already warning against this heresy (Hadiwijono 1967, 10).[13] The Javanese

---

[13] A good discussion of the problem of possible religious persecution in Java in the sixteenth and seventeenth centuries and its retelling in court literature can be found in Simuh 1988, who is suspicious of the veracity of Javanese tales of killings for heretical beliefs. One relevant passage from his book is quoted here:

> The *Serat Cabolek* [late eighteenth century] portrays the controversy between the understanding of Haji Mutamakin from the village of Cabolek, a follower of the teachings of the belief "God-in-myself" with its claims to become God-like, and Ketib Anom and all the Muslim scholars who reject this doctrine while upholding the purity of Islamic law. The story of this conflict of understanding is inspired by the symbolic story of the death sentences imposed upon Syekh Siti Jenar, Sunan Panggung, Ki Bebeluk, and Syekh Amongraga. All were charged because they were adherents to the doctrine of the unity of mankind and God, and claimed

tendency to merge Tantric philosophy with mystical Islam has resulted in increasing polarization, hostility, and intolerance between followers of reformist Islam and large segments of the Javanese Islamic population in the twentieth century. In earlier centuries, the doctrinal conflicts were between those who were orthodox Sufi mystics versus those who were unorthodox Sufi mystics. Since the nineteenth century and the strengthening influence of a fundamentalist, legalist, scripturalist Islam, the conflict has shifted to a polarity between any kind of mystic, orthodox or not, and those who claim to be the true followers of Islam.

Conversely, a growing number of Javanese who formerly called themselves Islamic, whose beliefs were tolerated within a syncretic interpretation of Islam, now feel alienated. Conversions to Christianity, to modern Hinduism, and to Buddhism are increasing. Mystical groups such as Sumarah, many of which could formerly be subsumed under an inclusive Islam, feel pressured to look for a

---

to be God; Siti Jenar in the era of the kingdom of Giripura, Sunan Panggung in the era of the kingdom of Demak [sixteenth century], Ki Bebeluk in the era of the kingdom of Pajang [sixteenth century], and Amongraga in the era of Sultan Agung [seventeenth century].

Later, under the government of Amangkurat [1645 c.e.] until Paku Buwana [1705 c.e.] (Kartasura until Surakarta), once more there was one who claimed to be God; that was Haji Mutamakin from the village of Cabolek. But after his defeat in the debate with Ketib Anom, Haji Mutamakin realized the error of his religious understanding and eventually received forgiveness and was not sentenced.

The story of the death of Syekh Siti Jenar, Sunan Panggung, Ki Bebeluk and Syekh Amongraga because of their adherence to the belief "God-in-myself" is a work of great beauty / importance (*indah*). But the contents of the story are very odd. It is difficult to understand how within the court circles of Java there were men who were condemned to death by the sword, burned alive and drowned for following the doctrine of the unity of mankind with God. The kings of Pajang and Mataram, along with all the poets and writers were usually also followers of the doctrine of "God-in-myself." The courts of Java were the protectors and promoters of Javanese literatures and Javanese traditions that were usually inspired by the "God-in-myself" doctrine. (Simuh 1988, 27–29. Translated by J. Becker. "God-in-myself" is Simuh's English translation of *kesatuan kawula-Gusti.*)

different designation, sometimes under the rubric of Hinduism or Buddhism, sometimes as spiritual study groups, and sometimes as philosophical study groups (Stange 1980, 47).

The decade of the 1980s has seen yet another shift in the ongoing dialectic between mysticism and orthodox Islam, between acceptable Sufi mysticism and non-acceptable Tantric mysticism, between theism and an immanent divinity, dualism versus monism. Recent writings by Stange (1986) and Woodward (1989) strongly suggest that Islamic modes of discourse, Islamic frames of interpretation, and Islamic terminology are gaining ascendancy over Tantric rhetoric and terminology, even in those *kebatinan* groups that do not consider themselves affiliated with Islam. Particularly, the belief in one transcendent deity seems to have been accepted as the ground upon which all religious formulations are built.

All this is part of the tacit background, the context, the prior texts of Soerachman's *Larasing Gendhing* on the relation between gamelan, *gendhing*, and meditation. One can discern the carefulness with which the author maintains the distinction between himself and the Divine. In the opening paragraph he uses the word *mohon*, "to ask," "to implore," a verb which implies no control over the Divine. In the closing paragraph this idea is emphasized by his saying that one receives divine blessing "without willing it to be so," "beyond imagination" (*tidak terkira-kira*). There is no heresy here. On the other hand, he avoids the term *Allah*, using instead the Javanese honorifics *Pangèran* "prince," *Gusti* "lord," and *Tuhan*, which is often used by Christians to refer to their God.

The phrase in Soerachman's text indicating the kind of concentration that leads to the sound of the gamelan surging "until it touches the heart" can equally be interpreted as referring to the Islamic "refined essence" within the *qolbu*, "heart," or the Tantric *rasa sejati*, within the heart *cakra*. Soerachman's use of the term *semedhi* [*samādhi*], the Old Javanese term for the ultimate meditative state, invokes pre-Islamic Tantrism, as does the practice of meditation while listening to the gamelan.

Gamelan Music as a *Yantra*

Soerachman's description of the spiritual practice involving gamelan music is strongly suggestive of the Tantric practice of the *yantra*. A *yantra* is an external object—a statue, a *maṇḍala*, a *mantra*, a poem, or a piece of music—that the religious practitioner uses for meditation, in which or through which to visualize the deity. Zoetmulder has written of the poem as a *yantra* in Java.

> For it is apparent from a careful study of the *manggala*s [intro-
> ductory stanzas] that we are dealing with a form of religious practice
> and experience in which the striving after union with the deity is
> central. The poet's worship of his *istadewata,* the god [or Buddha]
> of his choice, is an attempt to attain such union and the poem itself
> plays an essential role in this. It is a *yoga* practice, and in order to
> understand it we must have an understanding of the perception of
> the relation between god and man which underlies it. . . .
>
> Although its immanence is all-encompassing, the divine Abso-
> lute may nevertheless choose certain objects for its special mani-
> festation, descending into and inhabiting them in a special way,
> either continuously or for a certain limited time or in certain special
> circumstances. [In Tantrism, it is the practitioner himself, not the
> "divine Absolute," who "chooses."] Such objects may include holy
> formulae or sounds [*mantras*], statues, or men and animals in which
> the god is incarnated. . . . The person engaged in this, the *yogi*,
> knows that the deity resides in the depths of his own being. . . .
> What happens is less a unification than the realization of an existing
> unity. (Zoetmulder 1974, 177–78)

Later on in his discussion of the purpose of a *yantra* for realization of the deity, Zoetmulder says:

> The *yogi* uses palpable media such as hymns of praise (*stuti*),
> flower-offerings (*puṣpāñjali*), mystical positions of the hands
> (*mudra*), sacred syllables and formulas (*mantra*). . . . These are all
> *yantras*, or instruments with which to effect contact with the deity
> as well as receptacles in which the deity may reside. Into these

flowers, *mudras*, holy syllables, formulas and songs, the god is caused to descend. Concentrating the mind on them is a form of preparation for the meditation which concentrates solely upon the god in the heart lotus, in which the *yogi* loses himself completely [*samādhi*]. (Zoetmulder 1974, 184)

The use of music and dance as *yantra*s to aid meditation has a long history in Buddhist practice, although today it is generally associated only with Vajrayāna Buddhism. According to Buddhist scriptures, only the most elegant, high-class music is appropriate for religious practice and the music performed should be a "sonorous icon" for the deity who is to be visualized. Referring to the use of music in Tibetan rituals, Ter Ellingson writes:

In order to produce a more perfect and compelling experience of the nature of the deities, the bases of bodily gestures [*mudras*] and vocalizations [*mantras*] are extended by dance and music to complete the mandalas of form and sound. The music used must be a "sonorous icon,". . .perfectly suited to the nature of the meditated deity. We have seen. . .that the idea that music should reflect the qualities of a Buddha goes back to Hinayana Buddhist thought, and that various symbolic models of musical perfection— the music of celestial and royal palaces, and of first-class urban communities—were considered suitable reflections of the perfection of a Buddha. Although both Mahayana and Mantrayana [Vajrayāna/ Tantrism] include much larger and more varied pantheons of Buddhas and "deities," the same symbolic models apply to the music played for most of them. (Ellingson 1979, 194)

A court gamelan ensemble qualifies as a symbol of Javanese musical perfection, and the pieces mentioned in *Larasing Gendhing* can be imagined as reflecting the qualities of a Buddha. In three of the four *gendhing* listed by Soerachman in *Larasing Gendhing*, the title of the *gendhing* itself suggests its use as an aid to meditation: *Kinanthi Teplek*, "sitting up straight"; *Laras Driya*, "focusing the senses"; and *Asmara Dana*, translated by Soerachman as "gift from the lord" (also possibly translated as "gift of love"). All four pieces mentioned by Soerachman are performed with the full gamelan ensemble, including the most important soft-playing instruments, the *rebab,* the *gendèr,* the *gambang,* and singers. The *gendhing* are played slowly, with no sudden changes, no loud sections, and with quiet, subtle drumming, in a style considered elegant and refined. The musical texture is smooth, homogeneous, and restrained.

The quality considered intrinsic to these pieces, their *rasa,* is further revealed by the theatrical contexts in which they are also performed. For the listener, these contexts provide cumulative memories of the situations in which each piece has been heard. Remembrance binds affect to sound.

In the early 1970s, in the court city Yogyakarta, the "Association for the descendants/ sons and daughters of Hamengku Buwana I" performed a dance-drama (*sendratari*) entitled *Pangèran Mangkubumi Hamengku Buwana I* (Prince Mangkubumi, Hamengku Buwana I). The music was arranged by Ki Wasitadipura.[14]

Pangèran (Prince) Mangkubumi was the first ruler of the kingdom of Yogyakarta after 1755, when the kingdom of Mataram was divided into two parts with two capitals, Yogyakarta and Surakarta. Upon his coronation, Prince Mangkubumi took the name Hamengku Buwana I, a royal line that has been maintained in Yogyakarta until the present day. The staging of a dance-drama by the members of the aristocracy to glorify the history of their own ancestors was as much a political as an artistic event. It can be interpreted as a reaffirmation of the values and beliefs of the "times of the Javanese kings" and the historical continuity of twentieth-century Java with Mataram, the Central Javanese kingdom founded in the sixteenth century.

In the dramatized version of these events, Pangèran Mangkubumi goes to the mountains to the retreat of a holy man for spiritual instruction and meditation before his successful insurrection. This episode, in which the hero retreats to the forest for meditation in

---

[14] My text for this description is a stenciled manuscript entitled "Sendratari *Pangèran Mangkubumi* oleh Sunarjadi; Gendhing-gendhing oleh Ki Wasitadipura, dibantu 1) Ki Soeprapta, 2) Ki Walika." Recorded by R. R. I. Yogyakarta, 1971.

preparation for his encounter with some difficulty, is a standard feature of any shadow theater performance. Javanese literature and histories reiterate the same theme of the hero's retreat to the mountains or forest for the acquisition of spiritual power before a fateful encounter. In this performance, when Prince Mangkubumi goes to the forest hermitage and makes obeisance to its holy occupant, the gamelan plays Ketawang *Laras Driya* while the male chorus sings the following:

> Thus it is that the world-renowned holy man
> resided in his forest retreat.
> Breathtaking, beautiful the view.
> Fragrant the various flower offerings.[15]

The piece, whose title means "to gather the senses" or "to focus the thoughts"—the preparation for the *dhyāna* meditative stage—is, appropriately, the music to accompany a scene at a forest hermitage.

In the theatrical setting given above, the prevailing *rasa* is *shānta rasa*, the *rasa* of tranquility, the favored *rasa* of Tantric Śaivites and Tantric Buddhists and, according to Abhinavagupta, the most important *rasa* for spiritual pursuit (Masson and Patwardhan 1969, 89).

As a *yantra*, the music of the gamelan is transformed into a temple into which the deity may descend. Focused listening, as at a Western concert, is a part of neither the theatrical nor the meditative tradition. In fact, in Javanese mystical practice, and in Tantric teachings, focused listening is believed to be strongly ego-involved. One is enjoined to relax one's perceptions, to be open to a wider, broader set of sensual input. The following is a quote from

---

[15] Ketawang *Laras Driya*
  Nihan padepokanipun
  Kalokeng rat Sang Maha Rsi
  Indah lukitaning puspa
  Sumerbak amantja warni. ("Sendratari *Pangèran Mangkubumi*" 1971, 5)

the teachings of a contemporary Javanese Buddhist who is also a teacher of Sumarah:

> We call the meditation that we do here "relaxed meditation.". . . There are two aspects to this practice. The first is called "daily meditation" and the second is called "special meditation.". . . Daily meditation refers to the way we use our five senses, our thoughts and our desires in daily life. . . . For example, when we use our ears, the basic character of it is reception; just to receive. The terms for this are to "hear" but not to "listen." When you hear my voice, you should receive it in your own place wherever you are. But if you listen and concentrate, it is as if you try to come to where I am in order to receive this explanation. So, when you "hear," it is relaxed, but when you "listen," it is tense.
>
> A second example is the sense of vision. When you "see" something, this is relaxed, but when you "look at" something, this is tense. Actually, our eyes are like the lens of a camera so that when we open our eyes, the scene in front of us just comes in. Later when you are watching a soccer game or a badminton match on the TV and you just watch and "see" it, then you are the viewer and the sports event is what is being viewed. This is relaxed. But, on the other hand, if you concentrate on "looking at" that event, you are no longer a viewer but have become like a participant. . . . When you do that, you have let go of your meditation and are no longer a viewer but have become a participant.
>
> Another example is the sense of smell. When you just "smell" something, this is right and relaxed, but when you "sniff," this is tense.
>
> Now, concerning the sense of touch, when you just receive the sensation that is there, this is relaxed, but when you try to feel something, this is tense.
>
> So the way to use the sense is to just receive what comes in. (Darno Ong as quoted in Howe 1980, 90–91)

The distinction made by Darno Ong between "hearing" versus "listening" is important in defining what *langö/ langen,* or "aesthetic experience," meant in medieval Java and India. What we call "losing oneself in the music" or what we interpret as "aesthetic appreciation" may not be at all what is intended by *langö*, or *rasanā*, or *camatkāra*. For us, "absorption" in a painting, a play, or a piece of music often means a careful focusing on details. When absorbed in a piece of music, we may pay particular attention to the minute aspects of the construction and execution of a phrase. Rather than "the perception of the object itself becomes vague" (Zoetmulder 1974, 172), our perception of the object more likely becomes sharply delineated. We are focused and pointed in our concentration.

Part of the preparation for *dhyāna* and *samādhi* is to restrain sensory input, to quiet the receptors, and to relax the mind. Tantric meditative practices are not for the uninitiated nor for the impatient. Only after prolonged practice does one become proficient enough to attempt *dhyāna*. Entering the stage of meditation called *dhyāna*, before *samādhi*, is to enter a psychological realm that leaves far behind the ordinary mental activity of a serious concert-goer. The following is a description of *dhyāna*—that which precedes *samādhi*—of an Indian Tantric worshipper of "the Goddess."

> The worshipper first salutes his teacher (guru) and then Ganesha [the elephant deity]. Then using his yogic technique and his highly developed powers of imagination and concentration, the Tantric practiser envisages all the ontological realities that go to make up his personality. He then proceeds to envisage within himself the process of cosmic creation (evolution) in reverse order (i.e., cosmic involution). He follows every single step, imagining the dissolution of each element into its preceding cause, until in the end he is ultimately dissolved or immersed in his cosmic source. He then envisages his own resurrection, retracing each step of cosmic creation. Only now, having burned away with cosmic fire and blown away with cosmic air all his human perfections and limitations, he experiences bliss and, permeated with it, remains immersed in the cosmic source. He actually pictures himself as bathed in *amṛta*. He now has a body made of pure substance (*sattvika*) identical with that of the deity's and he is free to invite her to descend into it—to invoke the divine ego to descend on to his ego. (Gupta, Hoens, and Goudriaan 1979, 136)

Serat Cenṭini

In the nineteenth-century court poem, the *Serat Cenṭini*, the method of approaching *dhyāna* and *samādhi* through hearing gamelan music, is explained. Music is to be a vehicle through which one is transported to the mystic union with the deity. The reader is enjoined not to "lose [oneself] in the purely sensual sound of the gendhing," precisely that which we would call the aesthetic experiencing of the music.

> *Serat Cenṭini,* canto 277
> stanza 28:
> Music is in harmony with *niat* (a striving after the sublime) in that, in both cases (i.e., in prayer as well as during the playing of music), the human heart tends toward inner peace and tranquility, which we should strive after with all our energy.
> stanza 29:
> We should, however, not merely lose ourselves in the purely sensual sound of the *gendhing*; its enchantment be only the means to making the heart receptive,
> stanza 30:
> and to cause a great longing for union with *Hyang Widi* "That which is True." In this way, the *gendhing* itself disappears completely, and nothing is left of it.
> stanza 31:
> This is the way one should go. The sound of the gamelan and the voice, let the sound be brought back with the source of sound
> stanza 32:
> to that which gives the sound of the gamelan, that responsible for creation, whatever is sounded return to its ground.
> (Translation based upon Kunst 1973, 1:268–69; and A. L. Becker 1987, xix)[16]

[16] *Serat Cenṭini,* canto 277
stanza 28:
>   tjampoehipoen lawan niat kang moelja noeng anoengge ing kanang kinengan koenenging ati a ingati-ati kelawan niat

In both the stanzas from the *Serat Cenṭini* and in the description of *dhyāna*, a kind of inversion, a returning to origins, to the beginning of things, is a way of understanding and clarifying the mind. "Let the sound be brought back with the source of sound" is a statement about the reversal of time, as in the meditation in which "he follows every single step, imagining the dissolution of each element into its preceding cause, until in the end he is ultimately dissolved or immersed in his cosmic source." "Returning to the source" is not only a Tantric trope but a Sufi one as well. The words of the Qur'an are to be imagined as they were heard for the first time, and the listener is to be projected back in time to the state of the Prophet who heard the verses from the angel Gabriel.

> I did not cease to repeat this verse until I could hear it from that same Angel who pronounced it for the Prophet. (Crow 1984, 31)

The kind of listening proposed in Soerachman's short set of instructions and in the nineteenth-century *Serat Cenṭini* differs profoundly from the ways in which Westerners normally listen to music. John Pemberton (1987) contrasts the responses of Javanese audiences to the popular genre *dangdut*, or to forms of village gamelan, with the responses of the audience to the court-style

---

stanza 29:
  ajwa koroep mring genḍing soeroepanipoen soerasaning raras kinarja pangresing kapti kang minangka pangatere tyas ing gagas
stanza 30:
  nganjoet-ngajoet paloete joening kalboe kasaban soebrangta nira marang ing Hjang Widi dadya genḍing kenḍang datan koemalenḍang
stanza 31:
  kang kadyekoe ḍi ragil pamoentoenipoen swaraning gamelan genḍing genḍeng swaraneki ingoelihken swara mring kang doewe swara
stanza 32:
  mring kang asoeng swara oenining paroenggoe gangsa kang rinengga sor-sore titahing oeni ing sa-oeni-oenining babagan lemah (Soeradipoera et. al., 1912–15, 8:205)

For a translation and discussion of earlier stanzas in the *Serat Cenṭini* that also concern music, see A. L. Becker 1987.

gamelan performances heard at official functions such as weddings. The author makes the point that listeners become irresistably, even kinetically involved in the popular and village music and largely ignore the court-style performances at official functions. Reception music, court-style music, is "not listened to" except by the musicians themselves.

As a descendant of Tantric ritual music, and of music for meditation, the refined style of gamelan music is not intended for "listening," only for "hearing." Traditionally, the music was not an end in itself but a means to an end considered to be greater than itself. If, today, the habit of "not listening" remains while the spiritual practice that fostered "not listening" has largely disappeared, the refined, court-style gamelan music finds itself in a cultural vacuum. Both Sastrapustaka's and Soerachman's texts are attempts to reclaim the spiritual priorities of gamelan music and to reinstate the old associations between court gamelan music and spiritual development, to refine one's understanding of the processes of consciousness.

Javanese and medieval Indian aesthetic theories as described above are part of the tacit knowledge, the realm of prior texts of "Knowledge of Gamelan Revealed," *Larasing Gendhing*, and *Serat Centini*. All three assert the possibility of an experience of gamelan music which goes beyond pleasure, beyond the normal experiential states of normal existence. They define for gamelan music an extraordinary interiority, an utterly private and personal relationship between music and hearer, a way of coming to understand what are believed to be the most subtle aspects of the human condition; the activation of *rasa sejati* is, ultimately, a way of approaching the state of enlightenment. The claim is extraordinary and, at the same time, precise. The smooth, soft, so-called refined style of the Central Javanese court ensembles is being redefined as "art," as "classic," to reestablish its legitimacy in an increasingly Islamic Java (J. Becker 1994). The old connections to Tantrism, to *rasa* theory, and to Sufi Islam and the spiritual power that accrued from those connections are fast receding into history.

Gamelan Musicians
(Photographs by Danielle Diffloth)

Gamelan Gong Player
(Photograph by Danielle Diffloth)

Gamelan Musician
(Photograph by Danielle Diffloth)

Gamelan Singers (in foreground)
(Photograph by Danielle Diffloth)

References Cited

Becker, A. L.
1987 "An Essay on Translating the Art of Music." In *Karawitan: Source Readings in Javanese Gamelan and Vocal Music*, ed. Judith Becker and Alan H. Feinstein, 2:ix–xx.

Becker, Judith
1993 *Gamelan Stories: Tantrism, Islam, and Aesthetics in Central Java*. [Tempe, Ariz.]: Program for Southeast Asian Studies, Arizona State University Press.
1994 "'Aesthetics' and the 'Artist': Universalism and the Court Arts of Central Java, 14th–20th centuries A.D." In *Europe and the Orient*, ed. Drew Gerstle and Anthony Milner. Canberra: Humanities Research Centre, Australian National University.

Becker, Judith and Alan H. Feinstein, eds.
1984–88 *Karawitan: Source Readings in Javanese Gamelan and Vocal Music*. 3 vols. Ann Arbor: Center for South and Southeast Asian Studies, University of Michigan.

Beyer, Stephan
1978 *The Cult of Tara: Magic and Ritual in Tibet*. Berkeley: University of California Press.

Crow, Douglas Karim
1984 "*Sama'*: The Art of Listening in Islam." In *Maqam: Music of the Islamic World and Its Influences*, ed. Robert H. Browning. The Alternative Museum.

Drewes, G. W. J.
1967 "Indonesia: Mysticism and Activism." In *Unity and Variety in Muslim Civilization*, ed. G. E. von Grunebaum, pp. 284–310. Chicago: University of Chicago Press.

Ellingson, Ter
1979 "The Mandala of Sound: Concepts and Sound Structures in Tibetan Ritual Music." Ph.D. diss., University of Wisconsin, Madison.

Gnoli, Raniero, ed.
1968 *The Aesthetic Experience According to Abhinava Gupta*. 2nd ed., rev., enl. Varanasi: Chowkhamba Sanskrit Series Office.

Guenther, Herbert V.
1976 *The Tantric View of Life*. Boulder and London: Shambhala.

Gupta, Sanjukla, Dirk Jan Hoens, and Teun Goudriaan
1979 "Modes of Worship and Meditation." In *Hindu Tantrism,* by S. Gupta, D. J. Hoens, and T. Goudriaan. Leiden, Köln: E. J. Brill.

Hadiwijono, Harun
1967 *Man in the Present Javanese Mysticism.* Baarn: Bosch and Keuning N. V.

Hooykaas, C.
1958 *The Old-Javanese Rāmāyaṇa: An Exemplary Kakawin as to Form and Content.* Verhandelingen der Koninklijke Nederlandse Akademie van Wetenschappen, n.s. 65(1).

Howe, David Gordon
1980 *Sumarah: A Study of the Art of Living.* Ann Arbor: University Microfilms International.

Hunter, Thomas, trans.
1989 "Aji Ghurnita." Museum Bali, No. IIIc.2390. Den Pasar. Bali, Indonesia. Unpublished.

Kartomi, Margaret J.
1981 "'Lovely When Heard from Afar': Mandailing Ideas of Musical Beauty." In *Five Essays on the Indonesian Arts,* ed. Margaret J. Kartomi, pp. 1–16. [Melbourne]: Monash University.

Kunst, Jaap
1973 *Music in Java.* 2 vols. The Hague: Martinus Nijhoff.

Masson, J. L., and M. V. Patwardhan
1969 *Śāntarasa and Abhinavagupta's Philosophy of Aesthetics.* Poona: Bhandarkar Oriental Research Institute.
1977 "The Dhvanyāloka and the Dhvanyālokalocana: A Translation of the Fourth Uddyota," pts. 1–2. *Journal of the American Oriental Society* 97(3):285–304; (4):423–40.

Muller-Ortega, Paul Eduardo
1989 *The Triadic Heart of Śiva: Kaula Tantricism of Abhinavagupta in the Non-Dual Shaivism of Kashmir.* Albany: State University of New York Press.

Nicholson, Reynold Alleyne
1914 *The Mystics of Islam.* London: G. Bell & Sons, Ltd.

Pemberton, John
1987 "Musical Politics in Central Java (Or How Not to Listen to a Javanese Gamelan)." *Indonesia* 44:17–29.

Pigeaud, T. G. Th.
1967–70 *Literature of Java.* 3 vols. The Hague: Martinus Nijhoff.
Robson, S. O.
1979 "Notes on the Early Kidung Literature." *Bijdragen tot de Taal-, Land- en Volkenkunde van het Koninklijkinstituut voor Taal-, Land- en Volkenkunde* 135:300–322.
Sastrapustaka, B. Y. H.
1953–78 "Wèdha Pradangga Kawedhar" (Knowledge of Gamelan Revealed). Yogyakarta. Unpublished manuscript.
1984 "Wèdha Pradangga Kawedhar" (Knowledge of Gamelan Revealed). Trans. R. Anderson Sutton. In *Karawitan: Source Readings in Javanese Gamelan and Vocal Music*, ed. Judith Becker and Alan H. Feinstein, 1:305–33.
1986 "Wèdha Pradangga Kawedhar." Yogyakarta. Revised unpublished manuscript.
Sears, Laurie Jo
1986 "Text and Performance in Javanese Shadow Theatre: Changing Authorities in an Oral Tradition." Ph.D. diss., University of Wisconsin, Madison.
Simuh
1988 *Mistik Islam Kedawen.* Jakarta: Penerbit Universitas Indonesia.
Soebardi
1971 "Santri-Religious Elements as Reflected in The Book of Tjentini." *Bijdragen tot de Taal-, Land- en Volkenkunde van het Koninklijkinstituut voor Taal-, Land- en Volkenkunde* 127(3):331–49.
Soerdipoera, R. Ng., R. Poerwasoewigna, and R. Wirawangsa, eds.
1912–15 *Serat Tjenṭini: Babon Asli Saking Kiṭa Leiden ing Negari Nederland.* 8 vols. Batavia: Ruygrof.
Sparshott, Francis
1983 "Prospects for Aesthetics." *The World of Music* 25(3):3–12.
Stange, Paul
1980 *The Sumarah Movement in Javanese Mysticism.* Ann Arbor: University Microfilms.
1984 "The Logic of Rasa in Java." *Indonesia* 38:113–34.
1986 " 'Legitimate' Mysticism in Indonesia." *Review of Indonesian and Malaysian Affairs* 20(2):76–117.

Stcherbatsky, Th.

1974   *The Central Conception of Buddhism and the Meaning of the Word "Dharma."* Delhi: Motilal Banarsidass.

Sutton, R. Anderson, trans.

1984   "Wedha Pradangga Kawedhar" (Knowledge of Gamelan Revealed). In *Karawitan: Source Readings in Javanese Gamelan and Vocal Music,* ed. Judith Becker and Alan H. Feinstein, 1:305–33.

Woodward, Mark R.

1989   *Islam in Java: Normative Piety and Mysticism in the Sultanate of Yogyakarta.* Tucson: The University of Arizona Press.

Zoetmulder, P. J.

1974   *Kalangwan: A Survey of Old Javanese Literature.* The Hague: Martinus Nijhoff.

World Musics and World Religions: *Whose World?*

Philip V. Bohlman

Introduction:
Sufis and That Global Old-Time Religion

In May 1993, Berlin's "Haus der Kulturen der Welt," the House of the World's Cultures, featured among its other concerts staging world music a series called "the Music of the Sufis." Centrally located in Berlin, the House of the World's Cultures took special pains to display its concerts of Sufi music as an emblem of openness to Islam and Islamic culture, thereby publicly repairing the damage caused by recent fire-bombings and attacks on Germany's Turkish population, some of which had led to death. In the pamphlet describing the "Music of the Sufis" and the ensemble of Sufi musicians, called "Sheikh Hamza Chakour and Al Kindi," the concert-goer is promised an encounter with a truly world music anchored in a truly world religion ("Musik der Sufis" 1993, 14–15):

> Sheikh Hamza Chakour and Al Kindi are experts of classical Arabic and Andalusian-Moorish music. Sheikh Hamza Chakour, head of the whirling dervishes of Damascus, sings the sacred and secular repertory with centuries-old tradition. Abdelsalam Safar is well-known as the most venerated among all Syrian players of the end-blown flute, the nay. Adel Shams Eddin, an Egyptian playing the tambourine-like instrument, the riqq, is the last specialist of

classical rhythms utilizing long, asymmetrical intervals. The Frenchman, Julien Jalal Eddin Weiss, already studied the music of Morocco as a young boy; he plays the qanun, the Arabic zither, with virtuosity. After they played a concert in Switzerland, the newspaper, *Berner Woche*, passed this judgment on the ensemble: "Their songs and instrumental pieces unite tremendous inner peace with the sensibility of a reserved beauty."

Sufi music had come of age in Berlin, come of age as a music mixing bits of Syria, Egypt, Morocco, and France, all in the future German capital city, itself containing the largest Turkish and Muslim population in Central Europe. But whose music was this? Was it the music of the residents of Berlin's Kreuzberg district, home to the Berlin Muslim community? The Turkish *Gastarbeiter* who were increasingly the objects of attacks from the German Right? Quite the contrary, ownership was marked by the construction of the title for these concerts: "Musik der Sufis," "Music of the Sufis." Ownership belonged to the Sufis, and it resided in the great age of the instruments and traditions of this international ensemble of musicians. Authority emerged from the great age of Sufism and its musical traditions, as well as from its capacity to transcend the boundaries of time and region. The structures of Sufi music itself— its "long, asymmetrical intervals"—enhanced the transcendent potential of Sheikh Hamza Chakour and Al Kindi, allowing the ensemble to mix and remix the instrumentarium of North African and Middle Eastern traditions. Classical Arabic music becomes spiritual Islamic music, universalized for international audiences in the waning years of the twentieth century.

In any musical or sacred sense, however, the "Music of the Sufis" is an invention, a mixture of sound and spirituality marketed for mass consumption. One might even argue that "the Sufis"—the definite article standing as an icon of community—are also an invention, albeit a much older invention, well canonized in the West, at least for the Germans, by the time of Goethe's *West-östlicher Divan* ([1819] 1988). Sufism, as a category in and of itself, stripped of local practice and the meanings conveyed through the individualized genealogies descended from specific sheikhs, has taken a place in the global imagination as a world religion.[1] As a religion effaced of local meaning, Sufism has been forced to represent a postmodern otherness, whose differences perforce disappear as those who gaze upon it draw it closer to the West in ways artfully executed by Goethe and the House of the World's Cultures.[2] In the past decade, Sufi music has been marketed globally on records, video-cassettes, and CDs, and tours by Sufi musicians regularly sell out concert halls throughout the world; the stars and superstars of Sufi music—for example, Nusrat Fateh Ali Khan—find themselves equally at home in the popular-music recording studio as on the stages of the South Asian Diaspora (see Ruby 1992).[3]

[1] By and large, the history and polity of Sufism are local, with patterns of worship and ritual determined through genealogies that extend from the influence of specific saints. Local musical practices often provide ways of maintaining the genealogy through performance, again with emphasis on individualized means and texts that encode and transmit specific versions of Islamic thought. Shrines in and around Delhi devoted to the Sufi saint and musical innovator, Amir Khusrau (1253–1325 c.e.), sustain musical and religious practices that connect the larger aesthetic of Hindustani music to the meanings of *qawwālī* about the life and family of Nizamuddin Auliya, the spiritual figurehead for these shrines (cf. Neuman 1990, 85–90 and Qureshi 1995, 20–23).

[2] Sufism is by no means the only case of an invented world religion with its own world music. Studies of African religion in Brazil and elsewhere in the African Diaspora, for example, rely not only on the notion that the Yoruba are a single culture and society, but that there is a set of religious practices recognizable as "Yoruba religion." Yoruba musical elements, furthermore, provide ways of documenting the connections between Nigeria and Afro-Brazilian cults. The Yoruba as a single society, nevertheless, is largely an invention of nineteenth-century colonialism and the consolidation of political power in Nigeria so that it would be held primarily by larger groups, rather than by hundreds of small groups (see Apter 1992). A "Yoruba music," such as *jùjú*, is itself a historical consolidation of many different repertories and styles that have developed through the extensive processes of exchange throughout the diasporic cultural area of the Atlantic (cf. Waterman 1990 and Gilroy 1993).

[3] Record stores often provide a field for examining the ethnography of world musics (see Nettl 1985, 61–64). At the main Rose Records shop in downtown Chicago, Nusrat Fateh Ali Khan's recordings immediately precede those of Frankie Yankovich, the Slovenian-American superstar of polka, the result of the alphabetical relation between the bins, "Pakistan" and "Polka."

During the twentieth century Sufi music has become fully
transformed into a sound-mix of world musics and world religions
(for the classic study of *qawwālī*, see Qureshi 1995). The earliest
recordings of musics from the Middle East and South Asia established a position for Sufism as a "devotional" music with markets
that were both local and international. Already in 1902, the
Gramophone Company included a significant representation of
*qawwāl*s (singers of *qawwālī*) in its first attempts to record Indian
music for the West (Qureshi 1992/1993,112; and Joshi 1977).
During the early decades of recording in South Asia, international
recording companies deliberately identified religious communities
as a potential market and created for these consumers of devotional
music an appropriate style and repertory. For the diverse Muslim
communities of South Asia, the Sufi genre, *qawwālī*, fitted the
purposes of the recording industry perfectly, and by the 1930s it
dominated the Muslim market (Qureshi 1992/1993,113). *Qawwālī*
was an egalitarian music, and its use of Urdu, a language understood
throughout Muslim South Asia, assured that it had the broadest
possible popular audience. When *qawwālī* recordings boomed in the
1930s, texts in a more or less vernacular Urdu far outweighed those
in Persian or literary Urdu (Qureshi 1992/1993,114; and Joshi 1988),
and the subject matter of most texts was such that it included rather
than excluded different sects. The popularization of musics connected to Sufi shrines in India and Pakistan during the twentieth
century, therefore, follows a trajectory created in large part by the
recording industry. Popularity itself had a distinctly global character,
thus making it possible for *qawwālī* musicians such as Nusrat Fateh
Ali Khan to establish their fame outside of South Asia rather than
because of their association with a local shrine, the traditional path
toward musical specialization.[4]

[4] The biographer of Nusrat Fateh Ali Khan bemoans the "sad saga" that the
popular *qawwālī* singer "has the singular distinction of getting recognition
overseas earlier than at home" (Ruby 1992, 10), but then claims that his artistry
results from "a quaint synthesis: Nusrat Fateh is the topical symbol of this
exquisite East-West synthesis and the growth of individual talent from an inherent
classicist to a 'mod-vocalist' of the orient, gaining growing appeal even to the
continental, Japanese and trans-Atlantic folklore and country-music" (ibid., 9–10).

Other world-beat Sufi musics have different histories, which demonstrate distinctive processes of mediation within international recording projects. The music of Mevlevi Sufis in Turkey, for example, already assumed forms subjected to the Western gaze through early Orientalist publications, which depicted "whirling dervishes," a form of representation taken up by recording companies in the twentieth century (e.g., d'Ohsson 1788). It was hardly surprising that the two-record set designed to accompany the 1987 traveling exhibit, "The Age of Sultan Süleyman the Magnificent," should have borne the title, *The Music of the Whirling Dervishes.* According to the author of the liner notes, this recording contained music inspired by the poems of "Rumi, the towering figure of Sufism (Islamic mysticism) in the 13th Century," and that the performances were based on "the rituals of Rumi's followers (known in the Western world as 'The Whirling Dervishes'), [which] are among the enduring as well as the most exquisite ceremonies of spirituality" (*The Music of the Whirling Dervishes*). The popularity of Sufi musics from the Middle East has assumed diverse forms. Whereas "dervish recordings" may attract non-Muslim consumption in the West, the Syrian Abed Azrié has released recordings aimed largely at Muslim audiences in Paris (see, e.g., *Les Soufis*). Azrié's style owes no particular debt to the sounds or practices of *dhikr*, the ceremony of remembrance, but takes on a wide variety of New Age sonorities and textures, over which he sings the traditional poems of medieval poets. Marketed primarily in France, *Les Soufis* represents a repertory for France's large North African and Middle Eastern population.

Although all these musics claim explicit connections to Sufi music, their sounds are vastly different. How might we describe Sufi music after listening to the countless recordings produced during the past century? Are there elements of musical style or traces of music history that these examples share? Are the religious practices they accompanied the same? Or, indeed, is it the singular level at which they demonstrate a form of unity—that of the markets for which they were produced—that leads to claims that they are world music representing a world religion?

The questions I pose here contain numerous paradoxes, as does the interrogative subtitle of this article. On the one hand, the invention of a "music of the Sufis" offers a particularly striking example of such paradoxes, and I have chosen to introduce the issues lying at the center of this article with the troubling paradoxes of invention in mind. Still, I might have taken other examples, and, during the course of the article, it will become clear that we are not wanting for musics and religions that have invented themselves into the global imagination; the invention of world musics and world religions have, in many ways, become normative in the late twentieth century. On the other hand, the "music of the Sufis" is also a complex instantiation of the problem I wish to investigate here. It is not quite so easy to unravel this problem as my opening critique of the concerts at the Berlin House of the World's Cultures might have suggested. Indeed, the tour of the Sufi musical soundscape is not only made possible by the ready availability of sound recordings on the contemporary marketplace, but it also appears in the intellectual cartography of standard ethnomusicological discourse. The long intellectual history of weaving the representational fabrics with which the West has used Sufism to clothe the Other, moreover, is by no means unrelated to contemporary representational practices; nor is it conveniently packaged as merely or fundamentally postmodern. Sufism has provided us with one of the most privileged of all Orientalist tropes. It has also become one of the primary ways in which regional and national intellectual traditions in the Middle East and South Asia represent themselves, for example, in song anthologies published by the Turkish government or the center of traditional Islam at the Seljuk University in Konya, Turkey (e.g., Türkmen n.d.; and Halıcı 1983). Scholarly recordings, too, have included Sufi musics among their musical offerings, thereby also contributing to the authentication of the category as a world music (see, e.g., *Qawwali: Sufi Music from Pakistan*, which established the Sabri Brothers as an ensemble well worth studying). Given the problematic position of music in Islamic thought, Sufism has even become a unique *Ersatz* for music in Islam, a way of comforting Orientalist anxiety.

Sufis, after all, have no country, no single country—nor do they inhabit single geographic regions—and yet they are presumed to exist throughout the Islamic world. Their presence is timeless, and their music exists in a timeless present. World-music slogans have also recontextualized Sufi music, claiming it to be "spiritual," not religious, music.[5] Stated somewhat differently, Sufi music represents spirituality, not religion, whereby it can enter a realm cohabited by other world musics, for example the New Age sound of Native American flute that surrounds one in the growing number of shops that sell Native American art.[6] Its spirituality is presumably accessible to many, if not all, which means, by extension, that one needs neither to be Muslim nor to engage in Sufi ritual practice to penetrate the spirituality Sufi music conveys.[7] As recording companies repackage Sufi music as world music, they often undertake a gradual desacralization of the music as a prelude to spiritualizing it for more general consumption. We witness this rhetorical shift in an advertising blurb for the first of two CDs of *qawwālī* released by JVC in its "World Sounds Series." Even the way in which God is named—essential to the process of remembering and efficacy in musical practices used by many Sufi rituals, for example, *zhikr*—passes from a specifically Muslim ("Allah") to a generalized ("the Lord") and then finally to a generic level ("god"), all in the space of two sentences.

Qawwali is one form of traditional Islamic music, by which Sufi mystics sought to draw closer to Allah. Through these ballads, interpreted here by the legendary Nusrat Fateh Ali Khan, melodies

[5] Mickey Hart, in a chapter devoted to Egypt and the drumming tradition of the *tar*, a frame drum, compares the response of an Upper Egyptian *tar* maker to Hart's own instrument, which was, not surprisingly, "finely crafted by a Sufi in Northern California" (Hart 1990, 192).

[6] Native American art has itself come to replace Indian crafts.

[7] Inscribed on the cover of a CD of *qawwālī* performed by Jaffar Hussain Khan (World Music Library KICC 5115) is the following invitation to "popular Islam:" "This disc is a recording of the Qawwali, a religeous [sic] song of the south Asian followers of Islam, as sung by Jaffar Hussain. His songs, supported by classical vocal techniques, draw the listener into religeous [sic] intoxication."

and rhythms combine to transmit the Lord's message and to assist
listeners in their attempts to reach a higher plane of unity with their
god (Nusrat Fateh Ali Khan 1994).

The world-music production of *qawwālī* at once depends on the aura
of spirituality surrounding Sufism and on the possibility that music
can specify meanings that consumers in a world market can
recognize as their own. As if the chain of signification, Allah–the
Lord–god, in the adverstisement above were not fully capable of
achieving this, its authors insert a musical, even ethnomusicological,
signifier at a strategic moment, identifying *qawwālī* as "ballads,"
thereby evoking familiarity, although *qawwālī* could not possibly
be classified as ballads. This strategy of mediation, however, is not
about classification but, rather, about ownership of musical and
religious practice, and ownership has passed to the consumer of the
music with the transformation of religious music to spiritual music.

Interactions and Intersections of Religious and Musical Practices: Cultural Spaces In-Between

In this essay I concern myself extensively with questions of
ownership and with the ways in which music and religion provide
domains in which ownership is contested. The essay is not, however,
an attempt to catalogue the ways in which world musics have
participated in the disenfranchisement of everyday religious belief
and practice through the commodification of a global music
economy. The opening section presents one example, and I prefer
to let this stand as Exhibit A. Rather than observing the globalization
of musical and religious practice with despair, I want instead to look
at the other side of the problem: the ways in which musical and
religious practices actually repair the disenfranchisement and resist
the crush of colonialism and global cultural economies. Accordingly,
I prefer to invite the reader to think of "world musics" and "world
religions" not so much as institutionalized structures of power—as
hegemonic forces, that is—but rather as local practices and belief

systems, dependent on each other for responses to the politics of globalism.

Whereas considerable recent research in cultural studies theorizes local culture through its ultimate connections to global forces, I contend here that musical and religious practice cannot be reduced simply to evidence for processes occurring at great distance from the rituals and everyday conditions that instantiate religion and music. In this sense, music and religion both depend on performance and the agents that bring it about. Considered at the moment of its most sacred, religion is not just belief, nor does it allow itself to be defined as taxonomic categories in a belief system. Local religious meaning emerges only through active participation and the experience upon which practice depends. Through ritual and the performance of liturgical texts, music broadens the possibilities for participation and experience. Music enhances the everyday aspects of religious practice, thereby localizing it. Music, as I consider it here, does not exhibit a global ontology, but is in fact at its farthest remove from the universal. Through its local instantiations, the music of religion is not "Buddhist music" or "Sufi music," but rather the composite of musical choices used to guide worship during a specific ritual at a specific shrine. Music combines with religious practice to look inward in order to specify meaning rather than outward to determine its connections to globalized constructs of meaning.[8]

I am not only encouraging a shift of attention from the global to the local, even the subaltern, level but a rethinking of the conditions of world musics that further resituate them into a much longer and more complex history. This shift in my thinking, quite frankly, is a

[8] Ethnomusicology has recently embraced many of the cultural-studies theories that explain the local in relation to the globalization of world culture. In particular, Mark Slobin has theorized world music, especially in Europe and North America, as occupying various soundscapes that connect the local to the global (see Slobin 1993 for the most developed statement of this theory). Whereas these approaches create a framework that accounts for as many musics as possible, they extend with difficulty to sacred musical practices, which do not lend themselves to the objective and bounded nature embedded in the term "musics" or "micromusics."

move away from invoking the "conditions of postmodernism" as explanations of the fissures and schisms in world cultures, as well as world music cultures. These conditions, too, collapse world musics and world religions to symptoms of a timeless present.[9] I argue instead that the responses of musical and religious practice are in themselves actively resisting this presumed timelessness of a postmodern age.

World musics and world religions come into contact and interact in contested moments and places (cf. Bhabha 1994). We witness their interaction, for example, in the contact of colonialism. We witness their interaction in the regions of juncture and disjuncture between world religions, for example, the centuries-long confrontation between Islam and Hinduism in northern India.[10] We witness their interaction in situations of domination and subjugation—apartheid in South Africa or the forced internment of Native Americans on reservations throughout much of American history. Historical moments of political instability, too, bring world musics and world religions into contact. The turbulence in the Balkans and the Israeli-Palestinian conflict are but two obvious examples. Subaltern resistance and ethnic revival, too, juxtapose musical and religious practices to voice and mobilize their responses to political

---

[9] The explosion of Gregorian chant's popularity that began in 1993, symbolized by the dramatic leap of Gregorian chant to the popular and world-music charts, exemplifies the ways in which the present becomes a timeless site for world music. Recordings such as the Angel release of performances by the Benedictine monks of Santo Domingo de Silos in Spain take local practices and package them for global consumption. The "chant experience," however, cannot simply be dismissed as devoid of sacred qualities. Katherine Bergeron brilliantly describes the timelessness of chant recordings as a sort of "virtual sacred," observing further that chant comes to occupy a "queer space of suspended faith, . . .an oddly comforting interval in which, neither believing nor disbelieving, we recognize the very experience we never expected to find as something already potentially lost" (Bergeron 1995, 34).

[10] The mass production of recordings of Muslim devotional music in the early twentieth century depended on and benefited from this conflict (Qureshi 1992/ 1993).

globalism, which they nevertheless do not consider to be ineluctable conditions of modernity or postmodernity.

These areas of contestation and interaction are unstable; indeed, they are defined by their instability. The religious and musical practices that constitute them—that further define them—are also unstable, or, I might say, changing and dynamic. Accordingly, it becomes necessary to examine the processes of musical change that participate in the religious transformations of such areas. In this essay I reflect upon three larger processes: resistance, historicization, and pilgrimage. By no means do these constitute the only religious-musical responses to historical and modern political globalism. I have chosen them to represent these responses, nonetheless, because they are themselves global, which is to say that, even though each must be examined locally, none is dependent solely on local conditions. I should add, furthermore, that I have myself researched aspects of these processes to varying degrees, which permits me also to interrogate them empirically. It is my concern, then, not to relegate these responses to the realm of high theory or to position them on globalist culture-scapes (e.g., Appadurai 1990; and Slobin 1993), but rather to identify areas of research that compel ethnomusicologists and historians of religions together to enter the field, the contested regions in which music and religion interact.

Process I:
Resistance in the Colonial and Missionary Encounter

Missionary hymnody provides one of the most powerful records of resistance to the colonial experience. This claim may, at first glance, astonish, not least because it contradicts many historiographies of the colonial experience, which identify missionaries as the agents of the political and economic concerns that power the engines of colonialism (cf. Comaroff and Comaroff 1991). It follows, then, that missionary hymnody itself subjugates; it disciplines and controls;

it is a text inscribing the act of colonialism itself. As a documentation of world religion, missionary hymnody would accordingly insinuate Christianity in the religious practices of a colonized people, thereby erasing their own.

This usual historiography of missionary hymnody—I hesitate to use "common," for missionary hymnody has been virtually neglected by scholars—this usual historiography makes several sweeping assumptions about world music and world religion, which I believe need to be rethought and redressed. First of all, in this historiography both religion and music assume the forms of systems, which compete for adherents and must supplant other religions and musics or be supplanted totally in any given society. Christianity, therefore, "takes over" indigenous religions, and the repertories of Jesuit ritual or Methodist hymnody become the sole occupants of the cultural space relegated to religious expression. The hymnbook, then, symbolizes the religious system: a bounded repertory of systemically prescribed practices (cf. Rhodes 1960).

Hymnody, however, is not just an object or bounded repertory. Quite the contrary, it serves as the basis for musical practices that express individual and community differences. In the moment of performance, hymns pass from the ownership of a colonial religious institution into the local religious practices (Draper 1982). Ownership has passed from the colonizer to the colonized, who transform music into a means of responding to domination. It is precisely for these reasons that missionary hymnody becomes one of the most important sites for resistance in the contested domains of colonialism. Hymns afford what James Scott has called "hidden transcripts," an "art of" and an "art for" resistance (Scott 1990). These hidden transcripts of resistance, according to Scott, function because the dominant and the dominated perceive their meanings in radically different ways. Music has a particularly powerful capacity to embody radically different meanings because of its complex forms of signification. In her study of the musics created by the Jesuits to convert indigenous Araucanian peoples of the southern Andes (present-day Chile) during the seventeenth and eighteenth centuries, Beth Keating Aracena has demonstrated that the Araucanians took the rather contained and bounded texts of a few lines provided by the Jesuits and transformed them through performance into hours of ritual. The Jesuit missionaries understood "music" as the text of conversion, whereas the Araucanians borrowed new musical materials, introducing and translating them into their own religious practices (Aracena forthcoming).

The colonial encounter in South Africa provides even more dramatic cases in which the music of missionaries became hidden transcripts for resistance. "Nkosi sikelel'i Afrika," the anthem of the African National Congress, and, before that, the anthem of most black political parties, was composed by Enoch Sontonga as a missionary hymn at the end of the nineteenth century (Rhodes 1962, 16–17). It is found in the hymnbooks of many Protestant churches in South Africa, where it seems innocuously to reproduce the themes common to the Christian experience, albeit in an African context.

> God Bless Africa!
> Let thy name be praised;
> Let our prayers be heard!
> God bless us; thou only art to be respected.
> Come Spirit! Come Spirit! Come, Holy Spirit!
> God bless us, thou only art to be respected.

One does not have to undertake exegesis too imaginatively to recognize the themes of authority that shoot through this verse of "Nkosi sikelel'i Afrika." The hymn moves resistance to the highest level, and it conflates the symbols of the coming of the Holy Spirit with that of the return of the land to black South Africans. The hidden transcripts of black resistance, moreover, overlapped with the liturgy and worship of the church service and were constantly instantiated in the structures of black political organizations (see Blacking 1981). That the structures of the hymns themselves came powerfully to provide paths and models of resistance against apartheid is, in fact, strikingly evident when we listen to the musics of black South Africans today. John Blacking has further observed that distinctions between stanzaic hymns and the singing of Psalms in black South African churches provided specifically musical

processes for distinguishing the layers of Christian meaning in the
political activities of many churches. Psalmody provided a template
of fundamental texts, which, nonetheless, opened new textual spaces
through performance that allowed for the embellishment of sacred
meaning, specifically the translation of religious symbols into
political meanings (Blacking 1995, 205–6). The ritual and social
organization of the black South African church, therefore, became
a site for political agency that the multivocal musical repertories
of the church had the power to mobilize.

Thus far, I have concentrated on the ways musical texts provided
the hidden transcripts for resistance to domination; it is no less
essential to consider the ways in which musical contexts serve as
sites of resistance. Such contexts assume various forms. The
performative nature of ritual, for example, frequently turns it into
a site for resistance, publicly performed, yet hidden because of the
ways conflicting meanings are juxtaposed. The confrontation of
religious practices in the Andes provides an outstanding example
of the ways in which ritual practice has historically provided a
context for political and social resistance. Within Peruvian ritual,
taking place, for example, on saints' days, musicians and dancers
enact the ways in which Indians and mestizos have confronted the
dominant, urban economy of Peru, the ways in which folklore is
invented as a way of resisting modernity, and the ways in which
religion itself becomes, to borrow Zoila Mendoza-Walker's concept,
a way of "shaping society" (1993). Ritual, therefore, combines the
political and the sacred through music and dance, not simply
juxtaposing them, but rather fusing them into a form of local and
ongoing resistance.[11] The history and politics of Peru, troubled and
unsettled for centuries, necessitated this ongoing resistance, and
ritual, as a context for hidden transcripts, became the performative
site for its maintenance.

Resistance to the situation of dominance refuses to disintegrate
because ritual creates a cultural space for it, and Peruvian mestizos

---

[11] The premodern basis for musical practices that negotiate "between worlds"
is the subject of Giese 1994.

perform that space through dance and music. This contextualization of resistance exists also in North America, where it derives from the contested space between Native Americans and the governmental and economic forces that dominate their society (Cornelius and O'Grady 1987). This is the space that the peyote songs and the Ghost Dance movement of the late nineteenth century articulated. Native North Americans, too, have transformed the texts of Protestant hymns, making them the locus for indigenous languages, despite the repeated attempts of church and political authorities to eliminate, say, the Oneida language from all churches in Oneida communities in the Upper Midwest (O'Grady 1991). Ann Morrison's examination of the history of Wabanaki musical practices, moreover, suggests that Catholic liturgies also resisted white domination, even as they became a ritual context that maintained Wabanaki identities in the face of Protestant missionizing (Morrison forthcoming). Again we ask the questions, why hymns and why music? Why, in fact, do Native Americans seem so voraciously to borrow from white musics in general, only to indigenize hymn repertories and country-western songs alike? This music, reconfigured as the texts and contexts of resistance, represents a different history, not that of the white genres themselves, but rather the meaning they express as the contested past that Native Americans understand as their own (cf. Seeger 1991). This music provides a means of remaking history, of writing and righting it as Native American history.

Process II:
Historicization and Revival: Recalibrating the Past

It is at this point that I move rather uneasily into the realm of history and to my second process, historicization. I make the move uneasily because, quite frankly, "history" so hegemonically insinuates itself into the contested domains that result from the contact of the West—and of Western religion—with the rest of the world (cf. Wolf 1982). My uneasiness perforce arises also when I figure music into this contact as itself a process of making history. This history is inscribed, in certain ways, by notational practices, which therefore permit the reproduction of Christian hymns at the expense of oral traditions in missionized cultures. I move into the realm of history, nevertheless, because histories come into conflict in the contested areas interrogated in this article. It is as a response to that contestation, however, that historicization emerges as a process articulated by sacred music.

Historicization is a process of internalizing the structures with which one religion connects itself to the past by another culture or religion. It is historicization that occurs when, for example, indigenous Latin American societies introduce historical events and figures into myth (cf. Hill 1988). The Aymara of contemporary Peru maintain myths in which Christ, usually as a conqueror, plays a role as the central figure (Dillon and Abercrombie 1988). This conquering Christ differs from a Catholic Christ, seeming in many ways like other figures in Aymara mythology. The significance of the myth of conquest, however, is obvious, not least because of the violent disjuncture in Aymara history that it represents. If, indeed, this disjuncture had disastrous consequences for the Aymara, the recounting of it, even as a new form of narration and historiography, has passed into their hands. Through the myth of the conquering Christ, the Aymara have repossessed their own past (Dillon and Abercrombie 1988).

Essential to the historicization that the myth of the conquering Christ illustrates is the conscious attempt to give alternative representation to colonial conquest and the persistence of colonial political and economic structures. Michael Taussig, in particular, has argued that confrontations between colonizers and Native South American peoples have produced vastly different ways of representing history (Taussig 1980 and 1987; cf. Lentz 1994). In one well-known essay, for example, he formulates a notion of historicization with the concept, "history as sorcery" (1984). These indigenous narratives are largely invisible to Western historians, who lack ways of reading them, much less interpreting them.

Similarly, many religious musics, particularly those of non-

Western religions, remain inaudible because they are presumed to be without history. The music of Islam is but one of many examples of a religious music whose historical contact with Europe has yet to be fully understood as exerting a fundamental impact on what we now think of as Western art music. In Europe itself—and during the past several centuries in the United States as well—the musics of religious minorities existed outside of history, despite the historical reality that the music of, to take one obvious example, Romas and Sintis constantly reconfigured local and regional religious musical practices throughout Europe. Roma and Sinti music is a striking case of historicization, for it internalized the structures of religious folk repertories and popular musics alike, performing European history as the quintessential Other.

Historicization also provides many religious musics with an ability to adapt to modernity, or at least to accommodate it. The explosion of the cassette industry in South Asia, for example, has produced a concomitant explosion in what are usually called devotional musics (Manuel 1993, 105–30). These explosions them-selves, however, parallel the ways in which Indian music and musicians have responded to the structures of colonization and modernization. Peter Manuel has even suggested that the cassette has effected an overall increase in religious observance and religious practices. Private and family devotion has increased, even if some forms of small-group devotional singing have decreased. Entirely new genres, such as pop *bhajan*s, have emerged and have come to have enormous appeal in Hindu areas. The explosion of religious music would only be possible with a medium of mass dissemination such as the cassette, which internalized the modes of production that the global music economy, especially through the companies EMI and His Master's Voice, successfully transplanted to India in the early part of the century. These processes of historicization are limited neither to Muslim nor to Hindu areas of the subcontinent. *Qawwālī*, a shrine-centered devotional music at the beginning of the century, has enormous appeal in North India and Pakistan, as well as in much of the world, as the several examples of *qawwālī* recordings discussed in the introductory section demonstrated.

Both *bhajan*s and *qawwālī* exemplify genres of religious music
that have been reconfigured for modern and different histories.
Other subprocesses of historicization, which have internalized other
aspects of local and world history, have come to characterize other
genres and repertories. Qur'anic recitation, to take an example
central to Muslim religious practices, has undergone processes of
historicization, again responding to various forms of colonial
conflict and to modernization. Because of the dominance of the
record and cassette industry in Cairo, individual devotional practices
in many places outside the Middle East are characterized by Cairene
styles of recitation. This has been the case in Paris for several
decades, leading to a creation of what might be called pan-Arab
religious practices, which by extension have effected a broad-
ranging consolidation in the Arab community of Paris, which,
because of French colonial history in North Africa and the Middle
East, is the largest ethnic group in the city. A different process of
historicization in Qur'anic recitation practices has taken place in
Israel and Palestine. This transformation is evident in a style of
recitation associated specifically with the Al-Aqsa Mosque, examples of which students in my classes at the University of Chicago
have increasingly used to illustrate their papers since the beginning
of the *intifada* in 1987. Accused of lacking a true history, Pal-
estinians have used recordings of Palestinian recitation to make that
history, connecting that history, not by accident, to the same site
that has served to anchor the long history of Jewish music, namely
the Temple Mount and the music of the Temple.

At issue here is not whether there was or was not a music history
of Palestinian recitation, but rather how one constructs that history,
once there is a demonstrated need to claim it. Historicization
provides a means of connecting the past with the present. In extreme
moments, those of rapid change and dramatic contestation, historicization becomes intensified, undergirding revival. The present is
precisely an extreme moment of this type in the New Europe, as
the new nations and regions of the continent struggle to grapple with
the historical transformations of the twentieth century. Revival—
musical revival—is everywhere. At one level, musical revival aims

to stake out new regions. At another, it seeks to recontextualize national histories. At still another, revival attempts to recapture the religions that the twentieth century virtually eradicated in many parts of Europe. This is the case in Bosnia-Herzegovina, for example, where Muslim popular-song genres, notably the *qāṣidah*, have undergone revival. The resurgence of Jewish music in Central Europe demonstrates a particularly extreme case of this form of revival. Klezmer ensembles and Yiddish song concerts are everywhere to be heard. Some revivalists are local and their endeavors modest, if also persistent. Others enjoy national prominence, as in the case of the most popular German singer-songwriter, Wolf Biermann, who has increasingly sung from Yiddish repertories in recent years. For the most part, the musics performed by the revivalists were not musics ever performed in Central Europe; Yiddish folk song was a secular music of Eastern Europe, as was klezmer music. But this illustrates the point exactly. Revival and historicization cannot actually create a Jewish European culture at the end of the twentieth century. As dynamic processes and responses to the racial and ethnic conflicts of the New Europe, they can represent the history of a continent whose past is inseparable from its response to Jews and Judaism. Through the revival of Jewish music, that past has won a significant presence in the New Europe.

Process III: Pilgrimage

Revival is by no means an isolated religious and musical phenomenon but, in fact, occurs throughout the world at the end of the twentieth century. I should even go so far as to say that revival is a phenomenon of world religion itself. It is religious revival, moreover, that serves as a bridge to the third response I wish to examine in this article: pilgrimage. Pilgrimage, too, is a phenomenon of world religions that is enjoying a remarkable resurgence. Pilgrimage sites throughout the world are in many cases overrun with pilgrims, and the importance of undertaking pilgrimages exerts itself at the most individual and local levels. I turn to pilgrimage at this point for several reasons. First of all, as a revival of religious practice, it demonstrates some very distinctive characteristics. Pilgrimage challenges authority, which is to say, it is a bottom-up movement in which individual belief takes priority over institutionalized structures. Second, pilgrimage does not exist without music. Pilgrims musically perform their spiritual journeys into existence; the sense of communitas that they evoke exists only through their acts of performance. Third, through performance, pilgrimage represents and takes place within the contested spaces that I have claimed as the sites for interaction between world musics and world religions. Finally, these local, performative conditions notwithstanding, pilgrimage is a form of religious-musical practice found in many, perhaps most, religions throughout the world.

Figure 1 represents a Marian song I recorded at a pilgrimage in

Figure 1: Pilgrimage Song Recorded near Mariazell, Austria

which I participated during September 1993. Though the melody of this Marian song is known in Catholic regions throughout the world, its contexts and performances were localized in September 1993 and transformed into a response to specific, but international, political concerns shared by the pilgrims.

This song was performed in numerous variants during the course of a pilgrimage in the eastern part of Styria, in Austria, as the pilgrims made their way along the Way of the Cross toward the basilica in Mariazell, the central pilgrimage site for much of Central and Eastern Europe. The pilgrims heard the Marian song performed in German, Latin, and Slovak versions and by a Slovak brass band from the village of Dolná Krupa.[12] The other participants on the pilgrimage came also from Eastern Europe, particularly from Slovenia, Croatia, Moravia, the Czech Republic, and Hungary, as well as from Austria and Germany.

Distinguishing this pilgrimage were not so much the ethnic, regional, and linguistic differences—these are not uncommon in Mariazell, or other pilgrimage sites—as the way in which the pilgrims deliberately subverted authority through the performance (cf. Eade and Sallnow 1991). Taking place on the three days prior to the "Week of the Foreigners," this pilgrimage moved in the opposite direction along the Way of the Cross, reversing, that is, the order of the Stations of the Cross. In so doing, they not only recalibrated the larger pattern of the pilgrimage—as well as the liturgy of songs that represents that pattern—but they supplanted some of the fundamental symbols of Christianity with a narrative of the immediate concerns in their own lives as residents of the New Europe.

This was a pilgrimage protesting the racism and intolerance that had spread across Europe. Far more than the empty statements of politicians and the promises for increased security, this pilgrimage transformed the protest against racism to the domain of the everyday. It did so by reversing the direction of the pilgrimage, which

[12] Known in some versions as "The Lourdes Song" or "The Great Lourdes Song," this Marian song has variant texts that localize and universalize pilgrimage.

moved not from the everyday world to the sacred site, but from the sacred site to the everyday world. It did so by deliberately juxtaposing musical repertories and by deliberately mixing the sacred and the secular, that is, the sacred and the everyday: the Slovak brass band was just one of several "village ensembles" that participated in the pilgrimage. The sense of community evoked by these juxtapositions was itself secular, intentionally symbolized by the mixing and remixing of musical repertories drawn from diverse religious and folk musical practices. The pilgrimage had reframed the questions central to the state-sponsored "Week of the Foreigners" by expressing them through the musical and religious practices central to their own lives.

Pilgrimage possesses the power radically to remap religious and secular territories alike.[13] The songs of pilgrimage often refer directly to the character of these territories, representing their meaning for religious communities in distinctive ways. The vocal repertories of the Bengali mendicant sect known as Bauls—a response themselves to the spread of Vaiṣṇava Hinduism in Bengal—includes songs that refer directly to the stations along the constant journeys the Bauls make (see Capwell 1986). Baul songs narrate a very different history and nationalism for the territories now bounded by West Bengal in India and by Bangladesh, a religious history whose saints and religious communities belie the alternative secular history of this region, which lies at one of the most complex interfaces between Hinduism and Islam. The perpetual pilgrimages of the Bauls come to represent the constant negotiation—and the persistent strife—that trouble this region, even by conflating the musical practices derived from the different forms

---

[13] Pilgrimage sites are often located in border or otherwise contested areas. Mariazell, as the primary pilgrimage site for Slavic-speaking peoples and Hungarians, is in eastern Austria. Lourdes lies relatively close to Spain, as well as to Basque country. Andean pilgrimage sites are located in regions occupied by mestizos, but also near the boundary regions between nations, for example Peru and Bolivia. Jerusalem provides the classical example of a pilgrimage site whose position has been highly contested throughout history.

of pilgrimage that Indian Hindus and Muslims practice. The songs of Bengali pilgrimage, then, represent an alternative Bengal, one performed historically through everyday musical and religious practices.

Conclusion:
Reclaiming Worlds with Music and Religion

Pilgrimage, like the other responses I have examined in this article, depends on the scaffolding of meanings and the actions that motivate religious belief. Music, through its capacity to reorder time and signify meaning in especially complex ways, has become one of the primary agents of this scaffolding. Music also remixes these scaffolded meanings at different sites of production. Pilgrimage, I have tried to show, combines the sacred with the everyday, thus endowing religious practice with the power to reconfigure the sacred as the everyday itself. During the course of this essay, I have also moved, sometimes gradually, sometimes disjunctly, from the plane of global cultural and market economies to the individual and local sites in which music-making constitutes religious practice. Clearly, the initial problematizing of Sufi music took place on the global plane; in the previous section the unpacking of a single pilgrimage in eastern Austria was local. I have concerned myself, then, far less with the globalist "-scapes," the ineluctable transnationalism imposed by many cultural-studies scholars on global culture (e.g., Appadurai 1990), than I have concerned myself with the local events themselves in which religious practice remixes religious musics, re-configuring them as responses to change. The contestation within world musics and world religions at the end of the twentieth century does not take place on these global "-scapes," even though it necessarily responds to global conditions. It is a contestation between everyday religious practices, performed through song and bodily practices that themselves constitute the cultures of contested sites—pilgrimages, fairs, markets—sites where exchange and musical performance are not simply the products of transnational forces.

This article is not, however, simply an attempt to argue that world musics and world religions interact in ways that may well be confused by the ways we have allowed the label, "world," to be used. Nor do I simply wish to content myself with the identification of responses that take place in the cultural spaces where religious and musical practices intersect. Ultimately, I am urging us to be far more concerned with how we can listen to the musics and understand the religious practices that take place in these spaces precisely because they are so crucially contested. It would be too easy to ignore or traverse these areas because they discomfit, or because their precarious positions lie outside our too-often unprecarious disciplinary practices. These contested areas, moreover, may pose new questions, for which we are at a loss to find quick answers: To what extent are the practices and structures of world religions and world musics changing? To what extent does music—as performative and embodied practice—empower those believing in religions throughout the world to challenge, to resist, or otherwise to "respond" to the worlds in which they live and believe? To what extent does the interaction of musical and religious practice afford the individual the opportunity to understand and reclaim the worlds of world music and world religions? The cultural spaces this article attempts to open also represent, I believe, discursive spaces, which is to say, they lie at the interstices between the fields ethnomusicologists and scholars of world religion practice. These discursive spaces, too, pose new questions, few of which we have asked before. These are, nonetheless, increasingly crucial questions. We must ask them and respond to their unsettling answers if we hope to come closer to knowing of just "whose world" we might speak in our future studies of world musics and world religions.

Bibliography

Appadurai, Arjun
    1990   "Disjuncture and Difference in the Global Cultural Economy." *Public Culture* 2(2):1–24.

Apter, Andrew
    1992   *Black Critics and Kings: The Hermeneutics of Power in Yoruba Society.* Chicago: University of Chicago Press.

Aracena, Beth Keating
    forthcoming
        "Singing Salvation: Jesuit Musics in Colonial Chile, 1600–1767." Ph.D. diss., University of Chicago.

Bergeron, Katherine
    1995   "The Virtual Sacred." *The New Republic* 212(9) (27 February):29–34.

Bhabha, Homi K.
    1994   *The Location of Culture.* New York: Routledge.

Blacking, John
    1981   "Political and Musical Freedom in the Music of Some Black South African Churches." In Ladislav Holy and Milan Stuchlik, eds., *The Structure of Folk Models*, pp. 35–62. London: Academic Press.

    1987a   *'A Commonsense View of All Music': Reflections on Percy Grainger's Contributions to Ethnomusicology and Music Education.* Cambridge Studies in Ethnomusicology. Cambridge: Cambridge University Press.

    1987b   "Intention and Change in the Performance of European Hymns by Some Black South African Churches." In G. Moon, ed., *Transplanted European Music Cultures: Miscellanea Musicologica. Adelaide Studies in Musicology* 12:193–200.

    1995   *Music, Culture, and Experience: Selected Papers of John Blacking.* Ed. Reginald Byron. Chicago Studies in Ethnomusicology. Chicago: University of Chicago Press.

Bohlman, Philip V.
    1996   "Pilgrimage, Politics, and the Musical Remapping of the New Europe." *Ethnomusicology* 40(3):375–412.

Capwell, Charles
    1986   *The Music of the Bauls of Bengal.* Kent, Ohio: Kent State University Press.

Comaroff, Jean, and John Comaroff
1991   *Of Revelation and Revolution: Christianity, Colonialism, and Consciousness in South Africa.* Vol. 1. Chicago: University of Chicago Press.

Comaroff, John, and Jean Comaroff
1992   *Ethnography and the Historical Imagination.* Studies in the Ethnographic Imagination. Boulder: Westview Press.

Cornelius, Richard, and Terence J. O'Grady
1987   "Reclaiming a Tradition: The Soaring Eagles of Oneida." *Ethnomusicology* 31:261–72.

Dillon, Mary, and Thomas Abercrombie
1988   "The Destroying Christ: An Aymara Myth of Conquest." In Hill, *Rethinking Myth and History*, pp. 50–77.

Draper, David E.
1982   "Abba isht tuluwa: The Christian Hymns of the Mississippi Choctaw." *American Indian Culture and Research Journal* 6(1):43–61.

Eade, John, and Michael J. Sallnow, eds.
1991   *Contesting the Sacred: The Anthropology of Christian Pilgrimage.* New York: Routledge.

Eberhart, Helmut, Edith Hörandner, and Burkhard Pöttler, eds.
1990   *Volksfrömmigkeit.* Buchreihe des Österreichischen Vereins für Volkskunde. Vienna: Verein für Volkskunde.

Giese, Claudius
1994   "Gesang zwischen den Welten." In Max Peter Baumann, ed., *Kosmos der Anden: Weltbild und Symbolik indianischer Tradition in Südamerika*, pp. 335–58. Munich: Eugen Diederichs.

Gilroy, Paul
1993   *The Black Atlantic: Modernity and Double Consciousness.* Cambridge, Mass.: Harvard University Press.

Goethe, Johann Wolfgang
[1819]1988
        West-östlicher Divan. 8th ed., enlarged. Frankfurt am Main: Insel.

Gold, Ann Grodzins
1988   *Fruitful Journeys: The Ways of Rajasthani Pilgrims.* Berkeley: University of California Press.

Halıcı, Feyzi, ed.
1983   *Mevlâna: Yirmi alti bilim adamının mevlâna üzerine arastirmaları.* Konya: Ülkü Basımevi.
Hart, Mickey, with Jay Stevens
1990   *Drumming at the Edge of Magic: A Journey into the Spirit of Percussion.* San Francisco: Harper Collins.
Hill, Jonathan D., ed.
1988   *Rethinking History and Myth: Indigenous South American Perspectives on the Past.* Urbana: University of Illinois Press.
Ireland, Emilienne
1988   "The Cerebral Savage: The Whiteman as Symbol of Cleverness and Savagery in Waurá Myth." In Hill, *Rethinking Myth and History*, pp. 157–73.
Joshi, G. N.
1977   "The Phonograph in India." *National Centre for the Performing Arts* 6(3):5–27.
1988   "A Concise History of the Phonograph Industry in India." *Popular Music* 7(2):147–56.
Lentz, Carola
1994   "Die Konstruktion kultureller Andersartigkeit als indianische Antwort auf Herrschaft und ethnische Diskriminierung: Eine Fallstudie aus Ecuador." In Max Peter Baumann, ed., *Kosmos der Anden: Weltbild und Symbolik indianischer Tradition in Südamerika*, pp. 412–46. Munich: Eugen Diederichs.
Manuel, Peter
1993   *Cassette Culture: Popular Music and Technology in North India.* Chicago Studies in Ethnomusicology. Chicago: University of Chicago Press.
Mendoza-Walker, Zoila S.
1993   "Shaping Society through Dance: Mestizo Ritual Performance in the Southern Peruvian Andes." 2 vols. Ph.D. diss., University of Chicago.
Morrison, Ann
forthcoming
        "Medeolinuwok, Music, and Missionaries in Maine." In Philip V. Bohlman and Edith Blumhofer, eds., *Music in American Religious Experience*.
"Musik der Sufis"
1993   "Musik der Sufis." In May program announcement, *Haus der Kulturen der Welt*. Berlin: Haus der Kulturen der Welt.

Nettl, Bruno
  1985   *The Western Impact on World Music: Change, Adaptation, and Survival.* New York: Schirmer Books.
Neuman, Daniel M.
  1990   *The Life of Music in North India: The Organization of an Artistic Tradition.* Chicago: University of Chicago Press. Original edition, Detroit: Wayne State University Press, 1980.
O'Grady, Terence J.
  1991   "The Singing Societies of Oneida." *American Music* 9(1):67–91.
d'Ohsson, Constantin Mouradigea
  1788   *Tableau général othoman.* 2 vols. Paris: F. Didot.
Önder, Mehmet
  1990   *Mevlâna: Jelaleddin Rûmî.* Series of Culture Trace. Ankara: Publications of Culture Ministry.
Qureshi, Regula Burckhardt
  1992/1993 " 'Muslim Devotional': Popular Religious Music and Muslim Identity under British, Indian and Pakistani Hegemony." *Asian Music* 24(1):111–21.
  1995   *Sufi Music of India and Pakistan: Sound, Context and Meaning in Qawwāli.* Chicago: University of Chicago Press. original edition, Cambridge: Cambridge University Press, 1986.
Rhodes, Willard
  1960   "The Christian Hymnology of the North American Indians." In Anthony F. Wallace, ed., *Men and Cultures*, pp. 324–31. Philadelphia: University of Pennsylvania Press.
  1962   "Music as an Agent of Political Expression." *African Studies Bulletin* 5:14–22.
Rouget, Gilbert
  1985   *Music and Trance: A Theory of the Relations between Music and Possession.* Trans. Brunhilde Biebuyck. Chicago: University of Chicago Press.
Ruby, Ahmed Aqeel
  1992   *Nusrat Fateh Ali Khan: A Living Legend.* Trans. Sajjad Haider Malik. Lahore: Words of Wisdom.
Scott, James C.
  1985   *Weapons of the Weak: Everyday Forms of Peasant Resistance.* New Haven: Yale University Press.

1987   "Resistance without Protest and without Organization: Peasant Opposition to the Islamic *Zakat* and the Christian Tithe." *Comparative Studies in Society and History* 29(3).

1990   *Domination and the Arts of Resistance: Hidden Transcripts.* New Haven: Yale University Press.

Seeger, Anthony

1991   "When Music Makes History." In Stephen Blum, Philip V. Bohlman, and Daniel M. Neuman, eds., *Ethnomusicology and Modern Music History*, pp. 23–34. Urbana: University of Illinois Press.

Slobin, Mark

1993   *Subcultural Sounds: Micromusics of the West.* Music/Culture. Hanover: Wesleyan University Press.

Swadish, Morris, Floyd Lounsbury, and Oscar Archiquette, eds.

1965   *Onayodaaga Deyelwahgwata* ("Oneida Hymnal"). N.p.

Taussig, Michael

1980   *The Devil and Commodity Fetishism in South America.* Chapel Hill: University of North Carolina Press.

1984   "History as Sorcery." *Representations* 7:87–109.

1987   *Shamanism, Colonialism, and the Wild Man: A Study in Terror and Healing.* Chicago: University of Chicago Press.

Türkmen, Erkan

n.d.   *Rumi as a True Lover of God and on the First Eighteen Verses of Rumi's Masnevi.* Cultural Publications, 1. Konya: Department of Eastern Languages and Literatures, Seljuk University.

Wallis, Roger, and Krister Malm

1984   *Big Sounds from Small Peoples: The Music Industry in Small Countries.* Sociology of Music, 2. New York: Pendragon Press.

Waterman, Christopher A.

1990   *Jùjú: A Social History and Ethnography of an African Popular Music.* Chicago Studies in Ethnomusicology. Chicago: University of Chicago Press.

Wolf, Eric R.

1982   *Europe and the People without History.* Berkeley: University of California Press.

Discography

Azrié, Abed. Les Soufis: *D'apres les textes mystiques du ixe au xiiie siècle.* Le roseau 81021–81022.

Chant: The Benedictine Monks of Santo Domingo de Silos. Angel

Jaffar Hussain Khan. World Music Library KICC 5115.

The Music of the Whirling Dervishes. Finnadar 90606–1.

Nusrat Fateh Ali Khan—Qawwal and Party. *Shahen-Shah.* Realworld. Carol 2302–2.

Nusrat Fateh Ali Khan. *Qawwali: The Vocal Art of the Sufis (I).* JVC VICG 5029.

The Sabri Brothers and Ensemble. *Qawwali: Sufi Music from Pakistan.* Nonesuch H-72080.

Music and Historical Consciousness among the Dagbamba of Ghana*

John Chernoff

The Dagbamba people of northern Ghana have been studied from a number of vantage points, but their main claims to fame in the scholarly literature have had to do with politics. First, they have been the focus of several projects that inquired into the nature of their traditional political system and into related issues of state formation in West Africa because, more than five hundred years ago, the Dagbamba consolidated one of the earliest centralized political states south of the Niger bend, the traditional state of Dagbon.[1] Second, they have been a focus for journalists as well as scholars because of an extended and continuing chieftaincy dispute that highlights the interplay between the traditional political system and the Ghanaian government.[2] One can occasionally see coverage of the situation in magazines like *West Africa*.

---

* Sections of this essay were developed in an earlier publication, "The Relevance of Ethnomusicology to Anthropology: Strategies of Inquiry and Interpretation," in *African Musicology: Current Trends*, vol. 1, *A* Festschrift *Presented to J. H. Kwabena Nketia*, ed. Jacqueline Cogdell Djedje and William G. Carter (Los Angeles: African Studies Center, UCLA; African Studies Association and Crossroads Press, 1989), 59–92.

[1] *Dagbamba* is the plural form; an individual is a *Dagbana*. Their language is *Dagbani*. The traditional state is *Dagbɔŋ*.

[2] J. D. Fage, "Reflections on the Early History of the Mossi-Dagomba Group of States," in *The Historian in Tropical Africa*, ed. J. Vansina, R. Mauny, and L. V. Thomas (London: International African Institute and Oxford University Press, 1964); Phyllis Ferguson and Ivor Wilks, "Chiefs, Constitutions, and the British in Northern Ghana," in *West African Chiefs: Their Changing Status under*

Nearly twenty-five years ago, I went to Dagbon to study music,[3] and my research is an example of how the study of music can lead into broader ethnographic concerns.[4] I hope to earn for the Dagbamba another type of distinction that will be based on an appreciation of the way they use music to articulate images of their history and then act out those images within their community life. In their traditional state, music and dance play an important role in bringing historical meaning down to the level of participatory social action. The foundation of their musical repertoire and their historiography is an epic body of historical knowledge known as *Samban' luŋa*, literally, "outside drumming," because it is sung and drummed outside the house of the chief in major towns. The

---

Colonial Rule and Independence, ed. Michael Crowder and Obaro Ikime (New York: African Publishing Corp., 1970); Ghana Government, *Report of the Yendi Skin Affairs Committee of Inquiry* (Accra, Ghana: Ghana Publishing Corporation, 1974); Paul Ladouceur, "The Yendi Chieftaincy Dispute and Ghanaian Politics," *Canadian Journal of African Studies* 6 (1972):97–115; Paul Ladouceur, *Chiefs and Politicians: The Politics of Regionalism in Northern Ghana* (London and New York: Longmann, 1979; Emmanuel Forster Tamakloe, ed., *A Brief History of the Dagbamba People* (Accra, Ghana: Government Printing Office, 1931), also in A. W. Cardinall, *Tales Told in Togoland* (Westport, Conn.: Negro Universities Press, 1970 [London: Oxford University Press, 1931]); H. A. Blair and A. C. Duncan-Johnstone, eds., *Enquiry into the Constitution and Organization of the Dagbon Kingdom* (Accra, Ghana: Government Printing Office, 1931); Martin Staniland, *The Lions of Dagbon: Political Change in Northern Ghana* (Cambridge: Cambridge University Press, 1975).

[3] John Miller Chernoff, *African Rhythm and African Sensibility: Aesthetics and Social Action in African Musical Idioms* (Chicago: University of Chicago Press, 1979); John Miller Chernoff, "Music-Making Children of Africa," *Natural History* 88, no. 9 (November 1979):68–75; "The Drums of Dagbon," in *Repercussions: A Celebration of African-American Music,* ed. Geoffrey Haydon and Dennis Marks (London: Century Publishing, 1985); John M. Chernoff, *Master Drummers of Dagbon,* vol. 1 (Cambridge, Mass.: Rounder Records 5016); John M. Chernoff, *Master Drummers of Dagbon,* vol. 2 (Cambridge, Mass.: Rounder Records 5046).

[4] John M. Chernoff and Alhaji Ibrahim Abdulai, *A Drummer's Testament: The Culture of the Dagbamba of Northern Ghana,* 3 vols. With the collaboration of Kissmal Ibrahim Hussein, Benjamin D. Sunkari, Mustapha Muhammed, and Alhaji Mumuni Abdulai (to be published by the University of Chicago Press).

Samban' luŋa is one prototype of what we might call a "drum history." To me, a *Samban' luŋa* performance recalls an image of preclassical Greece, when Homer and his colleagues were singing epics about the Trojan War. It is not easy to see something like that anywhere in the world. I once attended a drum history performance with a poet. He fantasized himself appearing before such a forum, and he kept mumbling, "This is incredible! This is incredible!" Actually, it is normal for a drummer who is about to sing a *Samban' luŋa*, particularly for the first time, to be quite worried, and it is no wonder. He has to sing more or less non-stop for about eight hours, finding his way through his story and remembering countless details. And, he is not just entertaining the people: he is singing about history and conveying historical knowledge to people who are already knowledgeable themselves.

I would note that when I first went to Dagbon in 1971, I knew virtually nothing about the complex relationship of music and history in that society. I merely started working in Dagbon with the idea of taking Dagbamba music as one example within a broader framework that would use the study of music as a way of looking at social relations in general. My early work in Dagbon and in other cultural areas led to a book called *African Rhythm and African Sensibility*.[5] The main point I tried to make in that book is that in many African societies, music is an agent for the articulation of generative cultural themes and for the socialization of indigenous values. My argument hinged on demonstrating that the stylistic elements in African musical idioms exist within contexts of interaction that sustain and socialize particular modes of participation. Despite a number of significant works by symbolic anthropologists on the influence of cultural systems of meaning on social structure and history,[6] the area of musical culture has not

[5] Chernoff, *African Rhythm and African Sensibility*.

[6] For example: Clifford Geertz, *Negara: The Theatre State in Nineteenth-Century Bali* (Princeton: Princeton University Press, 1980); Marshall Sahlins, *Islands of History* (Chicago: University of Chicago Press, 1985); James W. Fernandez, *Bwiti: An Ethnography of the Religious Imagination in Africa* (Princeton: Princeton University Press, 1982).

received much attention from social anthropologists because music has seemed so far from the political and economic realities that are the basis of functionalist perspectives on social systems. I believe that in Africa, because of the way that musical style or communication can influence or even dominate situational interaction, because of the particular modes of participation that musical settings institute, and because of the aesthetic sensitivity and contextual awareness required of musicians and participants, ethnomusicologists and ethnographers may hope that attention to musical data can lead to significant generalizations about culture and that these generalizations can be grounded in social action, that is, in performances.

When I decided to continue my research in West Africa, I returned to Dagbon with the idea of elaborating on the broader themes of my early work through detailed investigation of a single society. Essentially, it was because of my involvement with music that I began to have access to historical data and to the types of issues historical knowledge presents to those responsible for passing it on. Thus, rather than looking at the drum history primarily from the standpoint of an historian interested in reconstructing Dagbamba history or a classicist critic interested in its poetic form and improvisational dynamics, I looked at it in terms of its symbolic and social meanings and how those meanings are expressed in musical contexts. This perspective was a nice fit with my original interest because, instead of dealing with historical knowledge as we do, Dagbamba bring it down to participatory contexts and express it through music and dance.

In an African context, the Dagbamba are not really all that unique in this regard. In many African societies, music fulfills functions that other societies delegate to different types of institutions. In Africa, music is an agent for the socialization of indigenous values.[7] Music serves a crucial integrative function within many types of

---

[7] Chernoff, *African Rhythm and African Sensibility*; Robert Farris Thompson, *African Art in Motion: Icon and Act in the Collection of Katherine Coryton White* (Los Angeles: University of California Press, 1974).

institutionalized activities,[8] and musicians perform a complex social role in community occasions.[9] Music and dance sometimes provide the generative dynamics of large- and small-scale social movements.[10] In many African societies, musicians are the acknowledged authorities on history and custom[11] and, particularly in the Western Sudan, often have important political functions.[12] In Dagbamba

[8] A. M. Jones, *Studies in African Music*, 2 vols. (London: Oxford University Press, 1959); Charles Keil, *Tiv Song* (Chicago: University of Chicago Press, 1979); Alan P. Merriam, "African Music," in *Continuity and Change in African Cultures*, ed. William R. Bascom and Melville J. Herskovits (Chicago: University of Chicago Press, 1959); Alan P. Merriam, *The Anthropology of Music* (Evanston, Ill.: Northwestern University Press, 1964); Hugo Zemp, *Musique Dan: La musique dans la pensée et la vie sociale d'une societé africaine* (Paris: Mouton and École Practique des Hautes Études, 1971).

[9] S. Kobla Ladzekpo, "The Social Mechanics of Good Music: A Description of Dance Clubs among the Anlo Ewe-Speaking People of Ghana," *African Music* 5, no. 1 (1971):6–22; J. H. Kwabena Nketia, *Drumming in Akan Communities of Ghana* (London: University of Ghana and Thomas Nelson and Sons, 1963).

[10] John Blacking, "The Role of Music in the Culture of the Venda of the Northern Transvaal," in *Studies in Ethnomusicology*, vol. 2, ed. M. Kolinski (New York: Oak Publications, 1965); John Blacking, "Music and the Historical Process in Vendaland," in *Essays on Music and History in Africa*, ed. Klaus P. Wachsmann (Evanston, Ill.: Northwestern University Press, 1971); T. O. Ranger, *Dance and Society in Eastern Africa, 1890–1970: The Beni Ngoma* (London: Heinemann Educational Books, 1975).

[11] David W. Ames, "A Sociocultural View of Hausa Musical Activity," in *The Traditional Artist in African Societies*, ed. Warren L. d'Azevedo (Bloomington: Indiana University Press, 1973); David W. Ames, "Igbo and Hausa Musicians: A Comparative Examination," *Ethnomusicology* 17 (1973):25–78; Ayo Bankole, Judith Bush, and Sadek H. Samaan, "The Yoruba Master Drummer," *African Arts* 8, no. 2 (winter 1975):48–56, 77–78; Paul Berliner, *The Soul of Mbira: Music and Traditions of the Shona People of Zimbabwe* (Berkeley and Los Angeles: University of California Press, 1978).

[12] Charles Cutter, "The Politics of Music in Mali," *African Arts* 1, no. 3 (spring 1968):38–39, 74–77; Roderic Knight, "The Manding Contexts," in *Performance Practice*, ed. G. Behague (London: Greenwood Press, 1984); Gordon Innes, *Sunjata: Three Mandinka Versions* (London: School of Oriental and African Studies, 1974); Thomas A. Hale, *Scribe, Griot, and Novelist: Narrative Interpreters of the Songhay Empire* (Gainesville: University of Florida Press and Center for African Studies, 1990).

society, these musicians are drummers, with distinct lineage groupings and hierarchical chieftaincy organizations. Indeed, during the chieftaincy dispute that I mentioned, when issues concerning Dagbamba custom were brought before national government committees of inquiry, the expert witnesses for the contesting parties were drummers. Dagbamba drummers undergo formal training for years and, like most intellectuals, continue their acquisition of knowledge throughout life.[13] Not only do Dagbamba assert that drummers have "the facts" about historical and social realities, but they also assert that, "If something is happening and there are no drummers present, then you should know that what is happening is not something important."

By way of background, let me note that according to most reckoning, the Dagbamba entered their present traditional area sometime during the fourteenth century. Since its founding over five hundred years ago, the traditional state of Dagbon[14] has been ruled by a single family in one line, making Dagbon perhaps the oldest continuous dynasty in the world. The Dagbamba have influenced the surrounding peoples of northern Ghana, and they played a role in the routing of precolonial trade and the penetration of Islam into southern Ghana.[15] Early studies by colonial officers emphasized the political sector, focusing on historical data in an effort to clarify and even codify chieftaincy succession patterns as an adjunct to indirect rule.[16] Recent research has had the same focus, an aspect

[13] Chernoff, "Music-Making Children of Africa" and "The Drums of Dagbon"; Christine Oppong, *Growing Up in Dagbon* (Accra-Tema, Ghana: Ghana Publishing Corporation, 1973).

[14] Fage, "Reflections on the Early History of the Mossi-Dagomba Group of States."

[15] Ivor Wilks, *The Northern Factor in Ashanti History* (Legon, Ghana: Institute of African Studies, University of Ghana, 1961); Ivor Wilks, *Asante in the Nineteenth Century: The Structure and Evolution of a Political Order* (London and New York: Cambridge University Press, 1974).

[16] Tamakloe, *A Brief History of the Dagbamba People*; Blair and Duncan-Johnstone, *Enquiry into the Constitution and Organization of the Dagbon Kingdom*; Staniland, *The Lions of Dagbon*.

of interest in and response to an extended chieftaincy dispute with national political implications.[17] Other discussions of Dagbamba life have been only brief sketches within works that attempted to deal with all the diverse peoples of northern Ghana or with selected aspects of social processes in the Volta Basin.[18] The historical literature has been reviewed,[19] and the process of Islamization has also received detailed attention.[20]

The Dagbamba entered their present traditional area as conquerors. With horses, spears, and arrows in their military technology, they subjugated the indigenous stateless tribes under an elaborate and competitive hierarchy of chieftaincies. They gradually intermingled and became agriculturists. Their staple crop is yams, but they do multiple plantings in their fields, and they rotate crops. Their other main food crops are sorghum (guinea corn), corn, millet, and beans; recently, intensive rice cultivation has been encouraged by the national government. The Dagbamba are patrilineal, virilocal, and polygamous. Marriages are relatively unstable, and divorce is common. Funerals are elaborate, and there is an annual cycle of festivals. Just over a majority are Muslim, and the remainder practice animism and what is often called "ancestor worship," focused to a great extent on local and household shrines, land-

[17] Ferguson and Wilks, "Chiefs, Constitutions, and the British in Northern Ghana"; Ghana Government, *Report of the Yendi Skin Affairs Committee of Inquiry*; Ladouceur, "The Yendi Chieftaincy Dispute and Ghanaian Politics"; Ladouceur, *Chiefs and Politicians*; Staniland, *The Lions of Dagbon*.

[18] A. W. Cardinall, *The Natives of the Northern Territories of the Gold Coast: Their Customs, Religion, and Folklore* (London: George Routledge & Sons, [1925]); R. S. Rattray, *The Tribes of the Ashanti Hinterland*, vol. 2 (Oxford: Clarendon Press, 1932); Madeleine Manoukian, *Tribes of the Northern Territories of the Gold Coast*, Ethnographic Survey of Africa: West Africa, pt. 5, ed. Daryll Forde (London: International African Institute, 1952).

[19] Brigitta Benzing, *Die Geschichte und das Herrschaftssystem der Dagomba* (Meisenheim am Glan: Verlag Anton Hain, 1971).

[20] Phyllis Ferguson, "Islamization in Dagbon: A Study of the Alfanema of Yendi" (Ph.D. diss., University of Cambridge, 1972); Nehemia Levtzion, *Muslims and Chiefs in West Africa: A Study of Islam in the Middle Volta Basin in the Pre-Colonial Period* (Oxford: Clarendon Press, 1968).

priests, soothsayers, medicine men, and witchcraft. There are several craft-guild lineages, such as drummers, and within the cohesive political framework of Dagbon, there are a number of groups that retain a degree of foreign lineal identity—assimilated Islamic scholars being one such group and many court officials of slave origins another.

In Dagbamba culture, seemingly divergent customs are layered into integrated patterns of institutionalized relationships and activities. The major strata can be broadly distinguished as: 1) the surviving customs of the original and assimilated inhabitants who are representative of the indigenous culture base shared in varying degrees by many small cultural groups in the region; 2) the political and technological innovations brought by the Dagbamba conquerors related to the Mossi, Mamprusi, and Nanumba peoples; 3) the Islamic customs introduced in the early eighteenth century through contact with Wangara and Hausa missionaries; and 4) the Western influence of the twentieth century. Significant complexes of customs have also developed through contact with Asante, Guruma, and Konkomba people. The complex integration of these many cultural trends within Dagbamba society has resulted in a thoroughly distinctive culture; yet, to an extent, Dagbon may be characterized as a cultural laboratory of the pre-colonial Volta Basin. Much of our knowledge of this highly structured traditional society has bearing on our understanding of the closely related states of Mossi, Mamprusi, and Nanumba and also has varying degrees of general application to many societies of the Volta Basin that share a number of cultural traits, most notably Tampolensi, Kantonsi, Talensi, Frafra, Kusasi, Wala, and Dagaba.

A performance of the *Samban'luŋa*, or drum history, normally occurs twice a year, and only in towns or villages ruled by a major chief. The two occasions are during the festival for breaking the fast at the end of Ramadan, on the evening when the new moon appears, and during the festival in the pilgrimage month, on the evening before the sacrifice. The drum history can also be beaten for the installation of a chief. After the evening meal, from around eight o'clock, the people of the town begin to gather outside the house of the chief. The town's drummers assemble opposite the entrance, and several take turns praising their own ancestors in lengthy introductory sections. This prelude to a performance is referred to as "sweeping outside the compound" or "pounding [preparing the vegetables for] the soup." By around ten o'clock, the chief, accompanied by his wives and his elders, will come outside and sit. One of the chiefs of the town's drummers, or his delegate, will then take over the singing and begin the part of the history chosen for the performance. The drummer who sings stands alone and faces the chief across the compound. Holding an hourglass-shaped drum (*luŋa*) over his shoulder, he is accompanied by as many as fifty to one hundred drummers seated behind him, beating responses to the verses of his song. Most of the drum history is recounted through the medium of stories about the lives of past chiefs, their ancestry and progeny, what they did and how they got their proverbial praise-names. A performance normally focuses on one particular chief or period, although, because the drummer will sing about that chief's forefathers and descendants, the performance can cover a lengthy time frame. The actual historical account in the *Samban' luŋa* depends on the extent of the drummer's knowledge and also on the particular path the drummer chooses to take through the material. I was told, "The *Samban' luŋa* tells Dagbamba how they were living in the olden days, and it also tells a chief what is inside chieftaincy."

To give an idea of the sort of people the Dagbamba were and what was "inside chieftaincy" in the olden days and, presumably, the type of character they believe they have inherited up to now, I shall summarize one of the better-known stories from the *Samban' luŋa*. The story of Naa Luro, that is, Chief Luro, is quite long, and here I will only recount parts of it. Naa Luro lived several hundred years after the founding of the state. The story of Naa Luro begins in the early seventeenth century during the reign of his predecessor, Naa Dariʒeɣu. At that time, the Dagbamba were faced with an external threat from the Gonjas. The Gonjas had just entered northwestern Ghana and were pushing against the western boundary of Dagbon. They started acting up at Dagbon's westernmost market, at the village of Tolon, where there was considerable intermingling.

The way the drummers sing it, the Gonjas were coming to the market with "hard eyes" and were catching some Dagbamba and selling them. The paramount chief of Dagbon, the Yaa-Naa, is praised with the epithet, "son of a lion": Naa Dariʒɛyu, however, did nothing. The Gonjas even carried off some of Naa Dariʒɛyu's own wives. When his elders asked him what he was going to do, Naa Dariʒɛyu—like many Dagbamba when they want to say something serious—gave a proverb: "A ram walks backwards before it's going to charge." Unconvinced, the elders told him that, "A Yaa-Naa does not run from fighting." Thus reminded of who he was, Naa Dariʒɛyu went to war against the Gonjas, who killed him. The Gonja chief was named Kaluysi Dajia, and Kaluysi Dajia cut off Naa Dariʒɛyu's hand at the wrist and put the hand into a bag which he carried around on his shoulder. After that, things cooled down.

When Naa Luro succeeded to the chieftaincy, he did not seek revenge. What finally made him annoyed and woke up the war was the way one of his wives abused him. Because of her good example, many Dagbamba women like the story of Naa Luro. Her name was Koyibgaa, and she was Naa Luro's most beloved wife. The way the drummers sing it, some of Naa Luro's in-laws came to visit him, and he sent his messenger into the compound to tell his best wife Koyibgaa to prepare food for his guests. Two hours later, there was still no food. Naa Luro sent the messenger again, only to have the messenger come back to say that Koyibgaa was just sitting down sucking her cheeks, and that she did not answer him. So Naa Luro went together with the messenger into the compound, picking up his whip on the way.

The type of whip the Dagbamba had in the olden days was called *barazim*: it was made by taking the phallus of a slaughtered bull and stretching it, then cutting the end of the phallus into strips, like a cat-o-nine-tails, and then drying it. All things considered, therefore, it was a pretty nasty whip. Anyway, when Naa Luro and his messenger reached Koyibgaa in the compound and asked about the food, Koyibgaa still refused to answer, so Naa Luro gave the *barazim* to his messenger and told him to whip her across the ears. The way the drummers sing it, after three times, Koyibgaa finally jumped up and grabbed Naa Luro and cried out, "Look at a useless chief! It's food that's worrying you! If not food, what do you know? The chief who died and you came to take his chieftaincy, do you know where his grave is? If you say you're strong, go and see his grave!"

At that point, according to the drummers, Naa Luro's nose started smoking. He went to war the same day, despite the fact that it was the rainy season at the time. The story goes on in great detail to describe many difficulties of the campaign, including a lengthy scene in which the Dagbamba are stranded at the bank of a river and find blacksmiths to build a bridge. The campaign concludes with Naa Luro reaching Kaluɣsi Dajia's village and killing everybody in it, until they were lying on the ground like "so many dead flies," and finally, in an epic battle scene, fighting Kaluɣsi Dajia and killing him. Then, Naa Luro cut off Kaluɣsi Dajia's head, signifying the end of the war. There is a rather interesting denouement. Naa Luro called Koyibgaa to come and look at Kaluɣsi Dajia, and then he cut off her head, too. He built a big fire and burnt both of the heads until they were ashes. Naa Luro collected the bag containing Naa Dariȝɛɣu's hand and took it back to Dagbon, along with the ashes of Kaluɣsi Dajia and Koyibgaa. There he built a room, buried the hand in a grave inside the room, and smeared the ashes of Kaluɣsi Dajia and Koyibgaa like paint on the walls of the room. That grave is still in Dagbon, at a village called Pong Tamale.

I have gone into some detail because telling the story is one way of presenting what many Dagbamba have to contemplate when they ask themselves about the type of past they come from. In this respect, the drum history does what any history does in representing the past. The *Samban' luŋa* is one of the ways Dagbamba deal with their past, but it is only one aspect of a very complex response. What I shall describe next is the way in which the Dagbamba have made a musical event like the drum history the center of a constellation of customs that link history to political and kinship institutions within a number of communal musical events. In that regard, as much as the Dagbamba drum history resembles history as we know it, there are some ways in which it is not quite the same as history because it has a different kind of dynamic in its cultural context. It relies on different cultural means, different types of media, different types of knowledge, and different types of sensibilities. Therein lie not only its interest but also a number of methodological problems.

The general ambience of Dagbamba social life and gatherings contrasts quite a bit with the image one might develop of them based on the story of Naa Luro. The complementary human values that Dagbamba admire are patience and shyness, which is conceived as a sense of shame. They say "Patience gets everything," and they also say "Shyness is a human being." Together, as a basis for social action, the two values address ideals of cooperativeness and interdependence and ethics of respect and obedience within the many hierarchical structures that coordinate an individual's life and social position in Dagbamba society. At the other end of the axis is pride or impudence exemplified by the notion of "showing oneself." Dagbamba do not like people who are proud or who boast, who get annoyed or who argue, who bluff others or who show themselves to be "more" than others. Given these values, the social atmosphere in the Dagbamba traditional area is, as one might expect, restrained and tranquil; the people are reliable, temperate, and generous; the pace of life is relaxed.

A sense of history is central to the integration of Dagbamba culture and to the Dagbamba musical heritage. In contrast to societies in which political offices or scientific-technological establishments control and authenticate information transfer, Dagbamba tradition is transmitted through artistic specialists, that is, musicians. A Dagbamba drummer is a political figure whose influence extends from conferring varying degrees of respect on chiefs to discriminating the status of individual lineage identities at social gatherings. As such, drummers acquire high respect not only for their historical erudition but also for their detailed knowledge of the kinship patterns of their local communities. Considered even against other African societies where music has a significant function in the institutionalization of tradition, Dagbamba society illustrates a further elaboration of this tendency into the maintenance and validation of political and historical information.

Regarding the rest of the Dagbamba musical repertoire, the drum history is extended to lend meaning to Dagbamba social dances, which themselves are based on the proverbial praise-names of the paramount chiefs, who sit at the town of Yendi, and the chiefs of other traditionally important towns. Different dances have associations that relate aspects of centralized political power with family origins, since drummers say that there is no Dagbana whose ancestry cannot be traced to a former chief. Although a typical Dagbana's preference in dancing is not necessarily overtly political, and although dance preferences can vary, many Dagbamba may demonstrate their relationship to historical figures by dancing to the name of a great forefather. The important musicological point is that the different dance beats are themselves rhythmic elaborations of the proverbial praise-names of former Dagbamba chiefs.

A dance called *3im Taai Kurugu* can serve as an example of how a name becomes a dance beat. *3im Taai Kurugu* is a praise-name for Naa Alaasani, who was Yaa-Naa at the beginning of the twentieth century. At the time he became the chief, there was a civil war between him and his brothers over the chieftaincy. Naa Alaasani's rivals were what we would call his cousins, the children of one of his father's younger brothers who was the Yaa-Naa who had just died. Naa Alaasan' 3im Taai Kurugu's full name was *3im Taai Kurugu, ka chinchansi wɔlinjɛ*, which means "Blood touches iron: rats will try to eat it and fail." Obviously, the name refers to the way in which Naa Alaasani ascended to the chieftaincy—by asserting his strength over his rivals: the "blood" is the chieftaincy, and he is the "iron"; the "rats" are his rivals who were not able to get or "eat" the chieftaincy that had come and "touched" him. The name also refers to the element of contestation within Dagbamba chieftaincy succession, and it makes an allusion to the civil war. In that sense, one can see why drummers sometimes say that the chiefs "throw their names at each other." Employing the well-known practice of using a drum to duplicate speech patterns, drummers set up a responsive alternation between the first and second phrases of the proverb. The text of the proverb itself therefore becomes the basis for the rhythms of the drumming, and a dancer picks up on these rhythms as he or she moves, embodying the proverb, so to speak. Drummers may beat other phrases or improvisations on the rhythms of the main phrases, and a good dancer can apply the variations as well to improvised dance movements.

A dance called *Nantoo Nimdi* serves as another example. *Nantoo Nimdi* is a praise-name for Naa Yakuba, who was Yaa-Naa in the mid-nineteenth century. *Nimdi* is "meat," and *nantoo*, defined by Dagbamba as a very poisonous flying creature, is a disease vector of anthrax. The praise-name means that meat which has been touched by *nantoo* cannot be eaten or approached. With regard to Naa Yakuba, the praise-name therefore asserts that he is the *nantoo* who has come to touch the chieftaincy, the meat his rivals wished to eat. On a general level, in addition to obvious respect for the power of chieftaincy, the name implies that whatever a chief's hand touches becomes a dangerous thing; thus, the name cautions that citizens should not do anything bad or should not become involved in a matter that will come before the chief. The name the drummers gave Naa Yakuba is not only appropriate to his violent career: it has a good dance beat. Drummers beat the name *Nantoo Nimdi* and improvise on its rhythm, and people dance to it.

Dances such as *3im Taai Kurugu* and *Nantoo Nimdi* are danced individually inside a circle of spectators. A dancer may dance several dances inside the circle, while friends and relatives press coins onto the dancer's forehead or place coins into the dancer's hands, publicly demonstrating their relationship. At a typical Dagbamba community celebration—whether a funeral, a wedding, a festival, or a chief's installation—music, dance, and proverbial praise-naming are integrated with status encounters, concerns of social control, and genealogical and historical elucidation.

In an actual community situation, what do the dances look like? How are they performed? I mentioned that Dagbamba do not like people who "show themselves"; the social realm in which people do show themselves, however, is dancing, though they do so in quite a limited way. In music and dance, Dagbamba provide a format for the display of character and, in both music and dance, character is represented as the flexible expression of individuality within the rigidity of structured affiliations. At a musical event like a funeral, a person seated in a circle of friends and relations is invited to a solo dance by a drummer who squats and beats and sings praise-names of that person's ancestors, who are traced to some point on a chieftaincy line. "A person does not praise himself," Dagbamba say, but thus identified and addressed by the drummers, the dancer stands up, looks around, smiles, arranges his or her clothing, then comes into the dance circle and "shows" himself or herself briefly with a solo dance before being surrounded by people who, as I noted, publicly demonstrate the dancer's integration into the community.

Observations of Dagbamba dancers as well as indigenous critical comments from master dancers indicate that Dagbamba dancers attempt to balance inward and outward movements to enlarge and contract their dancing space. Dynamic and expansive body movements that epitomize the force of personality are alternated with shifts into concentrated and precise movements that balance or freeze the body and establish the head and the eyes as the focus of the dance and of character. I have even seen dancers concentrate all movements into the eyes alone, which moved from side to side. Changes of direction and focused body movements engage the rhythms of the drums, while composed control and release of the body demonstrate awareness of what I sometimes call the subtleties of presence and projection in artistic and personal expression. Dagbamba say—to use their way of talking about dancing—that to dance nicely is to dance "coolly," "according to the tradition": like a drummer, a dancer must "cool the heart and use patience and sense to dance." A dancer who follows the "crying" of the drums, so that the dance "fits," makes a gesture of respect to the tradition of the particular dance, and the dance becomes an embodiment of the tradition in which improvisation, the personal expression of the unique insight and imagination of the dancer, projects, in their words, "beauty" and "happiness" and exemplifies and "adds to" or "increases" the tradition's continuity and vitality. At a community celebration, therefore, praise-drumming, music, and dance are integrated into a dramatic presentation of self on multiple levels of projected and expressed reality.

There are quite a few divergent and subtle themes held in balance when a Dagbana dances. It is not just one thing that he or she is expressing regarding the presentation of historical consciousness and the representation of social values. It is too simple, though undoubtedly true in many respects, to say that Dagbamba musical events validate the political and social status quo. Obviously, the conservative function of Dagbamba drummers is to elucidate genealogical relationships at community events and to provide a framework for asserting both social integration and status differentiation. The status of the drummers themselves fosters and preserves their lineal identity and their effective professionalism, as do other factors such as ritual sanctions on the recruitment of children into the profession. The drum history itself unites Dagbamba in learning about their past and enhancing their sense of their community as both a tribe and a family. Social dances like *3im Taai Kurugu* and *Nantoo Nimdi* as well as praise-names based on historical allusion augment concerns of political and social control and elucidate the nature of the chieftaincy.

But to an outsider, there are several peculiarities about the drum history and its influence on the Dagbamba musical repertoire that seem to require analysis on other levels. To someone raised on the exemplary myths of historical figures—like George Washington chopping down a cherry tree and Abraham Lincoln teaching himself to read in a log cabin—the first curious point about the drum history is that it presents a reality that is almost antithetical to the laid-back Dagbamba lifestyle. Many of its stories are tales of war, civil violence, and familial enmity, and many of its personages are treacherous, willful, vengeful, and proud, their characters and their praise the epitome of what Dagbamba would consider antisocial. Many of the praise-names flaunt the strength of a chief and abuse the weakness of his rivals; the praise-names also highlight the presence of jealousy, mistrust, and wickedness in human affairs. The enjoyable ambience of community celebrations, where people present themselves at their best, stands on an incongruous foundation of dances whose names and whose drum language say things like: "I Will Not Know a Person and Let Him Know Me," "A Wicked Man's Trap Catches His Own Child," "If You Trust a Human Being, You Are Lying Down Naked," "Someone Who is Recovered from Illness is the One Who Says that the Medicine is Finished," "Wind is Blowing Clay Pots, and Calabashes Should Not Be Proud."[21] These are all fine dance beats, but in short, the reality represented by the social dances and drum history is poles apart from the pleasant daily lifestyle and values of the people. Yet there is also an element of reality in the dramatized transformation of an amiable farmer or petty trader into the actual blood descendant of a great leader, a flash of remembrance, commitment, and capability expressed in a dance that is bounded by initial shyness at its start and by an enveloping community at its finish.

In Dagbamba musical events, therefore, there are obvious discontinuities of the type that cause students of culture to salivate. On the one hand are the violent historical reality represented in the drum history and the amoral and disruptive social presences memorialized in the praise-names of chiefs; on the other hand are the dance repertoire and social ambience of public gatherings, when the disturbing dimensions of Dagbamba history are enacted and transformed through aesthetic display into a communal ethos that expresses, as I have noted, the social values of respect and patience, interdependence and modesty.

There is another point worth noting. When the drum history is beaten, or when certain stories from the drum history are told, an animal is sacrificed. Depending on the circumstances and the particular story, the animal might be a sheep or even a cow, or both, and sometimes other animals as well. For the *Samban' luŋa*, this sacrifice is made by the chief who has sponsored the performance.

---

[21] In order given, these dances are: *Baŋ nira*, a name of Kari-Naa (chief of Karaga) Alaasan; *Zambalan' tɔŋ*, a name of Kari-Naa Abukari; *Sal' ka yɛda*, a name of Savelugu-Naa (chief of Savelugu) Bukari; *Ŋum biɛ n-kpaŋ*, a name of Savelugu-Naa Yakubu; *Pɔhim ʒɛri*, a name of Savelugu-Naa Ziblim.

The sacrifice is made early during the performance, and food is prepared with the meat of the sacrificed animal; later in the performance, the drummers will be given that food to eat. The indigenous explanation for the sacrifices is twofold. First, because many of the stories in the drum history concern war and bloodshed, the blood of the sacrifice is necessary as commemoration. Second, the spirits of the past chiefs are still around: I was told, "They are not the kind of people who are buried and stay in the ground; they roam." They are dangerous because they did bad things and they do not like to be talked about, but they can be placated with the blood of the sacrifice. And that is about as far as people go to explain the sacrifices.

Beyond these points, there are ritual sanctions that exclude explicit historical discourse from everyday life and from community celebrations other than the drum history performance; in fact, the drum history performance is the only time in which detailed accounts of the past are presented openly. In Dagbamba terms, the "old talks"—their word for history—are "forbidden" and "hidden." Drummers acquire historical knowledge only after years of effort. It was four years after I started learning drumming that I was told about some of the more serious dances, and it was seventeen years before I was told a definitive account of the founding of the state. Many drummers only learn Dagbamba history to a comfortable extent, and most do not even want to answer questions about it. Someone who talks about Dagbamba history can be accused of "revealing the anus of Dagbon." Such control of information is supplemented by the notion that the "forbidden talks" are dangerous, and drummers can easily justify lying or giving false information as a way of avoiding the dangers of mentioning "forbidden" matters. Talking about "forbidden" matters or performing the drum history must be accompanied by gifts and sacrifices whose expense is borne by the one seeking knowledge. If appropriate sacrifices are not made, bad luck or trouble will come to either the chief who sponsored the history or the drummer who sang it, and drummers can run off a list of examples to prove the point. Drummers and chiefs generally meet in advance to discuss the extent of the drum history that will be beaten and what sacrifices will be needed. There are as well parts of Dagbamba history that are not sung in the *Samban' luŋa*: only a very few drummers—the drum chiefs of certain towns—ever have to know them and most drummers do not even want to ask about them. "What good is knowledge," they told me, "if you get it and die?"

The fact that historical knowledge is hierarchically classified according to its degree of secrecy and danger is one of many cultural dimensions supporting drummers' lineal and social identity. What might be considered methodological problems by a Western historian are experienced as such by Dagbamba drummers who must deal, however, with an added dimension of concern for their lives. I have been in situations where one drummer was pressing to learn something with a stream of probing questions while another drummer was begging us all to leave the place. The context of knowledge in which drummers work—where they are continually making judgments about appropriate boundaries for demonstrating respect or undermining bluffing or dealing with actual fear—is certainly very intriguing in comparison with Western models, though it can also be encountered in several other African societies. Certainly, another issue that makes the Dagbamba stimulating from a comparative standpoint is how incredibly conscious they are about their past, about who they are and where they stand.

The drum history brings together many themes of Dagbamba culture. One notion in particular is worthy of reflection in this context. The facts of the sacrifices and the taboos, the physical and temporal structuring of the drum history as a performance, its repetitiveness and occasional periods of monotony, its mythic elements, its isolation from normal discourse: all these elements indicate that the event probably should be considered as a ritual. Anthropologists and other social scientists have generally discussed rituals as events based on a body of shared beliefs, in which concrete actions and things have symbolic meaning, functioning to affirm or realign a community's place in the cosmos, or, in the case of ritual healing, the place of the individual within the collectivity. The central communal metaphor of ethnographic studies is quite evident in interpretations of ritual as the reification of order or structure in the face of chaos; in more contemporary interpretations, the study of the relationships of ritual symbols reflects indigenous perceptions of a community's functional or structural order as well. To a musician, though, the portrayal of ritual meaning as established by the emotive force of comprehended symbols is somewhat uncomfortable: the perspective is a bit too close to the aesthetics of writing, including scholarly writing; the religious imagery as well resembles Western religious notions that project an "objective" view of chaos as something "out there." It is not surprising after all that the music which plays such an important role in rituals is often excluded from analyses oriented to the cognitive, symbolic, or iconographic dimensions of participation. It would seem as well that the Dagbamba case is one example among others that could help open up our perspectives on the nature of religious mediation toward models of action and engagement, particularly because general aspects of musical style and sensibility often convey ritualized presentations of order and participatory modalities beyond ritual boundaries into other contexts of social experience and cultural meaning.

In this regard, I would like to note that what is significant to me about looking at the artistic aspects of Dagbamba communal rituals is that, instead of posing a sense of community in terms of a covenant of the faithful or the blessed, Dagbamba look at aspects of uneasiness in their sense of history. When they dance at funerals or weddings or festivals, or when they assemble for the drum history, Dagbamba establish dramaturgical settings in which the unthinkable and the unknowable, the amoral and the disruptive, are incorporated into an expressive dialogue in which people define boundaries that enable them to feel involved with their society while they achieve a distanced perspective on some of its realities. Yet that distance is also challenged, for to dance with the identity of a forebear elicits the equivocal question: is the dancer up to the standard of his or her father or grandfather? The answer is a recurrent motif in the drum history: I am also capable of doing what my father or grandfather did. The drum history chronicles the destinies of individuals and families and the foundations of the social order in an ambivalent comparison of past and present. There is no sweeping affirmation of either the past or the present in the Dagbamba assessment of the drum history: "It tells a chief about his forefathers and lets a chief know what is inside chieftaincy." And we might note the sacrifices Naa Dariʒɛyu, Naa Luro, and Naa Luro's beloved wife Koyibgaa had to make to know what was inside chieftaincy. I was told, "And for any Dagbana, whether man or woman, the drum history tells that person who he is. The drum history will open his eyes to the old talks that are inside his family, and it is inside his praise that he will know his relationship to chieftaincy."

Sacrifice typically has been understood as a gift and a kind of communion, a symbolic substitution in which one gives something of oneself in order to receive something back or to continue receiving benefits. Thus do the Dagbamba place themselves into a relationship of continuity with their tradition as they address the dead ancestors in their sacrificial prayers: your grandchild is coming to get your benefit. Within the Dagbamba ritualization of history, the sacrifices make a bond with power and with the violence and frustration that underlie political form and social stratification: to use a psychoanalytic analogy, the need for sacrifice can be interpreted as a memorialization of the pain of structural trans-formation.[22] Dagbamba come to terms with their history by incor-porating and beautifying this ambivalent acknowledgment within participatory musical contexts that counterpoint and engage the "forbidden" through the generosity and communicative clarity of mature art and through the balance and control of personal ex-pression. One may wonder whether the greatest achievement of Dagbamba civilization lies in the organizing genius articulated in a complex political system that has continued for more than five hundred years under a single dynasty; or one may also wonder whether the Dagbamba's greatest accomplishment exists in the

---

[22] This phrase is borrowed from David Bakan, *Disease, Pain and Suffering: Toward a Psychology of Suffering* (Boston: Beacon Press, 1971).

artistic genius that turns people into allusive proverbs and reconciles an awareness of the necessity of terrifying greatness in politics, sophisticating it until it turns to play. Dagbamba drummers answer, "Without drumming, there is no chieftaincy in Dagbon."

To most Dagbamba, music remains a meaningful vehicle of historical perspective and a foundation for moral awareness; such abstracted insights into the role music plays in their lives are relatively unnecessary. There are also others who have become partial outsiders to their tradition and who might find in the preceding thoughts a degree of historical sympathy to help them overcome the destructive and totalizing tendencies of the anomie and frustration that can be unleashed by the loss of historical perspective. When the mythopoeic function of the drum history as an elaboration of cultural values has become morally problematic in life situations, they might find, and many do, that artistic sympathy is also a guide to authenticity in social relations. A number of my Dagbamba friends have explained to me how they are able to address issues of self-consciousness and alienation within a participatory framework of music and song and particularly through dancing. They are not alone in apprehending the times when the cultural ordering of their existence fails or is displaced by destiny or death. Like myths and rituals, music provides a structure for the transformation of symbols; but, like art, music also provides a context for experiencing and enhancing a mature sense of historical location and personal meaning. Many Dagbamba continue to resist Western influences, but even for Westernized Dagbamba, music and dance continue to be relevant vehicles of individuation and perspective even when the mythopoeic thrust of the drum history is compromised. Nonetheless, for many Dagbamba drummers, mythopoeic and historiographic problems are aspects of their professionalism. They have struggled with problematic issues of historical meaning and the relationship between history and myth: when they learn their historical tradition in enough detail to question its objectivity, they must reconcile its contradictions in matters of factuality and evidence and in terms of different interpretations and presentations; they also must work to find ways to extend their traditional medium on its own terms while making it appropriate to their changing society. To my knowledge, the drummers have expanded their role' throughout Dagbamba history and particularly during the twentieth century.

A focus on the artistic and expressive aspects of Dagbamba social rituals reveals a different dimension of cultural actualization that complements and expands other types of symbolic interpretation we might apply. An aesthetic focus can provide an essential complementary perspective that significantly enlarges our capacity to portray Dagbamba culture. A picture of Dagbamba society based solely on the privileged hierarchy of institutions in an orthodox functionalist analysis would be one of incredible tensions: a rigid and patriarchal feudal state that is characterized by political conflict and contestation within the elite; a stratified population of diverse origins; emphasized attention to status concerns among both elite and commoners; cultural conservatism and backwardness with regard to development; the exploitation of women and mistrust in social relations as evidenced in conjugal jealousy and witchcraft problems; and so on. Dagbamba life provides many manifestations of structural tension, even though the social ambience presents a calm surface. Without the musical data, however, the portrait of Dagbamba society remains a conflict portrait of difficult social and personal tensions, and the question of how these tensions are resolved or sublimated is left unanswered. It is not enough to refer the integrity of the Dagbamba state to an abstracted conception of something called culture as a unifying element that binds structural tensions. We have to characterize *how* contestation and conflict are culturally sublimated and *how* cultural representations achieve their effectiveness. As an element of culture, music does not inherently express anything functional, and music can be linked to social forms in many ways. But if it *is* music and dance that bind the tensions, then these aspects of expressive culture are not insignificant epiphenomena but are rather constitutive realities at the essence of the system.

It is tempting to speculate on the extent of influence that musical events have as vehicles and validators of historical and political information. Can the way in which this information is actualized in public gatherings and formalized in repertoire and process be said to exert meaningful influence on the traditional state? Although the details of Dagbamba cultural actualization are unique to Dagbamba society, it is my impression that in the broader culture area of which the Dagbamba are part, there are parallels in the use of music as a medium for articulating indigenous insight into patterns of social organization. In the Dagbamba case in particular, though, one cannot help but be impressed by the cultural creativity inherent in their institutional continuity. It is clear that the political aspect of Dagbamba music is not only a matter of using music to enhance institutional motives in political contexts, thus validating the status quo. Dagbamba spend a lot of time in contexts that present particular views of the relations between chiefs and commoners and the relations among various chiefs. These views elaborate a number of checks and balances in the relations of the paramountcy and the aristocracy, illustrated by stories of constraints on both the power of the divisional chiefs and the authority of the paramount chieftaincy. Beyond rationalizing the role of contestation within the political sector, musical events also designate channels of access and patterns of relationships that link persons and groups to centers of power in the social structure. In Dagbon, the social territory within which the drummers move is the political structure, but beyond the drummers' knowledge of history that people respect so highly, the drummers have applied their art so that historical data resonate through many aspects of Dagbamba social life.

To recapitulate: even given the sheer amount of historical thought that has permeated the society, the basic issue that makes the Dagbamba case interesting from a comparative standpoint is the way in which, through music, historical knowledge is brought down to the level of participatory social action—dancing, praising, and giving money—by the Dagbamba themselves. There is a significant distinction, I believe, between the Dagbamba situation and what we normally see in most societies, where historical knowledge achieves its functional effect primarily through the ideological comprehension of cognitive information or through the emotive or ritualized force of cultural symbols. Such means are there in Dagbon, of course, but Dagbamba augment those means within participatory modes that envelope their lives not only during events such as festivals, weddings, or funerals, but also in such mundane contexts as going to the market and being praised by market drummers or understanding the proverbs that people use on each other in family quarrels. More important, Dagbamba learn history not only as words but also as songs, and they not only listen to it but also dance to it and place themselves in relation to it at public gatherings where people look at them. These latter aspects of their historical consciousness distinguish them even from contemporary bardic traditions of epic history in such places as the Balkans, Turkey, Finland, Indonesia, the Philippines, and from the better-known Western models of preclassical Greece.

An effort to understand participation in Dagbamba musical contexts points toward musical expression as a dynamic style of mediating deep structures of meaning, the nexus of the complex institutionalization of history, politics, family, and community in Dagbon. Music is a permeating presence of symbolic and aesthetic forms in many types of participatory communal events where the actual translation of knowledge to social action takes place. In musical contexts, Dagbamba act out social identities with a self-conscious focus on origins that affirms archaic relationships and asserts a particular model of integration among the various layers of society and within the elite itself. Musical situations gather these elements and give them presence within a repertoire of historical allusion and concern. I believe that it is significant that musical events can give us access not merely to peripheral generalizations about expressive culture but perhaps to a more comprehensive overview of Dagbamba civilization, where history and historical consciousness have been refined to a sophisticated integration of perspective and practice.

When I noted above that the *Samban' luŋa* is only one aspect of a complex response to history, I was leading this essay into a description of the musical contexts that link history to political and kinship institutions. If the drum history is one foundation of the drummers' creativity, its imagery is a foundation of self-reflection and self-awareness for Dagbamba who must make their peace with the nature of their society and their place in it. The terrifying greatness of the chiefs who require sacrifices; the violence implicit in political form; the rivalry inherent in social stratification—these aspects of history are transformed through music. A drummer told me that *Nantoo Nimdi*—the name of Naa Yakuba—is a bad name, but in musical gatherings *Nantoo Nimdi* becomes something good, a dance that adds to the community and extends the family. In his comment lies an answer to a difficult question: a single ruling dynasty in Dagbon goes back more than five hundred years; what accounts both for the longevity of the Dagbamba state and for the reasons why this quasi-feudal political system has not developed into a more autocratic type of despotism? Students of social history generally answer such questions by looking for certain types of often complementary social and cultural elements: one is the presence of conservative factors that prevent changes in institutional forms and, particularly, provide checks against revolutionary or radical breaks with the past; another is the presence of ritualized communal forms and generative elements of social meaning that hinder the development of new patterns of institutional relations which might have effect on structural cohesion.[23]

In Dagbon, despite the historical themes with which the *Samban' luŋa* seems to challenge the cultural ambience, an image of contestation and conflict does not appear to the same extent in popular conceptions of the state. There is a high level of historical erudition among people who are not drummers. They are quick to give credit to the drummers for the role the drummers play, for most people know their history and family lines in great detail because they pay

---

[23] This formulation of variables owes much to Barrington Moore, Jr., *Social Origins of Dictatorship and Democracy: Lord and Peasant in the Making of the Modern World* (Boston: Beacon Press, 1967).

close attention to what the drummers do and say. In concordant terms, they identify and discuss themselves with continual allusions to their historical background. To Dagbamba, the Dagbamba heritage is handed down not as a fixed body of tradition but as a living body of thought.[24] Their past is part of their present, constantly reviewed and revised and acted out in cultural events, and what they are doing at their musical gatherings is connecting themselves to their family. With regard to questions about historical continuity, what one hears from knowledgeable people is a very basic concept of political cohesion based on a family model. In simplest yet most profound terms, what has held the Dagbamba together is the understanding that, whatever their problems with one another as they struggle with the vagueness of chieftaincy succession and their own status as a group, ultimately they are one family. This understanding is the foundation of the social cohesion that has prevented constant political contestation and even occasional civil war from destroying the unity of the state. Throughout Dagbamba history, whenever there was a civil war among princes and chiefs, the contesting parties would come together at the end to bury their brothers and move on, holding the idea that they were a family. That family includes the commoners, who also consider themselves and are publicly shown by drummers to be members of the conquerors' descent group. Such ritual relations between living and dead are an important aspect of the association of history and family, in which the past chiefs are ancestors with regard to whom the living stand in ambiguous moral relation. The history itself presents several examples of sitting chiefs, like Naa Dariʒɛɣu and Naa Luro, who are reminded of the dead chiefs, should they not rise to the level of the tradition they have inherited. Within the broader Volta Basin culture area populated by people who speak languages similar to Dagbani, the Dagbamba share a spiritual foundation with groups that have projected the family as the ubiquitous context for interpreting the vicissitudes of destiny and as a way of conceptualizing practical

[24] The phrase "living body of thought" is from Ivor Wilks, private communication.

morality, grounded in divination and sacrifice.[25] The *Samban' luŋa*
and the political culture it portrays may be considered in this vein
as a reflection of a descent group.

Given the regional culture base, it is no doubt prudent to
contemplate Dagbamba spirituality and religious sentiment with
regard to the precept that ritual and religion in that area of the world
typically have strong associations with the family. The significant
presence of ritual customs and sanctions within historical consciousness and political contexts points toward religious inspiration. The
view that the formation of a centralized and feudal patriarchal state
in Dagbon was an innovation brought by conquerors and imposed
upon the aboriginal inhabitants of the region has perhaps been
unduly influenced by Western scholarly interest in evolutionary
schemes of historical development. From another vantage point, it
is certainly logical to assume that the cultural capacity for that
development had to have been in place and that Dagbamba history
stands on that foundation. In Dagbon, the important transition that
distinguished the Dagbamba from the other cultural groups in the
region can be envisioned as much in religious motifs as in political
ones, as much in terms of ritual aspects of kinship structures as of
sanctioned authority structures. The unification of the towns and
villages under the rule of a centralized state was also the unification
of separate families into one larger family. The evolution of
hierarchical political form was also the evolution of an elaborately
segmented family.[26]

---

[25] Among the greatest ethnographic efforts ever undertaken are Meyer Fortes's
studies of the kinship system of a neighboring group, the Talensi, who speak a
closely related Oti-Volta language and who may therefore be presumed to share
elements of a regional cultural base with the Dagbamba. See Meyer Fortes, *The
Dynamics of Clanship among the Tallensi: Being the First Part of an Analysis of
the Social Structure of a Trans-Volta Tribe* (London: Oxford University Press,
1945); *The Web of Kinship among the Tallensi* (London: Oxford University Press,
1949); *Oedipus and Job in West African Religion* (Cambridge: Cambridge
University Press, 1959); *Religion, Morality, and the Person: Essays on Tallensi
Religion* (Cambridge: Cambridge University Press, 1987).

[26] The diffusionist model of the origin of the Dagbamba state (and perhaps
related Voltaic states), a model which presumes an imported link between

In Dagbon, musical situations represent in unique ways the strengths and weaknesses of the Dagbamba aristocracy as a whole and in their relations with one another. It is proverbial wisdom, however, that the strength of a chief is a commoner, and the strength of a commoner is a chief. Demonstrating the link between the commoners and the central institution of chieftaincy is the work of the drummers. Every Dagbana is the grandchild of a chief, the drummers claim, and they can use a drum to beat a praise-name for every Dagbana. In musical contexts, the historical continuity of the Dagbamba state is displayed as a dimension of the extended family. In musical contexts, as in many aspects of Dagbamba daily life, a sincere respect for older generations, for origins, and for the heritage of the past guides people's reasoning, their imagination, and their art. In the Dagbamba case, musical contexts are crucial to informing our perception of deep structures of meaning and refining our appreciation of the deliberateness with which the Dagbamba maintain their traditions. In the final analysis, one probably need not choose which type of cultural processes might have had the greatest significance in the development of Dagbamba society: what is impressive is the way in which the complex institutionalization of many cultural processes is manifested in Dagbamba music and made accessible to the Dagbamba themselves through participation in public events. Because of this cultural achievement, the Dagbamba merit a respected place on the world stage. I would also hope that for scholars in various fields, the ideas advanced in this

---

patrilineal descent and statist ideas of chieftaincy and which projects a process of usurpation, conflict, assimilation, and evolutionary stratification, has been critiqued by Skalník (Peter Skalník, "Early States in the Voltaic Basin," in *The Early State*, ed. Henri J. M. Claessen and Peter Skalník (The Hague: Mouton [1978]), 469–93; Peter Skalník, "The Dynamics of Early State Development in the Voltaic Area," in *Political Anthropology: The State of the Art*, ed. S. Lee Seaton and Henri J. M. Claessen [The Hague: Mouton, (1979)], 197–213). Skalník, working from a perspective inspired by Vansina, has argued the logic of asserting that the indigenous inhabitants of Dagbon were probably already well into the process of state formation before the arrival of Dagbamba horsemen.

essay indicate that a focus on music should not be the province of specialists, for musical events have the possibility to open a number of related and comparative dimensions to our perspectives on the people we meet in other cultures.

Historicism and the Quest for D/divine Music

Michael W. Harris

Historicism, Old and New

To the extent that academicians as a group can be said to debate any one topic, historians, anthropologists, literary critics, political scientists—and others willing to acknowledge philosophical dimensions of their respective disciplines—have been engaged in intense discussions over the merits of the New Historicism. In essence, this philosophy (more accurately, an array of critical studies) seeks to explain the ways in which scholars fail to achieve—in the words of H. Aram Veeser who has edited an anthology of New Historicist essays—the "disembodied objectivity to which humanists have increasingly aspired."[1] As expected of anything that purports to be both 'new' and iconoclastic, the New Historicism has prompted not only anguished criticism from traditionalists but, perhaps a sign of its poignancy, rancorous animosity from such representatives of the radical political right as William Bennett, Lynn Cheney, and Allan Bloom. These personalities have been prominent enough on the political scene over the last fifteen years that any of us can guess the institutions and ideas they perceive to be under attack: western civilization, truth, pure research, etc.

As a philosophy of history emerging in Germany during the middle to late nineteenth century, historicism (or historism) has been

---

[1] *The New Historicism* (London: Routledge, 1989), ix.

dogged by misunderstanding, most often generated by the often mutually exclusive definitions various historians have assigned to the word. In the late nineteenth century, on the one hand, it meant "that past events and situations are unique and non-repeatable" and thus can be understood only in their "particular contexts." On the other it meant "the discovery of general laws of social development" that apply not only to the present but beyond, almost to the extent that historicism can be employed to "predict future events."[2] Among United States historians in the 1930s historicism got tossed around in the (in)famous "New History" discussions with Charles Beard himself once using it to describe a historian's commitment to telling history "as it really was."[3] So confused was its meaning by mid-century that the *American Historical Review* in the "Notes and Suggestions" section of the journal sought not a definition but instead what could be regarded "as a 'proper' use of the word." The attempt proved futile, judging by the authors' conclusion that there were two definitions which they could "suggest" as the foundation "for the more systematic classification of other positions."[4] Historicism languished on the periphery of historiographical discourse until 1969 when Roy Harvey Pearce employed it to argue the use of literature as historical evidence, that is, "a literary work carries the past into the present."[5] The connection between history, via historicism, to literature was forged even further by Hayden White. He made a case for the historical text to be considered an account of "phenomena"; the account can be likened ". . .to the literal and figurative levels of imaginative literature. . . ."[6]

[2] Harry Ritter, *Dictionary of Concepts of History* (New York: Greenwood Press, 1986), 183.

[3] Ritter, *Dictionary of Concepts of History*, 185.

[4] Dwight E. Lee and Robert N. Beck, "The Meaning of 'Historicism'," *American Historical Review* 59 (1954):568, 577.

[5] *Historicism Once More: Problems and Occasions for the American Scholar* (Princeton: Princeton University Press, 1969), 5.

[6] "Historicism, History, and Figurative Imagination," *History and Theory* 14 (1975):55. For a complete explication of his historicism, see "Metahistory: The Historical Text as Literary Artifact," *Clio: An Interdisciplinary Journal of Literature, History, and Philosophy* 3 (June 1974):277–303.

In its "new" guise, historicism has hardly overcome its definitional crisis. Indeed, the broad range of scholars who profess some brand of "New Historicism" attests to the evolution of historicism from that of a contested term of historiography to a cross-disciplinary rubric for a widening array of critical perspectives on scholarship:

> . . .New Historicists muddy the formal walkways that criticism has up to now generally followed. They refuse to apportion the discussion of character, language, and theme to literary scholars, of primitive customs to anthropologists, of demographic patterns to social historians. By redistributing this disciplinary legacy, New Historicists threaten all defenders of linear chronology and progressive history, whether Marxists or Whig optimists. Those who would jealously enclose their private gardens against communal interference may well lock arms against a criticism that mingles disparate periods and upsets the calculus of Left and Right politics.[7]

In essence, this historicism shuns orthodoxy (except this one!) and seems to advance itself by enduring its own "internal stresses."[8]

Perhaps a historicism that consists of an admixture of the old and New and that thrives on a dynamic of self-destabilization could aid scholars' analyses of musics of various sorts, especially the musics that have been appropriated by various religious groups as suitable to their spiritual seekings. I have moved toward such a historicism in an effort not necessarily to devise a New Historicist critique of sacred music as to fashion a set of parameters for such a critique. Not surprisingly, I have found as my most useful sources the debates of the older historicism as well as the "internal stresses" of the New. Apparently the one hundred plus year tussle over terminology and the resultant community of 'new' practitioners celebrating their lack of consensus mean that historicism is still as ripe as any philosophy for making scholars reflect on their ways.

A word about parameters is necessary. Too often scholars premise

---

[7] Veeser, *The New Historicism,* xv.

[8] Veeser, *The New Historicism,* xv..

the success of their work on making findings. Thus, how scholars arrive at their findings is often relegated to the realm of methodology or, more often than not if there is an existing literature, to the realm of theory. If there is any one common goal of those who have pondered historicism of any sort, however, it is that the distinction between making findings and making conclusions about them is negligible if it exists at all. Hayden White dismisses as "conventional" the difference between "fact" (finding) and "interpretation" (conclusion about fact):

> The fact is presented where and how it is in the discourse in order to sanction the interpretation to which it is meant to contribute. And the interpretation derives its force of plausibility from the arrangement of the facts in the order and manner in which they are presented in the discourse.[9]

This shift of focus to the discourse throughout which findings and interpretations are deployed is the analog of my desire to shift attention away from a New Historicist critique of the music of Divinism. A critique would constitute a discourse about facts and interpretations and a finding of what I observed the music to be. The fashioning of parameters, on the other hand, constitutes a contemplation of the discourse and of the act of interpreting.

What follows is thus an exposition of the parameters—or constants—that investigators may utilize as they create their discourses and shape their interpretations of sacred music. The two categories of parameters below derive from the issues over which the proponents of the traditional historicism, and later those of the New, debated. To the former, historicism concerns itself with the position of the historian. If she believes that historical understanding arises out of the context of the past events, she sees it as her duty to place herself in that context. If she believes that history exposes immutable truths, she is obligated to explain the past in order to explain the present and perhaps the future. To the New Historicist, any sort of commerce provides the grist for historical understanding.

[9] White, "Historicism, History, and Figurative Imagination," 55.

But rather than merely locating and analyzing that which she finds engaged, the New Historicist seeks historical understanding from searching through and explicating the moment of engagement or intercourse itself—for example, the context of an exchange, the nuance of a negotiation, or the pattern suggested by the circulation of an artifact or idea. Thus our two categories, while rooted in rather disparate historicisms, provide for a common critique of the critic—in this instance those of us who set about observing and interpreting sacred music. One need not adopt one or both historicisms to welcome the prospect of having to reflect on our critical enterprise.

Positionality and D/divinity

Because he destabilizes two notions that are widely accepted as incontrovertible by our society, Major Jealous (Father) Divine and his Peace Mission movement highlight the historicist dilemma of positionality. By declaring himself to be GOD—the Judeo-Christian one, to be exact—and by refusing to acknowledge racial identity of any sort, he set himself at odds with a monotheistic and racially polarized America from 1918, when he first gained notoriety, to his death in 1965.[10] His declarations also fuel historicist debates over whether the past is unique or whether it reveals timeless truths. To

[10] Father Divine's notoriety—some would argue infamy—has spawned a number of studies. Some, like Robert Allerton Parker's *Incredible Messiah: The Deification of Father Divine* (Boston: Little, Brown and Co., 1937), border on the sensational; others, like Claude McKay's *Harlem: Negro Metropolis* (New York: E. P. Dutton, 1940), seem impressionistic. For an account of the social and political impacts of Divine, see Robert Weisbrot's *Father Divine and the Struggle for Racial Equality* (Urbana: University of Illinois Press, 1983). For the most recent, somewhat official (Mrs. Divine and the Peace Mission Movement endorse no outside studies) biography, see Jill Watts, *God, Harlem U.S.A.: The Father Divine Story* (Berkeley: University of California Press, 1992), which, however, like a number of recent studies, is problematical, given its unacknowledged positionality on Divine's godness and race. For a contextualization of Divine among popular religious leaders, see my essay, "Major J. (Father) Divine," in Charles H. Lippy, ed., *Twentieth-Century Shapers of American Popular Religion* (New York, Westport, London: Greenwood Press, 1989), 110–18.

the investigator of the music of Divinism, both his declarations and her position of observation challenge her analysis.

The eternality of 'God' (as opposed to a 'god') and the fixedness of racial heritage on the one hand and the social-/cultural-specific meanings assigned to both concepts on the other suggest the first positional parameter: neither position of classical historicism need work to the exclusion of the other. To Divine there was a simple cause-and-effect relationship between his divinity and racelessness: GOD has no color. His reasoning contains a combination of universalist/particularist (GOD/Negro) elements analogous to the transcendent/contextual (past exemplifies truth/past is unique) dialectic of historicism.

A correlative parameter follows: positionality is context-specific. The critic confronts this condition when, having accepted the possibility of both positions, she ponders which to argue as context-specific and which as overarching truth. This parameter homes in on what the observor finds to observe. Moreover, it challenges the assumption that what she finds questionable would be found so by any one. Is a human's proclamation that s/he is G/god of interest beyond the context in which G/god is not a human? Does one's denial of racial identity outside of a society in which every one is raced require examination? Given the fixedness of racial identity in the society Divine confronted and the continuity of that fixedness throughout American history to the present, no scholar, regardless of whether she regards Divine's racial identity as particular or universal, adopts such a position apart from her sense of her racedness. Despite his assertion to the contrary, he becomes either divine or Divine and either a racial other or brother to the person who would explain him.

The same paradox lies at the root of Divine's positioning on the eternal truth of his being. He, "God," was circumscribed by the other "God" and thus by the questioning, if not disbelief, of his "realness:"

If you refuse to let GOD be real to you, to you the realness of GOD may not be discerned, but to those whom the realness of GOD is revealed, to them it is real. . . . But if you close the way up—in

other words close the way behind you and before you as you go,
by your selfish ideas and opinions, by trying to measure GOD with
the measure of a man, it will be a matter of impossibility for GOD
to you to express HIS realness.[11]

The contextuality of the other transcendent truth he wanted to make
'real' plagued him as well. Indeed, he found himself having to carve
out his racial non-being by acknowledging race: "I AM NOT an
N[egro] and I AM NOT representing any such thing as the N[egro]
or C[olored] race. . . ."[12] In the racially bisected society of early-
to mid-twentieth-century United States, he saw it his task to de
racialize not only himself but his followers:

> Now I am not poor because I do not belong to a poor, downtrodden
> race. If I was attached to a poor downtrodden race like some of you
> think you are, . . . then I would be like some of you.

Even more adamantly he declined any association with African
Americans:

> The other night someone got up and said there were lots of c[olored]
> people from New Orleans [present]. . . . I don't care anything about
> c[olored] people. I haven't them in me. . .[and] cast them out of
> my consciousness and do not allow them to exist there.[13]

Relative to the contextuality of race, positional historicism may
not be as easily dismissed as anachronistic as would at first appear.
The rabid contemporary debates concerning racial constructivism
versus essentialism are premised—though not always explicitly—
on positionality as it was argued among nineteenth-century
historicists. Definitions that position race socially are not simply
intellectual exercises; they are regarded as betrayals of one's race:
"I do not understand how a Black critic aware of the implantations

---

[11] Quoted in Milton C. Sernett, ed., *Afro-American Religious History: A
Documentary Witness* (Durham, North Carolina: Duke University Press, 1985),
406.

[12] Watts, *God, Harlem U.S.A.*, 171.

[13] Watts, *God, Harlem U.S.A.*, 89.

of racist structures in the consciousness of Blacks and whites could accept poststructuralist ideas and practices."[14] A field of study, Critical Race Theory (CRT), has sprung up since 1989 to air positionality among legal professionals, particularly law school teachers, on race. One of CRT's major premises, a "call to context," stresses the position of legal theorists relative to the law:

> Most mainstream scholars embrace universalism over particularity, abstract principles and the "rule of law" over perspectivism. . . . For CRT scholars, general laws may be appropriate in some areas (such as, perhaps, trusts and estates, or highway speed limits). But political and moral discourse is not one of them.[15]

Before we particularize historicist positionality to Divine and race, we might turn our attention to the same discussions among feminist scholars. In *This Sex*, Luce Irigaray considers the mere question of whether she is a woman invalid and, in language startlingly similar to Divine's disclaimer of race, declares: ". . .I am not *one*."[16]

Turning from the issues of identity, we take up the last parameter of positionality, this one concerned with the notion of 'sacred'. We might think of it as the application of his identity. If so, we might broadly classify Divine's divinity into two categories. One is the proclamation of divine authority, i.e., his public claim to act as God. An example is the Peace Mission's "Righteous Government Platform," in which he asserts his power to save civilization:

> Just think of laws that are not according to the Constitution, and brought about under the Constitution, which are in complete

[14] Joyce A. Joyce, "'Who the Cap Fit': Unconsciousness and Unconscionableness in the Criticism of Houston A. Baker, Jr. and Henry Louis Gates, Jr.," *New Literary History* 18, no. 2 (1987):371–84. This article was one of several salvos between black scholars over the essence/construction of race in the 1987 volume of *New Literary History*.

[15] Richard Delgado, ed., *Critical Race Theory: The Cutting Edge* (Philadelphia: Temple University Press, 1995), xv.

[16] Quoted in Diana Fuss, *Essentially Speaking: Feminism, Nature and Difference* (New York: Routledge, 1989), 72.

violation of the Constitution. If GOD would allow it to continue, they would eventually undermine the Constitution completely, and the government of our civilization would be a failure.[17]

The other category is the exercise of his divinity, i.e., his power to sanctify—set apart as holy. An example is Woodmont Estate in Gladwyne, Pennsylvania, the Peace Mission's headquarters since 1953. Divine declared "and consecrated [it] as the Mount of the House of the LORD"; in accordance with biblical prophecy, one such place would be established "in the last days" (Isaiah 2:2–3):

> . . .the repetition of history. . .,as it was with the building of the Temple of the LORD in Jerusalem, in Mount Moriah, so it is in the rebuilding of the Temple of the LORD. . .at Philadelphia in Woodmont.[18]

Both categories pertain to positionality in terms of being historical acts which can be understood either as unique to their respective contexts or as universal truths. From the perspective of either position, we can frame historical acts and manipulate them for historical purposes: Woodmont was a spiritual space, designated so by Divine; or, Woodmont stands as another example of mankind's search for a holy place. But both categories of Divinity are more than historical acts; they signify, at least to Divine and his followers, the sacred. Positionality, however, fails as a tool for fathoming the significance of an act, sacred or otherwise. Regardless of what Divine declared Woodmont to be, we do not know what he intended Woodmont to mean. Hence the parameter: positionality and signification are irrelevant to one another. In other words, there can be no historicist understanding via positionality of Divinity.

At the root of historicist positionalism lies an explanation for this apparent mutual exclusivity of positionality and meaning. Positionality is predicated on nothing more than the *belief* that history

---

[17] [Mrs. M. J. Divine], *The Peace Mission Movement* (Philadelphia: Imperial Press, 1982), 158–59.

[18] [Divine], *The Peace Mission Movement*, 59.

can best be understood from one of two perspectives. Historicists, in other words, professed to find meaning positionally. Thus they argued rather than proved historical meaning. The acts were there; the meaning(s) gleaned from them, however, was declared. To the extent that one equates the declaration of Divine that he is and acts divine to that of classical historicists who declare the discovery of historical meaning, one ascribes an arbitrariness to both. Whether Divine is a savior of civilization or whether he sanctifies Woodmont are rejected or accepted arbitrarily by the researcher no differently than by Divinites. Quite simply, one assumption can not prove the validity of another.

One might ask what purpose a negative parameter serves for our study of sacred—Divine—music. In this instance the no-constant brings us to the point that historians faced when historicism got so caught up in itself that it ceased to generate history. My interpretation of this collapse is that historicists ultimately realized that arguments over whether one position might yield more meaning than the other were tautological at best. The logic—primitive as it is—that meaning cannot be rendered empirically had to prevail at some point. When it did, the shifting, "proper," and convoluted definitions ensued to the point that classical historicism collapsed into a solipsistic heap.

The negative parameter has important utility for this study because it classifies 'sacred' as unknowable beyond, perhaps, a specific act or articulated belief. Moreover, it frames 'sacred' as subjective to the degree that any location of it is arbitrary— tantamount, as it were, to building another Divine Woodmont. It thus directs us not to ask what is divine about Divine's music; instead, what is Divine about Divine's music. The redirection of focus from the discovery of 'sacred' to the making of it brings us to where New Historicists assumed the burden of the old—to search out historical understanding—but with the profound shift to the actions and interactions of historical actors.

D/divine Interactivity

The philosophies and methods of formal musicology echo those of classical historicism, especially its underlying positivism. Musicology expects music to yield an understanding of its context—for example, composition, performance, audience—and its timeless truths—for example, rules, classification of styles, and instruments of performance. Arising out of the same nineteenth-century German academic milieu as historicism, musicology is rooted in textualism and the notion that observations can be made and reported independently of the observer. Thus it has served to provide understandings of written, western European, composed music through analyses by critics trained to be 'objective' in the best of western European academic traditions. It is widely accepted that the closed circuitry of empiricist thinking and methods has been exposed by the failure of positivistic-driven criticism to plum the production of non-western European cultural traditions. Musicological analysis as a formal system is strongly challenged when it turns to non-notated musics and to music systems which, for example, are non-tonal centered. It is all the more limited when it turns to sacred music, especially D/divine music.

The parameters that I suggest for incorporation into a musicological critique of sacred music are premised on the focus on interactivity that seems axiomatic to New Historicist criticism. The isolation of any one component of a system from any other for the purpose of observing it ultimately distorts the element and may thus prove futile. Instead, one observes phenomena as they interact in what appears to be an organized or systematic manner. One seeks understanding of the organization—or economy—as part of the understanding of the phenomenon. This effort to explicate interconnectivity prompts historicists to use "marketplace" metaphors such as exchange, negotiation, and circulation.[19] Artistic production, whether material or conceptual, is intricately entangled in social and cultural networks, much as money is in capitalist economies. The

---

[19] Veeser, *The New Historicism*, xiv.

economist may be able to identify a piece of currency much as a
musicologist would a song. But the color and design of that dollar
or that which makes it money and capital—like words and harmony
make a song, and then a genre of music—can be ascertained only
by observing and interpreting its transformation as it interacts with
other components of the system. Via exchange, negotiation, and
circulation, the piece of paper makes transitions back and forth
between being a dollar, becoming money, and flowing as capital.

The concept of an economy helps to identify parameters for
understanding music, particularly of the Divine sort. By assuming
to isolate music from all that goes on around it, the analyst risks
particularizing it. Music was anything but specifically separable
from all the other sounds in a Divine context. Both the Sunday
church service and the holy communion banquet service, the only
congregational contexts of Divinism, are structured for individual
and communal expression:

> [Church services] consist of public singing of inspirational hymns
> and songs as the Spirit moves. . . . The services are conducted as
> in a great Spiritual Democracy which is what the Churches of the
> Peace Mission Movement really are. The privilege of free speech
> and volitional expression is preserved for everyone.[20]

True, there is something discrete about singing, especially when
alternated with speech as would have occurred in Divine's services.
But the question should follow: how discrete is music sound from
speech and all other sounds? This question suggests the most
fundamental parameter: avoid the presumptive particularization of
'music'. From an utterly reductionist standpoint sounds are sounds.
But we differentiate between them. Indeed, we assume a stark
discreteness between noise, music, speech, etc. The parameter,
however, has us consider how often sounds occur in isolation from
one another, even within our taxonomic structure of them. In
communal Divine events, streams of sounds flow in and out with

---

[20] [Divine], *The Peace Mission Movement*, 27.

one another. For example, at a communion banquet in 1936, a crowd of "thousands" voiced praises, burst into song, and then fell silent to the words of Divine:

> As they rejoiced in the realness and the genuineness of HIM Who said in the Body called Jesus, "All who ever came before ME are thieves and robbers," they sang with radicalness and enthusiasm. . . .
>
> Then speaking Words of Spirit and of Life, unfolding the science of salvation in psychological truths hid from the sages but condescending to speak in the language of men, FATHER arose speaking Personally as follows: PEACE EVERYONE! . . .[21]

Even conceding that there was a segmenting of sound into periods in which speech or singing prevailed does not obviate the need to put the "realness" of the crowd's rejoicing, the "radicalness and enthusiasm" of their singing, and the "speaking Personally" of Divine into one frame of analysis—one economy of sounds.

Divine alludes to a holistic deployment of sounds to reinforce his spirituality when he admonishes his believers to "speak" music "sincerely":

> When you sang the song, "GOD will take care of you," this is not a supposition, this in not an imagination, this is not merely to be sung for to be reiterated, and to be repeated and spoken as a melody, but it is a song sung. When it is reiterated spontaneously by the true and the faithful, if you say it sincerely and mean it sincerely, the very reaction of your conscious conviction according to your sincerity will respond within you. . . . That is why the vibrations [sounds?] are so high here; it is because the believers are sincere.[22]

Could it be that Divine music is anything but that which we particularize as divine music? I think the answer is yes, if we can agree upon how to focus new historicists' marketplace concepts on the economy of sounds that Father Divine favored in congregational settings. Take for example the notion of circulation. Because Divine

---

[21] Sernett, *Afro-American Religious History*, 405–6.

[22] Sernett, *Afro-American Religious History*, 409.

sought to de-racialize, he was forced to confront the presence of racially contextualized sounds which various believers not only brought to Divine gatherings but responded to in racially specific ways. The attempt to de-Africanize African American religious settings has a long history. Rabbi Wentworth A. Matthew, founder of the Commandment Keepers Congregation of the Living God, forbade his followers to engage in "'niggerations'" when singing and praying.[23] Nation of Islam founder, Elijah Muhammad thought of blues as "Nigger music." Those songs, along with all other traditional African American expressive culture, must be "rebuked" because they were manifestations of the "savagery inculcated within the blacks by the white man's teachings from slavery down to the contemporary world."[24]

Divine seems not to have taken such drastic measures. Rather than deny African American Divinites their cultural references, Divine encouraged a flow of religious African-Americanisms. At a meeting in 1933 at the New Star Casino in Atlantic City, over 6,000 were said to "sing, shout, and rejoice" in response to Divine's sermon on how to recover from the great Depression. At one point there was a saxophone solo "from one in the *orchestra* [italics supplied]." At another, the congregation sang an old African American hymn, "Take your burdens to the Lord and leave them there," followed by a Divinite hymn, "Put your trust in Father and everything will be all right."[25] This account strongly suggests a parameter: transmission of culturally specific sounds from one sacred context to another may provide some of the clearest indices of the construction of the sacred sound economy. Clearly, shouting, saxophone playing, and spirituals had deep roots in African American religious traditions before Divine allowed them into his services. Even more interesting is how he deployed these sound elements to instill belief in him instead of in the Christian God.

[23] Sernett, *Afro-American Religious History*, 399.

[24] Leon Forrest, *Relocations of the Spirit* (Wakefield, R.I.: Asphodel Press, 1994), 69–70.

[25] *New York News*, 11 February 1933, 1, 3.

More than any other factor, such an open passage between what should have been mutually exclusive contexts probably created the vibrancy of Divine worship.

Evidence of the way in which the marketplace concept of negotiation works to explicate the Divine sound economy can be found by sequencing the sources of various sounds. In official Peace Mission accounts of services, one notes a persistence of antiphonal dealings:

> "If you put your trust in Father, everything will be all right" ('It will Father', asserted the Audience). . . . "God will abundantly bless you, and first thing you know you have so much money you will not know what to do with it" ('Thank you Father', resound throughout the audience). . . . "There have been questions in the mind of the people, concerning my activities, and concerning My Followers recognizing Me as being the Infinite." ('Yes God',—came a shout from the Believers.)[26]

Another dialogue of sounds occurred when Divine, on rare occasions, chose to sing rather than speak. At a banquet in his Harlem headquarters in April 1934, Divine spoke a few words at the conclusion of the "communion meal." He then sang to the congregation while they left the hall:

There are millions, there are millions,
There are millions of Blessings,
Every day they are multiplied by
   as many, many more!

There are billions, etc., There are trillions, etc.
There are quatrillions, quintrillions,
sextillions, septillions, octillions,
duodecillions, and decillions, etc.

Peace everyone! . . .[27]

---

[26] *New York News*, 11 February 1933, 3, and 28 April 1934, 6.
[27] *New York News*, 28 April 1934, 6.

The parameter suggested by the antiphonal interchange of sounds in this manner is: negotiations of sounds occur in the alteration of roles between hearing and originating sounds. Even Divine, the master of his religious convocations, knew when to listen to his followers (or, at least, to appear to do so) and when to direct sound(s) at them. Moreover, his speech sound could be answered either with speech or song—perhaps at his choosing or spontaneously by the audience. He could reciprocate by answering in kind or by switching modes, that is, answering in song when his congregants had shouted back to him. Perhaps the most critical point to make regarding the negotiations in a Divine sound economy is that complete silence probably never existed. At a banquet the clinking of dishes, the scratching of chairs against the wood floors, and the muttered "thank you's" or "you're welcome's" that follow the passing of food all provided the ideal constant low-level din in which sound negotiations took place.

The new historicist concept of exchange offers the most comprehensive critique of Divine sound(s). At its most elemental level, a Divine service bartered noise for faith. During one of those classic Divine services in August 1934, when a believer's testimonial of faith included a spontaneous song—"Father Divine is all I need"—Divine forged the sonic link:

> That little Composition is well worth considering. Those of you that sung it, remember what you are saying. Do not think you are just playing! It is indeed Wonderful! You can tell by your daily actions, by your words, and your deeds, and by your personal appearances, if you really believe that I am Whom you say I Am,—and if you know, you will forsake everything for Me.[28]

The parameter suggested here assumes some sort of sonic transubstantiation: a melding of sounds to ideas—particularly those urging beliefs—is the presumptive dynamic of the sacred economy of sounds.

[28] *New York News*, 25 August 1934, 6.

One of the most fundamental beliefs of Divinism is that God had a body and that the believer, while in the presence of Divine, had the privilege of seeing that body. "The Body of God," became one of the most widely sung songs of the movement because it expressed the chief tenet of Divinism:

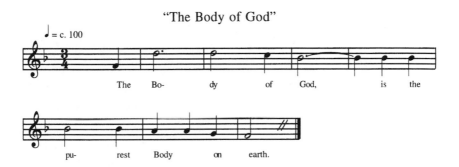

"The Body of God"

The extent to which a Divine adherent's belief in Divine's divinity could be either induced or affirmed by the inhaling and exhaling of air, the tightening and loosening of lungs and vocal chords, the ebb and flow of crowd sounds (e.g., shouting and clapping) in her ears, and, if at a holy communion banquet, her intermittent ingestion of food and drink (non-alcoholic) that occurred when 'singing' this song—these are the sort of probes this parameter suggests. The large initial melodic leap followed by the more than five seconds—at the highest level of pitch—spent generating the sound, "Bo-dy," becomes at some point to a believer the 'Body'. This is true, perhaps, of this song more than others because it has no verse-chorus structure. The music and speech patterns are expressed over and over.

A Conclusion

If nineteenth-century historicisms and the New Historicism have anything to offer the scholar of sacred musics, it is that her observations describe both herself and the sounds she seeks to explicate. The parameters suggested imply a relationship between sound-source and sound-seeker, whether or not they share the context of the sound or attempt to reconstruct it. Divine divined sounds that ultimately mean something to those who would discern the divine in Divine. The embrace of both historicisms seems to provide an analytical context for a deeper understanding of D/divine music.

"Musicalizing" the Other: Shamanistic Approaches to Ethnic-Class Competition along the Upper Rio Negro

Jonathan D. Hill

Introduction

In late July 1981, after having completed several months' fieldwork with Arawakan Wakuénai people living along the lower Guainía River in Venezuela, I was spending a few days in the river town of San Carlos de Rio Negro prior to taking a longer trip up the Guainía to begin working in a different village. As is often the case, the most interesting things happen when they are least expected. An indigenous acquaintance who lived across the river in the Colombian town of San Felipe stopped by my house to visit and told me that the people of San Felipe were preparing to perform ceremonial music and dances that evening. In the late afternoon of Thursday, July 22, I packed up my tape recorders, camera, and notebooks and headed across the Rio Negro to document the ceremonial activities.

The headman of San Felipe had organized a gathering of Wakuénai and Yeral people to perform musical dances in a small clearing on the outskirts of the town. In addition to his own following of local Wakuénai and Yeral families, the headman had invited a powerful shaman from a nearby village to help lead the musical performances. A core group consisting of the headman, the shaman, and several other elders performed most of the musical dances, while an audience of young people listened and applauded at the end of each dance.

The explicit purpose of these performances was to protest the political situation of indigenous families in San Felipe by demonstrating the collective identity of indigenous people living in San Felipe and by appealing to higher levels of power in the national political order. What had brought about this indigenous protest was the increasingly predatory economic practices of the town's merchants, who had settled in San Felipe during the mid-1970s at the same time as funds from the Colombian and Venezuelan governments began to flow into the region. These merchants had begun to intercept funds and materials, such as gasoline and cement, which had been donated by the Colombian government to the entire community, the majority of whom consisted of Wakuénai and other indigenous families. The merchants used these resources to build their own stores, and they sold the remaining materials to the Wakuénai for highly inflated prices. This economic exploitation went on for about five years, and by 1980 the indigenous families of San Felipe were heavily indebted to the merchants for materials which, they felt, had been originally sent into the region as a form of economic aid for them.

In early 1981, the local Wakuénai headman of San Felipe traveled to Puerto Inirida to protest his people's situation in front of authorities from the national government's Division of Indigenous Affairs. These officials passed the headman's complaint up to their central office in Bogotá, and within days the flow of funds and materials for the development of San Felipe had ceased. In response, the local merchants cut off electricity to the indigenous neighborhood. The Wakuénai families were by this time accustomed to having electricity in their homes, primarily for running lights, stoves, and refrigerators, so they reacted by repairing the electric lines. The merchants again cut the lines, and relations between them and the indigenous families soon intensified into open hostility. The Wakuénai headman organized a collective work party to clean up the neighborhood as a way of bringing people together and showing the strength of his following to the local merchants. This was the context of the ceremonial music and dances being performed in late July 1981; the power had been cut for several weeks, and people gathered at dusk to sing, dance, and play music. The performances in San Felipe in late July 1981 were also a rehearsal for the group of men who would travel to Puerto Inirida in August bearing a petition from the indigenous residents of the town.

In the opening performance at San Felipe, a group of male musicians and their female dance partners played the standard opening duet of *pudáli,* an indigenous type of ceremonial exchange between affinally related groups. The pairs of *máwi*, or *yapurutú,* flute players were later joined by the accompaniment of men singing and playing dance stomping tubes. The melody of *máwi* flutes was the same as that played in the first stage of *pudáli* ceremonies and consisted of a single descending melody played over and over with almost no variation in pitches or phrase lengths. Also, like the opening musical dances of *pudáli*, the opening performance in San Felipe was a relatively large ensemble of instruments and singers producing a decentered, chaotic-sounding mixture of voices, tones, percussive sounds, and rhythms.

After a short intermission, two senior men picked up flutes and began playing a duet. The two men danced in a counter-clockwise circle and were joined by two senior women until the end of the dance. The headman and several others referred to this particular dance as *viejita*, a species of small fish. A transcription of the melody reveals that the music was a simple variation on the theme of the melody from the first performance rather than a complex set of rhythmic and tonal variations based on a distinctly different theme.

In the third performance, a group of young men played *píti* whistles made from hollowed sticks of *yagrumo* (*Cecropia* sp.). These whistles produced only a single, high-pitched tone and were played in unison to make a loud rhythmic accompaniment for the dancers. The whistle players and their female dance partners moved quickly around in a clockwise direction, whirling around so that the tail of the procession became its head, and leaned backward and forward in unison. This performance evoked much laughter among the gathering of spectators.

This celebratory mood was quickly transformed back into the more somber, purposeful atmosphere with which the festivities in San Felipe had commenced. In a fourth, final performance, the visiting shaman led a song-dance accompanied by dance stomping tubes. The song which the shaman performed on this occasion was not one of the songs appropriate to *pudáli* ceremonies but a song called *kápetiápani*, or "whip-dance," that is usually performed only during male initiation rituals and sacred dances of *Kuwái* (*kwépani*). Dance-songs of *pudáli* do not explicitly evoke any sacred, powerful beings of myth, even though they implicitly embody some of the same symbolic processes as shamanistic curing rituals (see Hill 1983: 350–51). *Kápetiápani* songs, on the other hand, directly evoke the great fiery transformation of the mythic primordium into an expanding world of political and material relations among distinct people. In other words, *kápetiápani* dance-songs evoke the very beginning of indigenous historical time, the moment when men and women began to construct their own histories through the playing of sacred musical instruments that embodied the creative powers of the mythic ancestors.

The full significance of these ceremonial events in San Felipe only emerged gradually over the next several years as I learned more about the inner workings of ritual power, ceremonial exchange, and the history of revitalization movements led by shamans in the Upper Rio Negro region. With the advantage of hindsight, I can see now that the ceremonial activities were an example of what Sally Falk Moore has recently called "diagnostic events," or social situations that carry a heavy load of historical meaning and that reveal ". . .ongoing contests and conflicts and competitions and the efforts to prevent, suppress, or repress these" (1987: 730). An adequate interpretation of the ceremonial activities in San Felipe must understand them as a kind of semiotic "guerilla warfare," or a deadly serious game of restoring collective identities by taking symbolic control over the ways in which history is defined and acted upon in the present. Interpreting this symbolic struggle requires a knowledge of the cosmology of indigenous Arawakan Wakuénai peoples of the Upper Rio Negro region, the meanings of ceremonial exchanges (called *pudáli*) among intermarrying groups of people, the history of colonial and nation-state expansion in the Upper Rio Negro region, and the peculiarly (or perhaps multiply) ironic interminglings between indigenous processes of meaning construction and historical processes of political domination and resistance.

Mythic and Musical Groundings of Historical Consciousness

Mythic Origins of Political-Historical Consciousness

Wakuénai storytellers explain the genesis of ritual power and the coming-into-being of a specifically human social world in a cycle of myths about Amáru and Kuwái, the primordial human mother and son. The narrative cycle is composed of two distinct parts that are separated by the fiery death of Kuwái and his transformation into sacred flutes and trumpets. The Kuwái myth cycle describes two creations, or expansions, of the undifferentiated world of animal-humans living in the distant mythic past. In the first creation, Kuwái was a monstrous being whose body consisted of all material elements and whose musical humming and singing was a "powerful sound that opened up the world" (*kémakáni hliméetaka hekwápi*). Kuwái created all the species of animals and plants by musically naming them as he flew about the skies. After creating a vertically differentiated cosmos of upper and lower worlds, Kuwái was lured into returning to the ground at Hípana, the center of the world, where he taught the sacred *málikai* songs and chants of the jaguar-ancestors to Dzúli, the first chant-owner. Iñápirríkuli, the trickster-creator and father of Kuwái, led him outside to sing *kápetiápani* ("whip-dance") and pushed him into a bonfire. As Kuwái's body burned, the world shrank back to its original, miniature size.

In the second creation, the world opened up in the horizontal dimension as men and women played Kuwái's flutes and trumpets in various places. After his fiery death, the body of Kuwái transformed into an enormous tree connecting the sky and the earth. Iñápirríkuli knocked the tree down and made it into flutes and trumpets named after forest animals and birds. Amáru and the women stole these sacred instruments from Iñápirríkuli and took them far downstream. Whenever Iñápirríkuli caught up to Amáru, she escaped with Kuwái's flutes and trumpets through an underground passageway that led back to her home at Mútsipáni. Finally, Iñápirríkuli put a stop to this situation by assembling an army of men, disguised as *molítu* frogs, who together succeeded in capturing the flutes and trumpets and returning with them to Hípana. After holding the first dance of Kuwái (*kwépani*), Iñápirríkuli showed the men how to make the enormous jaguar-bone (*dzáwiñápa*) trumpets for male initiation rituals. Then Iñápirríkuli, Amáru, and Kuwái left this world to live in various regions of the sky.

In the most general terms, the Kuwái myth cycle is about the creation, or opening up, of two different dimensions of bodily, social, and cosmic space-time: 1) a vertical dimension of developmental-generational time; and 2) a horizontal dimension of political-historical time. Kuwái's first creation is a vertical opening up of the world that results in a differentiated, mediated structure of celestial and terrestrial regions and a ritual hierarchy of elders, ritual specialists, and initiated men who define their humanness in relation to the life-giving powers of the celestial jaguar-ancestors. Kuwái's powerful, musical voice begins the creation of vertical worlds in the skies above and outside the social space of people living on the ground at Hípana. Kuwái completes his first creation by coming down to the ground and inside the village at Hípana and by teaching his sacred songs and chants to Dzúli. The movement of Kuwái down and inside metaphorically creates the socialization of individuals and the passing down of mythic, ancestral power from one generation of people to the next. In parallel with this movement down and inside, the original process of creating natural species through the externalization of musical sounds is reversed into the prototypical act of internalization, or memorization, of musical naming power by the first chant-owner.

After Kuwái's fiery death, the world created in Part I of the myth cycle is turned upside down and inside out. The initial movement of Kuwái, who now takes the form of a palm tree, is a falling down to the ground, and the remaining myths show how this downward movement is reversed into Kuwái's movement back up into the sky. Also, the focus in Part I on bodily processes of internalization and externalization gives way in Part II to a concern for social processes of inclusion and exclusion among groups of people. The ambivalent status of women in a patrilineal, patrilocal social world motivates the second, horizontal creation of the world. Amáru and the women can take control of Kuwái's life-giving powers only if they go across the world from the center at Hípana to other places far downstream. In essence, the second creation is a metaphor for the opening up, or dispersal, of a single, hierarchically ordered patrilineal family into a collective order consisting of "we people here" and a plurality of "those other peoples there" with whom "we" have relations of trade and intermarriage. Whereas Part I of the myth cycle describes the transformations leading to a vertically differentiated cosmos of generations and developmental stages, Part II is about the creation of social others through the opening up of a horizontally differentiated world of historically developing political relations among a number of distinct peoples.

Part II of the myth cycle establishes a basic connection between women and the development of a historical consciousness of social otherness. This connection reflects the ambiguous status of women as affinal outsiders in the mythic order of patrilineal, patrilocal kin groups. The ambiguity of women is expressed in myth as an alienation, or horizontal displacement, from the center of the world at Hípana during the episodes in which Amáru and the women control Kuwái's sacred musical instruments.

The Musicalization of Mythic Power

In the mythic competition between Amáru and Iñápirríkuli, the ambiguity of women, spirits of the dead, and horizontal relations of exchange are all closely associated with the genesis of an indigenous mode of political historical consciousness. At a deeper level, the Kuwái myth cycle establishes the creative power of Kuwái's flutes and trumpets as the generative source of historical consciousness, since it is the sound of these instruments that opens up the world into a plurality of peoples and places. The connection between musical sounds and historical consciousness becomes clearer through comparison of the first and second creations of the world in myth. In the first creation, Kuwái's musical voice is a powerful, world-opening sound that is external to human social relations. Eventually, this extrasocial, natural, musical naming power is socialized by being brought down to earth and internalized into social consciousness in the form of mythically powerful genres of speech, called *málikai*. In short, Kuwái's first creation of the world is essentially a transformation of musical sounds into mythic speech in which the nuances of mythic meaning act upon and constrain musical sound.

In the second creation, Kuwái is no longer an independent being but a material object, or palm tree, that must be made into powerful musical instruments by human beings. Furthermore, these instruments have no creative powers without the active participation of adult men and women who use them to make music. Both the making of instruments and the making of music depend upon the abilities of human actors to transform deliberately the mythic body of Kuwái, the vertically defined relations of power between mythic ancestors and human descendants, and the structure of the cosmos. In Kuwái's second creation, the movements of men and women across the surface of the world powerfully transform the structure of mythic space-time. The activities of making musical instruments and sounds are thus root metaphors for social agency and a reflexive awareness of human actors' capacity to effect changes in the political order of society. For the Wakuénai, the musicalization of mythic power generates a historical mode of social consciousness.

Nowhere is this process of musicalization more powerfully and directly expressed than in the sacred *málikai* songs and chants performed at male and female initiation rituals. These performances consist of an opening song, a long series of chants, and a closing song that together musicalize the mythic descent of Kuwái from the sky to the ground at Hípana, the horizontal displacement of Amáru and Kuwái across the surface of the world, the return of Amáru and Kuwái back across the world to Hípana, and the return of Kuwái from down on the ground back up to the sky. The musical, horizontal opening up of the world in initiation rituals creates a socio-geographic image of the world of people and places occupying an immense region of riverine territories. The process begins and ends at Hípana, the place of mythic emergence and center, or "navel," of the world, where mythic beings are linked to the world of human beings via a cosmic umbilical cord (*hliépule-kwá dzákare*). Between opening and closing songs, a long series of chants outlines a horizontal journey across the world through the naming of places along the Aiary, Isana, Vaupés, Negro, Atabapo, Orinoco, Guaviare, Inirida, Guainía, and Cuyarí rivers. In these chants, the Wakuénai musically construct a mythic map of their world as the center of a much larger region, which corresponds almost exactly to the distribution of the Northern, or Maipuran, subfamily of Arawakan languages prior to the colonial period. The musical naming of places in *málikai* embodies a historical consciousness of a past when the ethnopolitical situation of the Wakuénai differed profoundly from that of the present.

The horizontal opening up of the world is also directly embodied in the organization of musical sounds in *málikai* songs and chants. The opening and closing performances are sung rather than chanted or spoken, and, by making use of exactly the same pitches, the two songs provide a stable, vertical tonal center around which the more dynamic chants, or "journeys," gravitate. Between these two songs, the names of all places and animal species are chanted in a long

series of performances that lasts for many hours. Horizontal
movement, or displacement from the center of the world, is
expressed in a variety of musical dimensions. The chants begin on
different pitches, and the starting pitch is gradually sharpened
through microtonal rising so that the final verses end on a totally
new pitch. The tempo is percussively sounded by striking *kadápu*
whips on a basket that covers the initiates' sacred food (*káridzamái*),
and the initial tempo is gradually increased during each chant. The
chants also exhibit contrasting dynamics between loud and soft
sounds, since the principal chanter's voice is doubled at the end of
each verse by a second chanter. From time to time, the chanters'
voices are accompanied by a collage of sounds made on the sacred
flutes and trumpets. In short, the musicalization of mythic power
uses tonal variation, microtonal rising, acceleration, and instrumental heterophony to embody directly the processes of horizontally
journeying to other places, or becoming other peoples, and back.

These same musical processes are used in shamanistic curing
rituals as a way of musicalizing the mythic boundary between the
world of living human beings and the dark netherworld (*íyarudáti*)
of the spirits of the dead. In their singing, shamans (*malírri*) begin
each song on a different pitch, and they gradually raise the pitch
through microtonal rising. Shamans make use of dynamic contrasts
between loud and soft voices to express their musical journeys to
íyarudáti. After singing each phrase aloud, the shaman, like a
ventriloquist, sings a faint echo of the phrase so that his song
appears to be coming from far off in the distance. Shamans also use
sacred rattles to produce a variety of percussive, rhythmic accompa-
niments to their songs. These sounds have the effect of speeding
up or slowing down the tempo at different moments of the curing
ritual. Thus, shamanistic musicalization is closely related to the
musical opening up of the world in *málikai* chants for male and
female initiation. In both contexts, movements of vocal sounds
through different tones and movements of percussive sounds
through different rhythms and tempos are the musical means of
mythically journeying across the world.

Like the *málikai* chants of initiation rituals, shamans' songs embody a collective consciousness of the historical past, since the shamans' journeys to *íyarudáti* are targeted at specific houses of the dead that belong to specific patrilineal kin groups and that have specific geographical locations within the ancestral territory of the phratry. Due to social changes of recent decades, the majority of Wakuénai social groups no longer live on their ancestral territories. The shamans' musical journeys to houses of the dead are thus more than a process of curing individuals; they are historical metaphors for the collective alienation of a people who have lost political and economic control over their own lands but who have nevertheless refused to forget the historical past and the sacred places that connect mythic ancestors to their descendants, both living and dead.

Pudáli: Musicalizing the Other

The historical mode of social consciousness embodied in initiation chants (*málikai*) and shamans' songs (*málirríkairi*) is put into practice on a collective level in *pudáli* ceremonial exchanges. Elsewhere, I have written detailed interpretations of *pudáli* as a sociopolitical and symbolic process of transforming the boundary between kin and affine through acts of giving, drinking, eating, dancing, and playing music together (Hill 1983, 1987). Here I will only sketch the bare outlines of *pudáli* exchange cycles and the internal transformations that unfold within each ceremony.

Pudáli is a two-part cycle of ceremonial food offerings between affinally related kin groups that begins when a male owner (*púdalímnali*) organizes the production of a large quantity of smoked fish and game meat. The guests transport the food gift to their hosts' village and perform musical dances with *kúlirrína* trumpets and a variety of flutes around the heap of food before offering it to their hosts. The hosts store the food inside during the night and invite their guests inside to drink manioc beer and perform song dialogues, called *pákamarántakan*. The male guests gather around the outside of the house and play *déetu* flutes to "ask" their hosts for drinks by imitating the natural sucking behavior of *déetu* insects. The hosts silence the *déetu* players one at a time by offering them drinks, which they are expected to imbibe until vomiting. Just before dawn, the guests play their *kúlirrína* trumpets around a bonfire before offering them to their hosts as reminders of the obligation to reciprocate for the food gift of smoked meat by a return gift of processed manioc pulp several weeks later. At daybreak, the smoked meat is redistributed to guest and host families alike, and individual men and women from the two groups join together to perform improvisatory flute-dances named after various animal species.

In a closing ceremony held several weeks later, the recipients of the first gift take a large quantity of manioc pulp to their hosts' village and perform song-dances with stomping tubes (*waanápani*) around the food offering. The basic, three-stage sequence of activities remains the same as in opening, male-owned ceremonies: 1) large, group ensembles of singers, flute players, and dancers circle around the food offering; 2) transitional performances center around the hosts' house and a bonfire during the late night period; and 3) small, improvisatory flute dances allow individual interaction between the two groups during a day of feasting and drinking. However, in closing ceremonies the guests' activities are organized by a female owner (*púdalímnaru*), and song-dances with stomping tubes (*wáana*) replace the *kúlirrína* trumpet-dances of opening, male-owned ceremonies.

The cultural origins of *pudáli* are two-fold. In myth, Káali, a younger brother of the trickster-creator and originator of all cultivated plant species, created the musical instruments, sounds, and dances of *pudáli* as a way of instructing his children how to ask for food and drinks from their affines (*apána náiki*, or "other people") in a socially appropriate manner. In this sense, *pudáli* is a secular process of using music and dance to cross the social boundary between potentially hostile, affinal groups.

The linkage of *pudáli* with spirits of the dead in *íyarudáti* is asserted in the general belief that the spirits of the dead spend all their time drinking and playing the musical instruments of *pudáli*. This general association hints at the more concrete, musical, and choreographic activities that metonymically include *pudáli* into the domain of shamanistic journeys between the living and the dead. The overall performative structure in *pudáli* is a process of movement from large, standardized performances with almost no musical variation to small, improvisatory flute duets that subtly explore tonal and rhythmic variations through the use of theme and variation (Hill 1987). Like shamans' songs and the chants for initiation, *pudáli* is a process of using tonal and rhythmic variation to embody horizontal "journeys," or transformations. The initial and final stages of *pudáli* are connected late at night by transitional performances, such as *dzúdzuápani*, *déetu* flute music, and drinking songs.

The movement from relatively fixed, collective performances to more improvisatory, individualized performances is best illustrated through a comparison of the music played on *máwi* flutes in the opening stage of *pudáli* with flute duets played in the final stage of the ceremony. In the opening stage of *pudáli*, the guests play *máwi* flutes together with other instruments as they enter the hosts' village with a gift of food. The guest musicians dance in a circle around the offering of food while the hosts watch from a distance. Guests and hosts are strictly forbidden to dance, speak, or play music together until the presentation of food has been formally made by the owner of *pudáli* to the hosts' headman. The *máwi* flutes are always played as part of an ensemble of singers and instrumentalists during this opening stage. There is little or no variation in the *máwi* flute music performed at this point. The opening music consists of a single descending melodic phrase that is repeated constantly through all the opening performances of the ceremony. This repetitive melodic theme runs like a continuous thread throughout the heterophonic collage of musical sounds and dance formations that guest men and women weave as they circle the offering of food.

Whereas the opening melody played on *máwi* flutes is highly repetitive and always forms part of larger musical performances, the *máwi* flute duets played in the last stage of *pudáli* (after the redistribution of food to guests and hosts alike) are highly improvisatory and allow pairs of men to exhibit their skills as musicians and dancers. The social boundary between guests and hosts has been transformed through drinking and singing together, and individual men and women from each of the two groups are free to dance and play music together.

These improvisatory duets are named after various species of forest animals, fish, and birds, and they are based on an underlying metaphor that relates the social processes of human courtship and marriage to natural processes of mating. The verb used to describe the action of musical-dancing in *pudáli* is *lirrápaka*, which is also used to describe the spawning behavior of fish species. Perhaps the clearest illustration of this metaphor is the *máwi* flute duet called *viejita* (*dzawírra*, Wáku), a species of small fish. In the dance, one male-female pair of dancers stands still while the other pair approaches and backs away several times, asking the *viejita* fish for permission to dance in its nest (i.e., spawn). The *viejita* fish gives its permission by raising its *máwi* flute high up in the air while the other pair of dancers passes underneath in several tight circles. The male musician-dancers continue to play their flutes in a continuous melody throughout these movements, and their music consists of a complex set of variations upon a simple theme.

The *déetu* flute performances implicitly evoke the power of shamans to remove illness through sucking and vomiting harmful substances from their patients' bodies. By imitating the *déetu* insects' natural feeding behavior of sucking sap from felled trees, the *déetu* flute players collectively enact the shamanistic activities of sucking and vomiting as a means of "asking" their hosts for drinks. When this metaphorical comparison between shamanistic activities and *déetu* flute performances is carried to its conclusion, it leads to an interpretation of the house full of drinking, singing men and women as a collective body that must be shamanistically cured. At the same time, the *déetu* flute performances shamanistically musicalize the mythic speech act of Káali's children "asking" their hosts to give them drinks.

In short, *pudáli* is a complex sociomusical process that simultaneously unfolds on two distinct levels. Explicitly, *pudáli* is a secular gathering of kin and affine for purposes of creating, or reproducing, alliances through reciprocal acts of giving and receiving foods. Implicitly, *pudáli* is a shamanistic musicalization of mythic speech that transforms the social gathering of kin and affine into a symbolic journey between the living and dead that alludes to the jaguar-ancestors' ambiguous gain and loss of life through horizontal relations of exchange. The musicalization of Others in *pudáli* forms part of a more general process of musicalizing mythic speech that generates and puts into practice a historical mode of social consciousness.

Interpreting the Events in San Felipe

The musical performances in San Felipe in July 1981 transposed the indigenous process of musicalizing the relations between affinally related groups in *pudáli* ceremonies onto the political relations between indigenous peoples of the Upper Rio Negro region and the white, or mestizo, merchants who controlled the regional trading economy. Musicalizing the Other is essentially a process of transforming mythic, verbally constructed categories of meaning into a dynamic movement through musically constructed "places," or configurations of pitch, rhythm, timbre, volume, and tempo. In *pudáli* ceremonies, the musicalization of mythic and social boundaries is accomplished gradually through a three-stage process of musical performances, beginning with large, standardized performances that restrict interaction between host and guest groups and ending with individual, improvisatory duets that promote integration of the two groups.

In San Felipe, the Wakuénai and Yeral creatively transposed the musical processes of *pudáli* to cope with an increasingly competitive situation of interethnic contact with local merchants and the Colombian national government. In *pudáli* ceremonies, the musicalization of Others is triggered by a periodic superabundance of economic resources (e.g., fish and game meat) and results in the extension of generalized and balanced reciprocity from one's own kin group to potentially dangerous "Others," or affines. In San Felipe, *pudáli* performances were set in motion by a series of activities that expressed an exceptionally negative reciprocity (e.g., the merchants' usurpation and manipulation of government aid to indigenous peoples) and that resulted in punitive deprivation. Given this set of social conditions, the meaning of ceremonial performances in San Felipe has to be understood as an ironic trope of the gradual series of transformations leading from formality to spontaneity in *pudáli* ceremonies. The Colombian merchants, unlike potentially dangerous affines, were the agents of an alien, unsocialized, and destructive power structure which was devouring the indigenous families of San Felipe by placing them into a system of crushing economic debt.

The irony of the social context of ceremonial performances in San Felipe went beyond the merchants' negative reciprocity to encompass a basic contradiction within the national cultures of Venezuela and Colombia: the paradox of official, institutional structures of the national governments (the Offices of Indigenous Affairs) charged with assisting indigenous minorities in the context of a spectrum of other governmental and private institutions which collectively denied the existence, much less the value, of cultural diversity within the two nation-states. What was new in the events that led up to the ceremonial performances of 1981 in San Felipe was not the debt fetishism of the merchants, a system with which the Wakuénai and Yeral had had a long, difficult historical experience. The new element was the emergence of economic aid specifically appropriated for indigenous peoples. The irony of the economic situation in San Felipe was thus double: the merchants' manipulations and stinginess were negations of an original act of generosity by the national government of Colombia toward the Wakuénai and Yeral families of San Felipe. It was this doubly ambiguous social situation of giving with one hand and taking away with the other that the Wakuénai and Yeral families were protesting and seeking to transform in their musical performances.

Like the double irony of the social context, the musical performances in San Felipe transformed the musical processes of *pudáli* in two important ways. In place of a gradual transition from collective, standardized performances to individual, improvisatory duets, the

Wakuénai and Yeral of San Felipe compressed the entire series of transformations making up *pudáli* into a dramatic juxtaposition of contrasting performances. The abrupt, unmediated, consecutive performances of musical dances selected from the opening and closing stages of *pudáli* gave concrete symbolic expression to the local indigenous peoples' desire for rapid social transformation. The compression, or juxtaposition, of formal collective action and spontaneous individual modes of expression was an indigenous representation of the transformative power of musical behavior, a synthesis of formality and spontaneity into a single ambiguous totality.

   This juxtaposition finessed the shamanistic dimensions of meaning implicit in *pudáli* ceremonies and set the stage for a second transformation of the music of *pudáli*. By performing *kápetiápani*, or "whip-dance song," in the context of *máwi* flute music and other performances from *pudáli*, the Wakuénai and Yeral of San Felipe were juxtaposing musical performances from two contrasting ceremonies. *Kápetiápani* evokes the fiery destruction, or transformation, of Kuwái's first mythic creation of the world. By performing *kápetiápani* in the context of musical dances from *pudáli*, the indigenous people of San Felipe were not merely representing the transformative power of musical behavior but enacting control over that power in order to socialize the history of interethnic relations. In myth, the fiery transformation of Kuwái transformed the supernatural, self-replicating process of musical naming power into human, collectively controlled processes of social reproduction through the making and playing of musical instruments. In San Felipe, the performance of *kápetiápani* was an attempt to harness, shamanistically, the mythic power of presocial, preverbal, animal-human nature into a humanly controlled musical power to create socialized history.

   The events of July 1981 in San Felipe form part of a long-term process of interethnic conflict and competition between indigenous peoples and non-native immigrants to the Upper Rio Negro region. Although this history was generally characterized by the colonial domination of indigenous groups, the extent to which indigenous

peoples have had to cope directly with political-economic domination by outsiders has varied at different points in time, depending
upon historical changes taking place outside the region at national
and international levels of organization. Like the Wakuénai and
Baniwa followers of Venancio Camico's movement[1] in 1858, the
Wakuénai and Yeral families of San Felipe in 1981 were faced with
a potentially disasterous loss of social and economic autonomy. In
both cases, the Wakuénai turned to powerful shamans to orchestrate
their collective resistance to external domination. In both 1858 and
1981, shamanistic musicalization was an attempt to rehumanize
relations of power and exchange by moving people from passive
acceptance to active resistance.

Conclusions

Interpreting the events and processes of interethnic relations
challenges us to develop new theoretical approaches for understanding the social histories of indigenous Amazonian peoples. In
recent years, the concern for integrating a historical perspective into
social analysis has become a central preoccupation in anthropology.
Where they once found reified structures, traditions, and cultural
systems, anthropologists today find historically situated processes
of social adjustment, accommodation, and resistance. For the field
ethnographer, the historical orientation of anthropology requires a
heightened sensitivity to ongoing processes of change that form part
of deeper, long-term historical processes. Ethnographic researchers
can no longer rely on simple classifications of old versus new but

---

[1] Venancio Camico was a Baniwa shaman and the leader of a major revitalization movement among the Baniwa and Wakuénai of the Upper Rio Negro
region in 1858 (see Wright and Hill 1986 for a detailed analysis). Although
Brazilian and Venezuelan authorities quickly suppressed the movement, Venancio
escaped from prison and lived among indigenous followers in a remote village
on the Caño Aki until approximately 1903. Baniwa and Wakuénai storytellers
commemorate Venancio Camico's resistance to exploitation during the Rubber
Boom through a variety of oral histories and legends (see Hill and Wright 1988
for interpretations of these historical narratives).

must search for better ways to answer difficult questions: ". . .how is the anthropologist to distinguish the transitory from the durable, cultural change from cultural persistence? . . . How can fieldwork be done as current history?" (Moore 1987: 728). Certainly, no methodology in the existing literature provides a guaranteed means of dealing with these basic issues.

Sally Falk Moore provides a partial solution by developing the concept of "diagnostic events," or social situations that carry a heavy load of historical meaning and that reveal ". . .ongoing contests and conflicts and competitions and the efforts to prevent, suppress, or repress these" (1987: 730). Researchers can practice ethnography as current history by choosing to focus upon events that are inherently destabilizing and that bring into play a multiplicity of levels and modes of social consciousness. Social relations are forever in transition and surrounded by indeterminacy.

What is lacking in Moore's definition of diagnostic events is a sense of how social groups have developed their own modes of social consciousness for interpreting and acting upon historical indeterminacy. In order to conclude that a given event or process is diagnostic of long-term processes of change, it is necessary to explore underlying modes of social consciousness that both constrain historical processes of change and can serve as resources enabling individual and collective action in situations of competition or conflict. The events of July 1981 in San Felipe were diagnostic of long-term historical processes not only because they epitomized the interethnic tensions between mestizo and indigenous groups of the Upper Rio Negro region but also because of their multivocal resonances with an indigenous historical consciousness rooted in diverse genres of narrative, ritual music, and ceremonial dance. By musicalizing interethnic competition in San Felipe, the Wakuénai redefined the contradictory gain and loss of economic goods in terms of the ambiguity of inclusive and exclusive relations in *pudáli* ceremonies, affinal relations, shamanistic journeys, and the musical opening up of the world in sacred narratives.

References Cited

Hill, Jonathan
    1983   "Wakuénai Society: A Processual-Structural Analysis of Indigenous Cultural Life in the Upper Rio Negro Region of Venezuela." Ph.D. diss., Indiana University.
    1987   "Wakuénai Ceremonial Exchange in the Northwest Amazon." *Journal of Latin American Lore* 13(2):183–224.
Hill, Jonathan, and Robin Wright
    1988   "Time, Narrative, and Ritual: Historical Interpretations from an Amazonian Society." In J. Hill, ed., *Rethinking History and Myth: Indigenous South American Perspectives on the Past*, pp. 78–105. Urbana: University of Illinois Press.
Moore, Sally Falk
    1987   "Explaining the Present: Theoretical Dilemmas in Processual Ethnography. 1987 AES Distinguished Lecture." *American Ethnologist* 14(4):727–36.
Wright, Robin, and Jonathan Hill
    1986   "History, Ritual, and Myth: 19th Century Millenarian Movements in the Northwest Amazon." *Ethnohistory* 33 (1):31–54.

Conceptualizations of Music
in Jewish Mysticism

Moshe Idel

Music and Models in Jewish Mysticism

Jewish mysticism is a variegated mystical lore that encompasses different religious models: those dealing with the spiritual world, be they divine, angelic, or demonic; those concerning the human world and its spiritual and corporeal constitution as well as its modes of behavior; and, finally, those involving nature and its relationship to the more spiritual worlds and to humanity. In many cases these models are not merely abstract conceptualizations—the offering of mental pictures of these realms—but, rather, provide active methods to interact with and even to influence the realms described in mystical literature. Convenient distinctions between the main activistic approaches to music would differentiate between the human attempt to have an impact upon the divine intra-structure—an activity which may be described as theurgy; attempts to manipulate nature, which could be described as magic; and, finally, attempts to shape the inner state of consciousness, which are more specifically mystical approaches.[1] This more varied view of the nature of kabbalistic thought and experience as constituted by

---

[1] See a much more detailed discussion on the three models in Moshe Idel, *Hasidism: Between Ecstasy and Magic* (Albany: State University of New York Press, 1995), 45–145, and my forthcoming *Messianic Dimensions of Jewish Mysticism*.

different modes and models is crucial for a nuanced understanding of many kabbalistic texts.[2]

Music, a human activity that was not part of the Jewish rabbinic rites, nevertheless has at times been integrated into medieval Kabbalah as aspects of the three domains of activity mentioned above; thus, different musical activities, as portrayed in Jewish mystical sources, may be described as having theurgical, mystical, or magical aspects or any combination of the three. The shared assumption of these models with regard to musical activity is the transitive power of music, related to its energetic quality. Musical activity is not only pleasant but also implies the possibility of transmitting power from the source to the object, thus exercising a certain type of influence on the latter. The two main assumptions

[2] Kabbalah is the body of literature related to mystical teachings in the Jewish tradition. Kabbalistic themes can be traced back to the period of the Second Temple, but extensive developments in Kabbalah took place beginning in the twelfth century and continuing on throughout the Middle Ages. This was thus a formative period for what is generally considered the bulk of Jewish mystical thought, incorporating traditions on ecstasy, esoteric knowledge, mystical theology and cosmology, and some ethical teachings.

The twelfth-century developments began primarily in Provence but in the thirteenth-century found a particularly fertile ground in the city of Gerona. These regions were, during the period of Muslim rule in Spain, culturally and religiously charged environments due to the ongoing mutual influence of and interaction between the religions of Islam, Catholicism, and Judaism.

By the late thirteenth century, the most important product of Spanish Kabbalah was the Zohar, a book of teachings and philosophies compiled by Moses b. Shem Tov de Leon. This seminal text incorporated the profound speculative influences of esoteric traditions and Geronese Kabbalism. Around the same time, various philosophers were interpreting kabbalistic thought as a canonical aspect of Jewish thought. This trend was exemplified by a formative kabbalist, Abraham Abulafia, who contributed greatly to traditions of ecstasy and the use of numerology (Gematria) but who also devoted much thought to kabbalistic readings of the thought of Maimonides.

After the expulsion from Spain (1492), Israel—and especially the cities of Jerusalem and Safed—became a major center of Kabbalah. In the mid-sixteenth century, Moses Cordovero emerged as a chief exponent of Safedian Kabbalah. His contemporary, Isaac Luria, however, is considered an even more influential representative of the Safed community. Luria's esoteric philosophies were based

that will be discussed here are: the attempt to relate musical treatments to an ancient, biblical activity in order to establish music's authority, despite its marginal role in the rabbinic literature; and the modes of influence through music, as found in the kabbalistic and Hasidic literature.

"Templar" Music and *Prisca Mystica*

Many of the earlier discussions of music in the thirteenth-century Kabbalah deal with attempts to establish a link between kabbalistic practices and ancient rituals in the Temple—attempts that were part of a much broader claim concerning the antiquity of kabbalistic topics: musical techniques were among those subjects deemed by the early kabbalists as sufficiently important to be endowed with a respectable pedigree. This practice is reminiscent of the much later Renaissance theory of *prisca theologia*, which allowed some Christian intellectuals to adopt crucial forms of thought stemming from what they believed were very ancient writings.[3] Examples for

on the notion of divine "sparks," which are trapped in "shells," and may be liberated through "tikkun"—literally, the word for fixing or mending, often applied to the human situation in the cosmos.

Kabbalists developed various philosophies based on the concept of *sefirot*. These are the ten, hierarchically ordered "spheres," or realms, comprising the cosmos, which early writings define as the stages of the hidden life of God. Meditation upon the *sefirot* is considered a form of mystical activity, a means of communion with the godhead. Numerous other meanings were developed by kabbalists throughout the formative period.

Much of kabbalistic thought became a source of tradition for the later Hasidic movement that began in Eastern Europe in the eighteenth century. Although Hasidic rabbis differ in their opinion of the Kabbalah as a basis for Hasidic thought, many attributes are derived from kabbalistic practices. The distinguishing characteristics of Hasidism, for example, include ecstasy, mass enthusiasm, and a strong emphasis on community cohesion.

[3] See Daniel R. Walker, *The Ancient Theology: Studies in Christian Platonism from the Fifteenth to the Eighteenth Century* (London: Duckworth, 1972); Charles Schmitt, "Perennial Philosophy from Agostino Steuco to Leibniz," *Journal of the History of Ideas* 27 (1966):505–32; "Prisca Theologia e Filosofia Perennis: Due temi del rinascimento italiano e la loro fortuna," in *Il pensiero Italiano del rinascimento e il tempo nostro* (Florence, 1970), 211–36.

the projection of modern practices on the templar rituals are numerous: here I shall refer only to a few; others will occur further on in the discussion. I should mention first that the view that the science of music had originated with Israel and was then lost appears in the *'Adnei Kesef*,[4] a work of the early fourteenth-century philosopher and devoted follower of Maimonides, Rabbi Joseph Kaspi. This view is also expressed in the important musical discussion by Rabbi Moses Isserles, a sixteenth-century rabbinic authority in Poland, who, in his book *Torat ha-'Olah*, writes, "the science of music which, due to sin, has been forgotten by us from the day on which the song-service[5] ceased to exist."[6]

My primary concern, however, is with some kabbalistic examples. We find in a text by Rabbi Isaac ben Jacob ha-Kohen, a mid-thirteenth-century kabbalist from Castile, who was also associated with the kabbalists of Spain and Provence, the following passage that combines the three main models (which I will elaborate upon below) in a description of the High Priest:

> The High Priest. . .[7] knows how to fully direct his concentration on all inner and outer emanations, in order to exert influence by means of the secret of the holy *Seraphim* [Angels]; his elevation is according to either his closeness or remoteness, and his power is awakened[8] by the sweetness of the song and the pure prayer. So do the musicians direct their fingers, according to their elevation and understanding, [placing them] on the key-holes of [wind instruments] *kinnorot* and [on] strings, arousing the song[9] and the melody to direct their hearts toward God. Thus the blessing is

[4] London, 1912, 2:120.

[5] Namely, the service in the Temple.

[6] Part 2, chap. 38. Cf. also Israel Adler,"Le traite anonyme du manuscrit Hebreu 1037 de la Bibliothèque Nationale de Paris," *Yuval* 1 (1968):15–16.

[7] In the passage I omitted, R. Isaac mentions the correspondence between the supernal and the lower high priests and temples.

[8] *me'orer koho.*

[9] *ha-mit'orerim ha-shir.*

aroused[10] and the *Shekhinah* [divine presence] resides in them, each one according to his performance and according to his understanding.[11]

This portion of the text deals with the correspondence between the lower and the supernal High Priest: in other words, the mortal influences the supernal structure.[12] Thus, in this context, the passage can be interpreted as describing a theurgical activity. There is a certain ambiguity in the way the ancient praxis is presented. The High Priest is said to enter a mystical experience by listening to the music. Music is portrayed as part of the rite, and it is quite plausible that the musical ritual of the Levites was conceived of as primarily enabling the ecstatic experience of the High Priest. However, what is less clear is the possible reverberation of this concept during the lifetime of Rabbi Isaac. Does the sentence beginning "So do the musicians" deal with what he believed to be a remnant of the Temple musical ritual? I intend to return to this issue later on, but it should be emphasized here that the ecstatic experience of the High Priest is only one of the aims of ritualistic, ancient—and perhaps also contemporary—music. The blessing, *Berakhah,* and the divine presence, *Shekhinah,* are mentioned as being aroused by the music, and perhaps also by the act of the High Priest, so that they then descend and dwell among the musicians. These two concepts are to be understood as forms of divine immanence present in this world, or, more precisely, within the musicians or the mystics. Indeed, this understanding of the blessing is well known in the Jewish and Muslim literature.[13] If the two sorts of impact music has are related—and this relationship is indicated by the sequence of the statements in the quote and the word "thus"—I would then propose the following scheme, or model:

[10] *ha-berakhah mit'oreret.*

[11] *Sod ha-'Ammud ha-Semali* (Treatise on the Left Emanation), in Gershom Scholem, *Madda'ei ha-Yahadut*, 2 (1927):247. See also his commentary on *Ta'amei ha Nequddot ve-Tzuratan*, in ibid., 267.

[12] Scholem, 2:247. For more on music and theurgy, see pp. 169–72 below.

[13] Idel, *Hasidism*, 72.

music enables the High Priest to achieve a mystical experience, and, during this experience, he is able to activate the supernal entities, *Berakhah* and *Shekhinah*. If this reading, which I see as quite plausible, is correct, then the passage expresses what I shall designate as a mystico-magical model—a model found earlier in the thirteenth-century Geronese Kabbalah of Spain, but much more evident in the later phases of this lore[14] which is conjoined with a theurgical one. This reading, as I shall explain below, is related to an understanding of the mystico-magical ritual of the *Shekhinah* (which was said in some biblical verses actually to dwell in the Temple), and so is also related to the Temple. It is thus a "templar" reading of a model that may well be one of the major models of Kabbalah in general. Another passage by the same kabbalist also points to an ancient templar vision:

> Those who served in our glorious Temple were expert in the subtleties of the *nequddot* [notations][15] which went forth from their mouths when they made music, with the known measure and references to the musical instruments of David—"the most pleasant of Israel's singers" [2 Sam. 23:1]—of blessed memory. At the moment when [the melody] emanates from their mouths with awe, reverence holiness and pleasant voice, rising and falling, extending and shortening—by the Holy Spirit, of specified measure— according to the prophets of blessed memory, and on the basis of the pattern of the notes[16] drawn according to the melodic [evolution] of the rising and falling sounds[17]. . .some of them of high [pitch] and others of low [pitch], some are small and others large [rhythmic

[14] Idel, *Hasidism*, 95–102.

[15] This term usually denotes vowels; here, the term was probably used to mean musical notes. Cf. Israel Adler, *Hebrew Writings Concerning Music* (Munich: G. Henle Verlag, 1975), 172 (the preface of 360/Ibn Sahula), and 173, sentence 3; see also ibid., index, 375: *nequddah*.

[16] *nequddot*.

[17] In ed. Ferrara and MS Paris BN 745 of R. Isaac ha-Kohen's work, *ha-beten*. Scholem suggests the correction, *ha'bittuy*. The original version may have been a Hebrew transcription of the term 'notes,' such as *ha-noti*.

values].[18] The measures and the drawings [of the notes according to] the melodic [evolution] of the sounds are all based upon and directed to the inner spiritual qualities—then the Holy Spirit awakens,[19] sparkles, and craves.[20]

In this passage, too, there is a certain affinity between the mystical ideas and a more theosophical, or even magical, effect generated by them. And, again, this hypothetical model is attributed to the Temple ritual, as can be seen in the works of other kabbalists, such as, for example, Rabbi Abraham ben Hananel of Eskira, a late thirteenth- or early fourteenth-century kabbalist, who wrote in his voluminous treatise, *Yesod 'Olam*, that

> When the [high] priest entered the Holy of Holies, which is the solitude,[21] his garment produced sounds from the thirty-two bells, as it is written, "and his sound shall be heard when he goeth in unto the holy place. . .that he die not" [Exod. 28:35].[22]

[18] Compare the very similar view of R. Isaac ben Shelomo ibn Avi Sahulah, a kabbalist who belonged to the school of R. Isaac ha-Kohen, who wrote in his *Commentary on the Song of Songs*: "the praiseworthy song is the sound emanating from the musician's mouth with awe, reverence, and holiness, rising and falling, extending and shortening, as if it were emanating from the song of the heavenly angels. By moving in known measures, which are understood by the pattern of the notes [*neqqudot*] which are drawn according to the melodic [evolution] of the sounds, they are directed towards the spiritual degrees, as is explained in the science of music." ed. Arthur Green, "Rabbi Isaac ibn Sahola's Commentary on the Song of Songs," in *The Beginnings of Jewish Mysticism in Medieval Europe*, ed. J. Dan (Jerusalem, 1987), 408.

[19] *mit'oreret*. See also fns. 7–9 above and fn. 75 below.

[20] Quoted, in the name of R. Isaac ha-Kohen, by Rabbi Shem Tov ben Shem Tov, *Sefer ha-'Emunot* (Ferrara, 1556), fol. 94a; also published in G. Scholem, *Madda'ei ha-Yahadut*, 2 (1927):277. See also R. Isaac ibn Avi Sahulah, *Commentary on the Song of Songs*: "All this was intended to awaken the soul to its loftiness, in order that it arrive at its true character. Then the Holy Spirit arises, sparkles, and craves with fondness, care, and great love, and then it achieves an even greater degree."

[21] *hitbodedut*. The nexus between the lonely presence of the high priest in the holy of holies and solitude occurs in other medieval texts.

[22] MS Moscow-Ginzburg 607, fol. 8a.

The mystical perception of the High Priest as entering states of ecstasy through music is worthy of a much more detailed investigation than can be done here. It is, at the very least, indubitably connected to much earlier views of the High Priest as undergoing mystical experiences, as we have learned from Philo's writings and from Midrashic descriptions of the High Priest [Exod. 28:35].[23] Nevertheless, the possibility that—and the extent to which—some kabbalistic material reflects much earlier concepts of music is still a matter of speculation and requires more research. The similarity between the ancient and medieval conceptualizations of the High Priest notwithstanding, I prefer not to commit myself to a historical filiation that may explain the emergence of the medieval concepts. We read in an anonymous kabbalistic text, written a generation or two later, that:

> The kabbalists say that this[24] note is like the lovely music which the angels sing and play before God, and that David received some of this music by means of the Holy Spirit. So also with the Levites [one of the Priestly tribes], who performed the holy songs in the

---

[23] See *Philo of Alexandria*, trans. and introduction by David Winston (New York: Paulist Press, 1981), 254. See also Joshua Finkel, "The Guises and Vicissitudes of a Universal Folk-Belief in Jewish and Greek Tradition," in *Harry Austryn Wolfson Jubilee Volume*, English Section (Jerusalem, 1965), 1:236–40, 242–43, where he deals with the possible relationship between Midrashic material and Philo on the ecstatic experience of the high priest. See also Maren R. Niehoff, "What is a Name? Philo's Mystical Philosophy of Language," *Jewish Studies Quarterly* 2 (1995):232–33. It should be mentioned that Philo is conceived as being of priestly origin: see Daniel P. Schwartz, "Philo's Priestly Descent," in eds. F. E. Greenspahn, E. Hilgert, and B. L. Mack, *Nourished with Peace: Studies in Hellenistic Judaism in Memory of Samuel Sandmel* (Chico, Calif.: Scholars Press, 1984), 155–71. On one author's explanation of the possible relation between the emphasis on the high priest's mystical experience and the priestly connection, see the end of this paragraph.

[24] Namely, the sign designated as *shalshelet*. On the mystical interpretations of the accentuations, see Elliot Wolfson, "Biblical Accentuation in a Mystical Key: Kabbalistic Interpretations of the *Te'amim*," *Journal of Jewish Music and Liturgy* 11 (1988/89):1–16, 12 (1989/90):1–13.

Temple, that is, the Psalms. They made their voice pleasant by singing the song in a lovely, pleasant, clear and good voice. They pronounced their speech with a significant melodic movement, with that same suspended pronunciation as with the great *shalshelet* [in this case referring to a particular cantillation mark], in order to elevate that speech with the note of the *shalshelet*, which is made at the beginning of the word, and before he ends that particular word, he makes a lovely turn with the small *shalshelet*. He would thereby elevate his tune higher, and then lower it a little, as, for example, in chanting according to the science of music. He would make this pronunciation while performing the good and pleasant song which he knows by tradition to be fit for the *shalshelet*. If he has received no tradition, and he knows how to innovate a pleasant tune on his own—a tune which will have a pleasant cantillation and a pronunciation similar to the enunciation of the *shalshelet*—then he must pronounce the Name in this order and with this sound, for this is what the High Priest used to do. He used to proclaim the Name with this tune while in the Holy of Holies, and he would vocalize it while employing a tune according to the rule of the *shalshelet*, so that he would swallow the letters of the Name. This was so that all those listening heard the pleasant melody and did not heed to understand the letters of the Name, so much were their souls enjoying listening to the melody. This can be done also by one graced by God to proclaim the Names, by one who know how to do this, and who directs the letters and performs the necessary activities, and this is the secret of "He within Whose dwelling there is joy." Joy comes only from the joy of music, and the joy of music comes from the Holy Spirit, as it is written, "and when the minstrel played, the power of the Lord came upon him" [2 Kings 3:15].[25]

[25] *Sod ha-Shalshelet*, found in the kabbalistic secrets extant in MS Paris BN 790, fol. 141a–b; On these secrets, see Ephraim Gottlieb, *Studies in the Kabbalah Literature* (in Hebrew), ed. Joseph Hacker (Tel Aviv, 1976), 120 n. 57. See also Moshe Idel, *The Mystical Experience in Abraham Abulafia*, trans. Jonathan Chifman (Albany: State University of New York Press, 1987), 60–61. For the context of this quote, see below, p. 179.

Music, or melody, is described in this text in a rather conspicuous manner, related as it is to the activity of the High Priest. However, what is emphasized specifically is the relationship of music to one of the primary acts of the High Priest: the pronunciation of the divine name. This nexus is, indeed, not accidental, as a term designating melody is mentioned in the Mishnaic description of the proclamation of the Name.[26] In this text, it is only the more mystical aspect of music that is invoked, as is also the case in the work of a later author, writing perhaps at the end of the fourteenth century:

> The musical service in the Temple, vocal and instrumental, [was intended] to draw hearts towards Blessed God, and to lift the souls to the supreme world, the spiritual world. This is the issue of the pleasantness of voice [required] in the synagogues for prayers, *qerovot* and *piyyutim*,[27] and in the Temple they had proper command of the science of music.[28]

Here the kabbalist suggests that the active belief in the mystical impact of music, found in the templar service, is still present in contemporary synagogues. This "templar" vision of music served, as mentioned above, to bestow upon music an aura of antiquity and authority. However, it should also be pointed out that already, in the early Kabbalah, there were attempts to envisage this lore as a substitute to the Temple rituals in general. This is evident in the rarer vision of Kabbalah as a body of lore dealing with divine names and their pronunciations—once the patrimony of the High Priest[29]—and in the assumption that the kabbalistic rituals—again dealing with mystical traditions concerning the divine names—have the same

---

[26] See *Qiddushin*, fol. 71a, and fn. 67 below.

[27] *Qerovot* and *piyyutim* are forms of Jewish liturgy.

[28] R. Solomon ben Samuel, *Pitehei 'Olam*, in Adler, *Hebrew Writings Concerning Music*, 301, sec. [1], n. 1. Cf. also ibid., 300–301.

[29] Moshe Idel, "Defining Kabbalah: The Kabbalah of the Divine Names," in *Mystics of the Book: Themes, Topics, and Typology*, ed. R. A. Herrera (New York: Peter Lang, 1993), 97–122.

effect once achieved through sacrifices in the Temple.[30] Because the substitute in both cases is a linguistic practice, it is more easily understood that music, which is, indeed, intimately connected to the pronunciation, will be recognized as both the ancient Jewish practice and the present-day effective mystical device. Even now, in the kabbalistic writings mentioned above, it is difficult to find convincing evidence of the existence of musical practices among those kabbalists. There is some logic to discussing in some detail music's pedigree despite this lack of concrete evidence: the fact that one of the kabbalists' younger contemporaries, Rabbi Abraham Abulafia, had indeed resorted, as we shall see below, to musical techniques as part of his Kabbalah may serve to advance the hypothesis that other kabbalists, somewhat earlier, also envisaged music as a practical part of their Kabbalah. It should be mentioned that at least one of the writers who embraced the templar vision of ancient music as conducive to ecstasy was a Kohen, namely, Rabbi Isaac ben Jacob ha-Kohen; this may also have been true of Philo. However, Abraham Abulafia, who influenced fundamental developments regarding ecstatic kabbalist thought, did not belong either to the family of Kohen or of Levi.[31] He relates his model not to the High Priest but to the ancient prophets and the paradisiacal experience.

Music and Theurgy

It would be appropriate now to explore how musical themes were used in describing the widespread kabbalistic view which assumes that human ritualistic actions have an impact upon the divine realm. Although this belief predated the kabbalistic literature that was

---

[30] See Moshe Idel, *Kabbalah: New Perspectives* (New Haven and London: Yale University Press, 1988), 53–54.

[31] Jewish families, up to the present day, continue to identify, with greater or lesser awareness, with one of the three main tribes: Kohen, the priestly tribe descended from Aaron, the brother of Moses; Levi, a priestly class who performed temple duties; and Yisrael, the largest group of the people of Israel.

produced in the Middle Ages, as we know from several discussions found in rabbinic literature, only in the mainstream of Kabbalah has the assumption that human actions and divine powers are closely related flourished.[32] The image that best illustrates the theurgical use of music is that of the two violins: when a string on one of the instruments is played, the same string on the second violin resonates. This principle of acoustical resonance may serve—and indeed has served—different models, such as the magical one.[33] Here, I shall resort to it in order to show how a kabbalistic vision has been accepted in early Hasidic thought. In the classic treatise, often designated *'Avodat ha-Qodesh*, of the sixteenth-century Spanish kabbalist Rabbi Meir ibn Gabbai, we read:

> David said: in order to [ensure that] the Glory—that is the secret of the Bride—will sing and chant to Thee, I shall thank you forever, incessantly, so that the Glory on high will also not be silent. Because just as I am arousing here below, so the arousal will also be on high. . . . And the secret is that the Kenesset of Israel, that is singing, is the harp of David. . . . And this is the reason that it is incumbent to arouse by means of a variety of melodies, so as to draw down the holy spirit and life from the source of life, to his attribute, and this is the reason why the first of his qualities was that he had known to sing.[34]

The clue to understanding this passage is the sympathetic relationship between the earthly David, the famous singer, and the last Sefirah, *Malkhut* (the kingdom). The king uses his harp in order to

---

[32] Idel, *Kabbalah: New Pespectives*, 173–99; Charles Mopsik, *Les grands textes de la cabale: Les rites qui font Dieu* (Lagrasse: Verdier, 1993).

[33] See Moshe Idel, "The Magical and Theurgical Interpretation of Music in Jewish Sources from the Renaissance to Hasidism" (in Hebrew), *Yuval* 4 (1982):35–37, 49–51, 57-60.

[34] *'Avodat ha-Qodesh* (Jerusalem, 1973), fol. 132c; Idel, The Magical and Theurgical Interpretation of Music," 46. On this kabbalist, see the monograph by Roland Goetschel, *R. Meir Ibn Gabbai; Le Discourse de la Kabbale espagnole* (Leuven, 1981).

induce a higher song, that of the corresponding divine attribute, symbolized by the name of David, which sings to an even higher divine attribute. The mundane harp, too, corresponds to the last Sefirah, which is also designated as a harp. In other words, the lower song ascends and provides a higher song, which, in turn, ascends to an even higher ontological level. The principle of similarity is quintessential in order to understand the sympathetic influence on the powers within the divine realm. The kabbalist ibn Gabbai formulates this issue, earlier on in his book, as an important theurgical principle:

> The supernal Glory[35] does not arouse but when a thing that is related and similar to it. . . . And so also David said: "God is thy shade on thy right hand" [Ps. 121:5]. What is the meaning of "God is thy shade"? Like a shade, just as when you laugh it laughs to you, and if you cry, it cries to you. . .since the supernal entities are aroused by the lower ones, and this is why they compared the lower and the supernal entities to the form and the shade respectively, because they are related and similar to each other."[36]

The power of music, like that of the human "form" that is able to manipulate its shade, confers on the ancient David an unprecedented quality. However, from the second quotation, we learn that it is not David alone who was able to activate the lower Sefirah; in fact, the human body corresponds to the higher Glory, by dint of its similar structure, and so the music of David is just one of the theurgical forms of activities.

I would like to emphasize the theurgical nature of ibn Gabbai's discussion of music, which fits perfectly his vision of the impact of the commandments on the divine realm. At the end of the first quotation from his work, he explicitly mentions the need to draw down life and holy spirit to the "attribute" of David, namely, to the

---

[35] This, in ibn Gabbai's book, is a technical term for the sefirotic realm.

[36] *'Avodat ha-Qodesh*, fols. 35d–36a. For more on issues related to this quote, see Idel, *Kabbalah: New Perspectives*, 174–78.

last Sefirah. The song is aimed, ultimately, at arriving at a divine attribute; thus, the divine realm is the most important goal of music, while the extradivine realms—namely, the mundane world—are not even mentioned in this context. For this reason I propose using the term "theurgy," rather than "magic," in this context.

Rabbi Israel ben Eliezer, Ba'al Shem Tov (or, Besht) and founder of Hasidism, writes in the first part of the eighteenth century:

> The Besht has interpreted the verse "God is your shade" [Ps. 121:5] that God, blessed be He, is behaving with man as a shadow does; just as the shadow does whatever man does, so the Creator, blessed be He, is behaving with man as he [man] does. Thus Israel said the poem[37] at the time of the redemption from Egypt, and so likewise did the Holy One, blessed be He, as it were, sing this poem. Behold that the [verbal form] *yashir* points to a causative [grammatical] form and this is the meaning of the verse "then He will sing," namely, the children of Israel caused, by means of their singing, this singing of God, namely, that God, blessed be He, as it were, also sang this song.[38]

The founder of Hasidism is playing upon a fine ambiguity: in Hebrew, it is difficult to distinguish between the regular understanding of the verb *yashir*, "he will sing," and the same construction which could also be the causitive verbal form (*hif'il*), translated as "he will cause [someone] to sing—and the someone is God. The children of Israel are therefore described here as great theurgians, able to cause God to sing, understood here as imitating man, an interesting case of *imitatio fidei*. In the kabbalistic theurgy formulated by Rabbi Meir ibn Gabbai, the Hasidic master sees man as a musical instrument able to cause the reverberation of his melody by the divine organ, conceived also as a musical instrument.

---

[37] *'amru shirah.*

[38] Quoted in Rabbi Levi Isaac of Berditchev, *Qedushat Levi* (Jerusalem, 1972), fol. 39d; Idel, *Kabbalah: New Perspectives*, 178.

Music, Ecstasy, and Paradise

The integration of music into much more complex techniques to achieve mystical experiences is well-documented in the writings of mystics. This integration is more evident in Muslim mysticism[39] but is also present in various forms of Kabbalah.[40] Music as a preparation for obtaining prophecy is mentioned several times in medieval Jewish philosophy and had an impact on kabbalists, a topic I have dealt with elsewhere.[41]

The most important proof text for many of the discussions of music as conducive to the mystical experience of revelation is a verse from the book of Kings related to the prophet Elisha: "And when the minstrel played, the spirit of the Lord came upon him" [2 Kings 3:15], may be a reference to the use of music to obtain prophetic revelation or may allude to the dwelling of the divine spirit reached by means of listening to music.[42] In the period approaching the emergence of Kabbalah, music returns again; so, for example, we find some views on music in the writings of R. Yehuda he-Hasid of Regensburg and his student, R. Eleazar of Worms, both early thirteenth-century masters active in the Rhineland, whose thought was perhaps one of the sources of the later, ecstatic kabbalists and an important source of tradition for the eighteenth-century Ashkenazi ethical Hasidic teaching. R. Yehudah claims that:

> It cannot be that the Glory speaks of His Own accord in the same way that man speaks of his own accord. Take the *nevel* as an

[39] See Jean During, *Musique et extase: L'audition mystique dans la tradition soufie* (Paris: Albin Michel, 1988); Amnon Shiloah, "The Role and Nature of Music in the Practice of *Sama'*," in *Report of the Twelfth Congress, Berkeley, 1977*, International Musicological Society (Kassel and Philadelphia, 1981), 425–28, 433–34; Arthur Gribetz, "The Sama' Controversy: Sufi vs. Legalist," *Studia Islamica* 75 (1991):43–62.

[40] Cf. Idel, *The Mystical Experience*, 53–71.

[41] Idel, *The Mystical Experience*, 57.

[42] Karl Erich Grözinger, *Musik und Gesang in der Theologie der frühen jüdischen Literatur* (Tübingen: J. C. B. Mohr, 1982), 102–3.

example; the man plays on it, and the sound is not of the *nevel*'s own accord.[43]

The divine Glory, one of the major modes of revelation in the systems of the Ashkenazi Hasidim[44] is understood here as a musical instrument used by the revealer, God, in order to communicate to the prophets. However, in the writings of R. Yehudah's student, R. Eleazar, we find a much more technical approach to music:

> And the prophet was singing songs to the Holy One, blessed be He, and out of the joy of the commandment[45] the speech was coming, as it is said: "I rejoice at thy word" [Ps. 119:162].[46]

Singing songs to God is by no means an extraordinary motif in Judaism.[47] However, the song mentioned here concerns the evocation of a kind of joy that induces the emergence of prophetic speech—a stance closer, perhaps, to some Midrashic[48] views, where prophets were described as those "who were like an instrument full of speech."[49] Elsewhere, when referring to the same talmudic

---

[43] In Joseph Dan, *Studies in Ashkenazi-Hasidic Literature* (in Hebrew) (Ramat Gan: Masadah, 1975), 179.

[44] See Joseph Dan, *The Esoteric Theology of Ashkenazi Hasidism* (in Hebrew) (Jerusalem: Bialik Institute, 1968), 104–68; Elliot R. Wolfson, *Through a Speculum that Shines: Vision and Imagination in Medieval Jewish Mysticism* (Princeton: Princeton University Press, 1994), 234–69; Daniel Abrams, "'Sod kol ha-Sodot': The View of Glory and the Intention of the Prayer in the Writings of R. Eleazar of Worms and its Reverberations in Other Writings" (in Hebrew), *Daat* 34 (1995):61–81.

[45] *Simhah shel mitzvah.* Cf. *Shabbat,* fol. 30a.

[46] *Sefer Sodei Razzaya,* MS Oxford 1572, fol. 130a.

[47] See Ps. 33:2, 47:7, 66:2, etc.

[48] Midrash refers to a particular genre of rabbinic commentary, comprising biblical exegeses, public sermons, and commentaries on specific books of the Torah. The term is used primarily with regard to a set of midrashic literature from the second to the twelfth centuries C.E.

[49] Cf. *Mekhileta'* on Exod. 18:19; cf. also Boaz Cohen, *Law and Tradition in Judaism* (New York, 1959), 24 n. 70.

passage cited in *Shabbat*, R. Eleazar describes the enhancing of the glory that is revealed to the prophets who praise God.[50]

These statements are reminiscent of those of the founder of ecstatic Kabbalah, Rabbi Abraham Abulafia. For example, Abulafia described "prophecy," a term that he often used to describe an ecstatic experience, in this manner:

> The proof that song indicates the degree of prophecy is that it is the way of song to make the heart happy by means of tunes, as it is said, "And when the minstrel played, the spirit of the Lord came upon him" [2 Kings 3:15], for prophecy does not dwell in him [unless there is] joy.[51] This was already hinted at in two words appearing at the end of Ecclesiastes where he says, "The end of the matter, all being heard: Fear God, and keep his commandments, for this is the whole duty of man" [Eccles. 12:13]. Join *yare'* with *shamar*, and you find *shir 'amar*.[52] There is a hint [of this] in "and they shall put my name upon the children of Israel, and I will bless them" [Num. 6:27].[53]

The last part of this passage is based upon the gematria of 751, by which *yare' shamar* = *shir 'amar* = *'et shemi*.[54] Abulafia equates the two verbs, *yare'* and *shamar*, which denote awe and obedience, to the recitation of the song on the one hand and to the divine name on the other. Here blessing stands for the descent of prophecy, in a manner that differs from the blessing in theosophical-theurgical Kabbalah. The nexus between the song, *shirah*, and prophecy is the culmination of a much longer discussion, which portrays the Song of Songs as Solomon's last and most sublime composition and

---

[50] Cf. Rabbi Eleazar of Worms, *Perushei Siddur ha-Tefillah la-Roqeah*, ed. M. Hershler and Y. A. Hershler (Jerusalem, 1992), 1:145 and 149.

[51] See *Shabbat* fol. 30b. Compare with the texts of Rabbi Eleazar of Worms, cited above, fn. 47.

[52] *yare'*, 'fear'; *shamar*, 'keep'; *shir 'amar*, 'say a song'.

[53] *Sefer 'Otzar 'Eden Ganuz*, MS Oxford 1580, fol. 62a; Idel, *The Mystical Experience*, 61–62.

[54] Fear, keep = say a song = My name.

points to the spiritual attainment of the author and to the mystical kiss of death.[55] In general, Abulafia assumes that the biblical songs, like the song of Moses and Devorah, for example, point to metaphysical topics and to the intellectual human faculty.[56] This view seems to be related to a theory found in an anonymous commentary on the Jewish liturgy, contemporary to Abulafia: in effect, the secret of the Song of Songs is the secret of the combination of letters, a central technique in Abulafia's Kabbalah.[57]

Abulafia's interpretation of the passage above, transforming somewhat negative terms into much more positive ones, is reminiscent of the kind of interpretation explored by eighteenth-century Hasidic hermeneutics. However, the introduction of the song in the context of Ecclesiastes, quite an artificial move, demonstrates that music or songs were part of Abulafia's mystical vision in general; music thus becomes a sort of hermeneutical grid in this type of Kabbalah. To what extent music was related to the prophetic, namely, an ecstatic experience, we learn from a detailed parable in which Abulafia compares the human body, wherein dwells the divine spirit, to a musical instrument:

> It is known that sound is heard more loudly in a place which is hollow or pierced, due to the purity of the spiritual air which enters therein, as in the case of the *kinnor* and similar musical instruments, which produce sound without any speech, and so also the concavities of the upper stories, caves, mountains, bathhouses, ruins, etc., whose interior is hollow. . . . By means of this secret you will understand the meaning of "Moses spake, and God answered him by a voice" [Exod. 19:19], i.e., in a voice similar to that of Moses.[58] You must know that the body of man is full of holes and cavities,

---

[55] MS Oxford 1580, fols. 59b–60a. On the kiss of death as a moment of ecstasy in other texts of Abulafia, see Idel, *The Mystical Experience*, 180–84.

[56] MS Oxford 1580, fol. 60ab.

[57] See MS Paris BN 848, fol. 7b.

[58] On this issue see Idel, *The Mystical Experience*, 65 n. 14, 83–95.

from which you may understand how the *Shekhinah* dwells in the body which is pierced and [contains] cavities and which produces speech.[59]

In lieu of the Temple as the dwelling place of the divine presence, the human body is now conceived as the place of the *Shekhinah*. This move is part of the same interpretation of Kabbalah as a substitute for the temple ritual, but now, in ecstatic Kabbalah, the experience rather than the ritual is conceived of as important.[60] This vision of the human body as a musical instrument is not uncommon in the mystical literature,[61] but Abulafia was more drawn to this image than any other mystic with whom I am acquainted. Thus, he writes in his last work, *Sefer 'Imrei Shefer*, that

Just as the owner of a garden has the power to water the garden at will by means of rivers, so does the one making music with the Name have the power to water at will his limbs by means of his soul, through the Almighty, Blessed Name; and this is [the meaning of] "and it came to pass, when the minstrel played, that the hand of the Lord came upon him" [2 Kings 3:15]—this is the *kinnor* [harp] hung above David's bed, which used to play of itself and "praise Him with the *nevel* [psaltery] and *kinnor*" [Ps. 150:3].[62] But

[59] *Sefer Mafteah ha-Re'ayon*, MS Oxford Heb. e 123, fol. 64b.

[60] For Abulafia's anomian stand, see Idel, *Kabbalah: New Perspectives*, 74–75.

[61] See Philo, *De Virtutibus*, par. 39, 217. Cf. also H. A. Wolfson, *Philo: Foundations of Religious Philosophy in Judaism, Christianity, and Islam* (Cambridge, Mass.: Harvard University Press, 1947), 2:29; M. R. Jones, *Studies in Mystical Religion* (London: Macmillan, 1919), 40; and the additional material collected by A. J. Heschel, *The Prophets* (New York: Harper and Row, 1962), 341 nn. 28–29, and Eva Meyerovitch, *Mystique et poesie en Islam* (Paris: DeBrouwer, 1972), 78, 88.

[62] The combination of the legend of David's harp with the proof text, 2 Kings 3:15, appears in several places in Midrash. Cf. *Pesiqeta de-Rav Kahana*, ed. S. Buber, chap. 7, fols. 62b–63a, and Buber's footnotes; and Louis Ginzburg, *The Legends of the Jews*, trans. Henrietta Szold (Philadelphia: Jewish Publication Society of America, 1946), 6:262 nn. 81–83.

this would only be after receiving the divine effluence, which is called the seventy-two-letter name, together with the understanding of its paths."[63]

It seems to me that the analogy of the garden to the body also extends to the *kinnor*: just as the garden and the body are passive, receiving the action of the gardener and the musician with the name of the seventy-two letters, so also does David's *kinnor* play "of itself" when the divine effluence reverberates within it. Abulafia here appears to suggest that David's *kinnor* resembles the human body: like the harp, man also makes music "of himself" when the wind, namely, the divine spirit, blows. Support for this interpretation may be found in another passage:

> The body is like a garden, which is the master of vegetation, and the soul is *'eden*, which is the master of delights; and the body is planted in it. The secret of *gan 'eden* [Garden of Eden] is *'ad naggen* [through playing], for prophecy dwells when *'eved naggen* [the servant plays?], e.g., "when the minstrel played [2 Kings 3:15], as in the case of Elisha."[64]

The expression *gan 'eden* in gematria equals *'ad naggen*, and *gan be-'eden* equals *'eved naggen*. The human body is a garden, *gan*, planted within the *'eden* and activated by it. Thus, the change in locus for the performance of ecstatic music from the ancient Temple (see below) to the human body is accompanied by a paradisiacal vision of mystical experience. The combination of the letters of the divine name is a practice intended to irrigate the garden, namely, the human body, and induce in it the soul, the *'eden*,

---

[63] MS München 40, fol. 246b, and also in the anthology of Abulafian texts found in the collectanaea of Rabbi Joseph Hamitz, MS Oxford, Bodleiana 2239, fol. 130a. The name of seventy-two letters—in fact, of three times seventy-two, namely 216—is one of the major topics in Abulafia's technical handbooks, especially *Hayyei ha-'Olam ha-Ba'*, where it stands for the means to bring about the opening of the mystic's consciousness to the divine influx.

[64] *Hayyei ha-'Olam ha-Ba'*, MS Oxford 1582, fol. 7a. For more on these issues, see Idel, *The Mystical Experience*, 56–57.

or the divine influx. Music is, therefore, an attempt to create in this world a spiritual individual Edenic experience. It is important in this context to mention the Sufi nexus between the mystical experience achieved by *samā'* and listening to the music of Paradise.[65] According to another point of view—that of Mircea Eliade—the mystical experience was understood as a "nostalgia for Paradise."[66] Abulafia's short discussion on music, and his longer discussion on Paradise, support such a position. I suggest, on the basis of this succinct discussion of his view of music and ideal figures, David and the prophets, that Abulafia was much less concerned with templar music; certainly, the High Priest does not figure prominently in his discussions on music. Given the options of returning to the Temple or regaining Paradise, Abulafia would definitively prefer the latter, while the theosophical kabbalists would eventually choose the former.

As seen above, musical performance was part of a mystical technique well represented in ecstatic Kabbalah. However, this brand of Jewish mysticism, inclined as it was to Aristotelian interpretations of mystical experiences, is not the only kabbalistic school that embraced this view. Other examples, whereby kabbalistic views were combined with Neoplatonic ones, do not depend upon ecstatic Kabbalah, yet nevertheless represent music as part of a mystical path. Abraham ben Hananel of Eskira, a late thirteenth-century kabbalist, writes that

When the soul craves solitude and to regale itself in the luxuries of the intellect, were it not that Nature stands in its way with a temptation of images, it would separate itself from the body. For this reason, the *kinnor* was struck in front of the altar at the time that the sacrifice was offered. . . .[67] It is known to those who speak

---

[65] See During, *Musique et extase*, 42–47.

[66] See, e.g., *The Quest* (Chicago: University of Chicago, 1971), 88–111.

[67] The phrase "the harp was struck in front of the altar" seems to be based on the Mishnaic phrase "the *halil* [flute] was played in front of the altar," in *'Arakhin* 2:3.

of the science of music that music is intermediate between the spiritual and the material, in that it draws forth the intellect at the time of its imprisonment, as it is written, "but now bring me a minstrel" [2 Kings 3:15], and as it is written, "awake, *nevel* and *kinnor*" [Ps. 57:8]. Nature drags the intellect, so to speak, to leave the intellectual [world] and to amuse itself with material things."[68]

Unlike Abulafia's writing, here the more Neoplatonic and templar attitude toward music performance is evident. Music, including its ritualistic performance, is a technique to liberate the soul from its prison, namely, Nature, rather than a technique to refine the intellect and prepare it for purer forms of intellections—the interpretation of Abulafia and some of his followers. In this context, let us return to the secret of the *shalshelet* (cantillation mark); the mystical impact of the melody is emphasized by describing the death during ecstasy:

Such also was the incident of the two young French girls in the city of Montpellier[69] in ancient times, who knew how to perform music, and had pleasant voices and excelled in the science of music. They began to recite [Ps. 45:1]: "To the chief musician upon *Shoshannim*, for the sons of Korah, Maskkil, A Song of Loves." They chanted, according to the straight path,[70] and they become united with the higher [entities], and they were so absorbed in song that before they finished half the psalm, God rejoiced at hearing the song from their mouths, as is his way, that the tune rose upwards, they achieved

---

[68] MS Moscow-Ginzburg 607, fol. 8a. This passage seems to be an adaptation from *Muserei ha-Philosofim*, I, 18 (8); cf. Adler, *Hebrew Writings Concerning Music*, 148; see also the emendations of the sequence of this passage in E. Werner and I. Sonne, *Hebrew Union College Annual* 17 (1942–43):515–16 and 525 (English translation). For the connection between music and sacrifice, see Ibn Falaquera's *Sefer ha-Mevaqqesh* (based on the music epistle of the *Ihwan al-Safa*); cf. Adler, *Hebrew Writings Concerning Music*, 165, sentence 3.

[69] In the original, *Har ha-Ga'ash*, literally, volcano.

[70] *'al ha-derekh ha-yashar.*

union, and their souls ascended to Heaven. See how God rejoices at hearing a tune done correctly, and how much power there is in good music! As proof, notice that when the cantor has a good appearance, a pleasant voice, clear speech, and good melodies, the congregation rejoices with him, and for this reason the souls, which are sublime, take pleasure. Souls come from God, and thus God rejoices along with them, concerning which they say, "making happy God and men."[71]

The ecstatic experience of the young women is described in terms of an ascent of the soul. I assume that the kabbalist resorted to a Neoplatonic view of *henosis* as found in some Muslim and Jewish sources which speak about the ascent of the soul on the "straight path" to their union with the supernal entities. In the above passage, the term that may point to the straight line that unites the lower soul with the higher powers is *derekh yashar* (straight path), a term that stands for the mode of singing. But I wonder whether we should overlook the possibility of relating this phrase to the *qav he-yashar* (straight line) and similar expressions that point to the ontological continuum that unites the lower and higher spiritual powers.[72] This is a rather rare example of the mystical attainment of young women, whose sole knowledge was the science of music, and thus they were able to attain the most sublime mystical experience.

[71] *Sod ha-Shalshelet* (see fn. 24) and Idel, *The Mystical Experience*, 60–61; Michael Fishbane, *The Kiss of God: Spiritual and Mystical Death in Judaism* (Seattle and London: Washington University Press, 1994), 31–32.

[72] See the important study by Alexander Altmann, "The Ladder of Ascension," in *Studies in Mysticism and Religion Presented to Gershom G. Scholem*, ed. E. E. Urbach, R. J. Zwi Werblowsky, and Ch. Wirszubski (Jerusalem: Magnes Press, 1967), 1–32. See also Idel, "The Ladder of Ascension: The Reverberations of a Medieval Motif in the Renaissance," in *Studies in Medieval Jewish History and Literature*, 2, ed. I. Twersky, Harvard Judaic Monographs, 5 (Cambridge, Mass.: Harvard University Center for Jewish Studies, 1984), 83–93.

Music and Magic in Jewish Mysticism

The magic model is the last, from the temporal point of view, to be accepted by the kabbalists. While the theosophical-theurgical model appeared in the first kabbalistic documents, and the ecstatic Kabbalah—in the 1280s—saw music as part of the mystical techniques, it is only at the end of the thirteenth century that the magical model has been integrated and become increasingly more visible in some forms of Kabbalah. However, although it appears later in Jewish mystical literature, this model is by no means less influential. It is especially evident from the end of the fifteenth century, and one of its earlier formulations is found in the writing of Rabbi Yohanan Alemanno, a mentor and companion of Pico della Mirandola. According to Alemanno's view of the performance of music:

> The material music can operate the operations related to it given its proportions, because of the spiritual force[73] inherent in it. Even if the performance of music is deficient, the music will [nevertheless] be able to operate its operations because of its proportions."[74]

The term "spiritual force," used in many of Alemanno's writings, refers to an astral power that is collected here below in material and spiritual structures that correspond to the entity upon which this power is appointed above. Thus, Alemanno's assumption is that the spiritual—which in this text means magical power—aspect of music is able to operate, even if the performance is not perfect. Alemanno's vision of music as magically effective was not an exception; this was upheld by other kabbalists of his generation and even by non-kabbalistic authors like Rabbi Isaac Abravanel, who subscribed to the templar vision of music and magic, and by the Safedian

---

[73] *ruhaniyyut.* On this term in magical sources, see S. Pines, "On the Term *Ruhaniyyut* and Its Sources and on Judah Halevi's Doctrine" (in Hebrew), *Tarbiz* 57 (1988):511–40; Idel, *Hasidism*, 427, sub voce *ruhaniyyut.*

[74] *Sefer Hesheq Shelomo*, in Adler, *Hebrew Writings Concerning Music*, 44; Idel, "The Magical and Theurgic Interpretations," 39.

kabbalists. Since I have dealt with those views elsewhere,[75] here I will take examples from a much later period. Rabbi Levi Yitzhaq of Berditchev, the eighteenth-century Hasidic master and the founder of Hasidism in central Poland, again quoted the Besht, the founder of Hasidism:

> Each angel has to recite his song in accordance to his particular aspect. . .and each of them says a song in accordance to his aspect, whether this is love, or awe, or victory and in accordance to the aspect that he worships our Lord, and says his song, so does he suck and so does he distribute [efflux] to his nation. . . . Know that if someone wants to change the heart of a certain nation toward Israel for good, and he knows the aspect of its song and in what way does it worship God, and what [divine] attribute does it praise, if the *Tzaddiq* [a righteous, often wise and revered, man] says this song, which is said by the angel [of that nation] and he worships our Lord by that aspect that angel is worshipping, the angel has to love this man who worships the Lord of Lords by his aspect he [himself] is worshipping and says his song is peculiar to him. Provided that the angel loves the *Tzaddiq* who says the song said by the angel, then he [the *Tzaddiq*] compels him to do the will of the *Tzaddiq* and there is no need to resort to "incantations of angels."[76]

Prima facie, this is an anti-magical passage, as it suggests the existence of a technique that does not resort to incantations. There are incantations, but in this instance they are addressed not to angels but to divine attributes. Because he has the knowledge to address a certain divine attribute with a song used by an angel of a certain nation, a *Tzaddiq* is said to be able to dominate that angel himself. Thus, in lieu of an angelic magic, we have here a super-angelic magic, able to control the angels themselves. Music is used in an enterprise that I consider to be part of my description of magic: although songs, divine attributes, and angels are being manipulated,

---

[75] Idel, "The Magical and Theurgic Interpretations," 42–45, 51–57.
[76] *Qedushat Levi*, fol. 118a.

the final goal is to control the efflux suck by the angel, an emanation
of power that the *Tzaddiq* can control and channel to his nation.

> The *Tzaddiqim* were causing,[77] by their good deeds, whatever
> [result] they want, [either] to impart [the influx] to someone, or to
> stop the influx from another.[78] This has been the worship of the
> Levites, who were playing the musical instruments sometimes they
> were raising their voice sometimes they were lowering it, as it is
> knowing to the sages of music. When they were raising their voice
> during their singing, it was in order to prevent the influx from the
> wicked. . .and when they were singing in a low voice their intention
> was to draw down the influx to all the lower and created entities.[79]

Here, the magic of drawing down the supernal influx through
music, or songs, is quite evident. A sympathetic form of magic is
involved: the high pitch is conceived of as preventing the descent
of the influx on the wicked ones, while the low pitch draws the
influx down to the lower beings. In other words, unlike the
theurgical function of music, which concentrated on efforts to affect
divine processes, the above passages are deemed to affect extradivine powers.

These passages do, indeed, deal with theoretical visions of music
and one may duly question their relevance for the floruit of the
actual practice of music in Hasidic circles. Indeed, it may be that
the coexistence of different models for understanding music in the
Hasidic writings—and here we have addressed only two, the
theurgical and the magical, although more ecstatic examples might
also be adduced—created a certain predisposition to see in the
musical performance meanings that were less important in non-
mystical Jewish milieux.

---

[77] *me'orerim.* See also fns. 8–10 above and fn. 82 below.

[78] It may be the issue of blessing and curse that is hinted at here. See also the
passage by R. Qalonimus Qalman Epstein of Cracow, *Sefer Ma'or va-Shemesh,*
discussed in Idel, *Hasidism,* 245–47.

[79] *Qedushat Levi,* fol. 17a.

Music and Power

Music is seen in all the above texts as influential. In the ecstatic Kabbalah, music induces a feeling of joy which contributes, according to the rabbinic literature, to the occurrence of the prophecy; or, according to other, more philosophically oriented views, music is perceived as able to soften the soul and open it to a more spiritual type of perception.[80] In the two other models, the power of music is more closely connected to an energetic sense that, by either descending or ascending, exercises different influences on the respective realms.[81] Let me adduce some texts that articulate energetic and ontic perceptions of music. Rabbi Moses Cordovero, one of the leading sixteenth-century Safedian kabbalists, describes the ascent of the songs in terms reflecting the inverse processes of the descent of the divine influx:

> Just as the supernal influx and the vitality descend from the [world of] Emanation, and there it is pure, but when it descends to [the world] of Creation, and from there to [the world of] Formation, it becomes coarse, so the supernal song and the arousal,[82] that ascends from below upward, is purified and ascends from the [world of] Formation to that of Creation and from Creation to Emanation, and within the Emanation—from one degree to another—until it reaches the chambers and attics, and there they will be purified and ascend to cause joy to the [supernal] union [between the *sefirot* of *Hokhmah* and *Binah*].[83]

The song is, therefore, no different from the divine influx. It is a mode of the divine produced here below; when sent on high, it becomes purified in a manner reminiscent of the ascent of the astral

---

[80] See Idel, *The Mystical Experience*, 63, 66–67 n. 28.

[81] See the discussion by R. Isaac ibn Sahulah in his *Commentary on the Song of Songs*, 408–9.

[82] *ha-shir ve-ha-hit'orerut.*

[83] *Shi'ur Qomah* (Jerusalem, 1966), fol. 16c.

body in the ancient mystical forms of literature. In other words, the song is a spiritual energy, a way to respond to the divine with a human activity that affects the union between the two higher *sefirot*. Elsewhere,[84] Cordovero speaks of the song of all the creatures which ascends to their creator in a manner quite similar to that of his contemporary, Rabbi Shimeon Lavi. Rabbi Shimeon, who was active in Tripoli, describes another form of ascent of the song of the creatures toward their source and originator:

> You should know that because all the lower worlds desire to see the face of the Lord, the Master of all the world,[85] in order to obtain their will and nourishment, each in accordance to the food that is appropriate to it, that desire and turn[86] is called *shirah* [song]. They know how to relate each cause to its cause, and they need it,[87] and their desire will arrive from cause to cause until the cause of all the causes, blessed be his name. This[88] is their song, each of them [of the worlds] according to its specialty they do and were appointed upon it, the firstborn according to his birth and the youngest according to his youth, from Michael, the great angel, to the smallest of the species in the great sea, because they have been created for this purpose. This issue, namely the collection[89] of all the desires, from the smallest [creature] to the greatest one, altogether, were called by the sages of inquiry, "the melody of the world," namely, the collection of all the voices in a harmonious manner. And this is the praise of God, blessed be He, which ascends from below

---

[84] *Sefer 'Elimah Rabbati* (Brody, 1881), fol. 43d–44a; Idel, "The Magical and Theurgical Interpretation," 52–53.

[85] *'Adon kol ha-'aretz*. According to Zoharic symbolism, the earth may stand for the last *sefirah*, that of *Malkhut*.

[86] *Teshuqah u-feniyyah*.

[87] *Hittztarekh*. I wonder whether a better reading might be *hittztaref*, which would mean that the lower worlds are joining the causes on their way upward to the higher causes.

[88] Namely, the desire.

[89] *Qibbutz*.

upwards, each and every category speaking in the language of its nation: "heavens tell the glory of the Lord"[90] in their language, though in that language there is no speech and words as in our language, by [means of] mouth and lips, as said in that psalm. Likewise, all the beings according to their species, birds, beasts, animals, trees, according to their quests a song was attributed to them, as mentioned in *Pereq Shirah*. But the song of Israel is more sublime then all the others, because of their comprehensive knowledge.[91]

The song is but another term for the desire of the creature to return to the creator, a mythical version of the neoplatonic *reversio*. The cosmic melody, namely, the impulse to reach the source, represents an ontic link beneath all the variety of beings and their emanator.

Finally, allow me to cite a Lurianic text that exemplifies the nexus between music and power. In his *Commentary on Luria's Songs*, Rabbi Israel Sarug, a student of the famous kabbalist, writes as follows:

You should know that just as those who descended to the *Merkavah* must say the song[92] and by dint of this song the gates of the [divine] chariot were opened and they entered into their palaces. . .and by dint of the songs that they were singing the gates were opened, [and] also the power of the descendants themselves was enhanced by their singing, thus being able to walk and so to ascend; without their singing they were not able to walk, because they walked [only] while singing, as in the case of [the verse] "Sun, stand still on Give'on" [Josh. 10:12], which means that should he not silence the sun, he would not be able to stop them. This shows that by virtue

---

[90] See Ps. 19:1. This verse has also been interpreted, using the Pythagorean view of the music of the spheres, by another North African Jewish author, the fifteenth-century R. Shimeon ben Tzemah Duran. See the text from *Magen 'Avot*, his *Commentary on 'Avot*, in Adler, *Hebrew Writings Concerning Music*, 133.

[91] *Ketem Paz*, fols. 416b–417a.

[92] Or, 'were singing'.

of the song, the sun is circulating every day from East to West. . . .
The song is empowering each and every spiritual being and celestial
body to walk.[93]

Sarug interprets the use of the song in different ways. The song
opened the gates of the celestial world so that the contemplators
would be able to enter and see God. However, the act of singing is
also conceived of as empowering the singers themselves and thus
gives them the power to ascend. This interpretation is described as
part of a more general principle, which attributes to the song the
power to move celestial bodies, such as the sun. Silence is thus
conceived of as deleterious, and the halting of the sun is related to
Joshua's termination of the act of solar singing.

An overtly lingual type of mysticism, which attributes so much
power to the performance of language, Kabbalah also implicitly
invests other sonoric activities with similar energetic qualities.[94] It
projects the energetic visions of language and music into the remote
past in order to invigorate the present.

---

[93] In *Ne'im Zemirot Israel* (L'viv, 1794).

[94] See Moshe Idel, "Reification of Language in Jewish Mysticism," ed. Steven
T. Katz, *Mysticism and Language* (New York and Oxford: Oxford University
Press, 1992), 42–79; and "On Talismanic Language in Jewish Mysticism,"
Diogenes 43, no. 2 (1995):23–41.

Music, Myth, and Medicine in the Choctaw Indian Ballgame[*]

Victoria Lindsay Levine

The most important repertory of Choctaw traditional music today is called Social Dance music; it is performed in diverse secular contexts, such as folkloric demonstrations and educational programs. However, this repertory originally belonged to the Choctaw Ballgame. The Ballgame existed in some form among virtually all Native Americans from the Eastern Woodlands and Great Lakes regions and was the forerunner of lacrosse (cf. Vennum 1994). The Ballgame involved a competition between two opposing teams; the players attempted to strike their goal post with a ball, which could be touched, carried, or thrown only with special rackets. But the Ballgame was much more than a sport. Framed by elaborate religious ritual lasting days or even weeks, the Ballgame constituted a complex, multivalent sacred festival[1] that integrated the work of

[*] I am deeply grateful for the Senior Fellowship I received from the American Council of Learned Societies during 1994–1995, which enabled me to research and write this paper. I wish to thank Claire Farrer (California State University at Chico) and Michelene Pesantubbee (University of Colorado at Boulder) for their helpful comments on various drafts of this paper. I am also grateful to Doug Fox, Gale Murray, and Dennis Showalter, my stalwart friends at Colorado College. Above all, I want to thank Mark, Scott, and Elizabeth Levine for their ongoing support at home.

[1] The festival has been defined as "a periodically recurrent, social occasion in which, through a multiplicity of forms and a series of coordinated events, participate directly or indirectly and to various degrees, all members of a whole

religious and medical specialists, individual power quests, and communal ceremony to effect curing, rites of passage, and world renewal (Fogelson 1971; Herndon 1971; Vennum 1994). For the Choctaw, the Ballgame became the most visible sacred ritual from the eighteenth through the early twentieth centuries. The Choctaw no longer perform the Ballgame as a sacred ritual, yet the Social Dance music that once played an integral part in the ritual continues to express religious feeling.

That a musical repertory can outlive the religious ritual with which it was associated suggests that, for the Choctaw, music is not merely an adjunct to ritual; it actually constitutes a discrete segment of the Choctaw sacred ideology. Choctaw religious traditions, like other Native American belief systems, consists of a number of distinct segments including mythology, medicine, and communal ritual cycles, as well as Christian observances. Each religious segment operates as a separate configuration of beliefs and has its own qualities and functions. The degree of integration among these religious segments varies from tribe to tribe and, in some cases, they are fairly independent of one another (Hultkrantz 1984). This feature of American Indian religious traditions can make it a challenge to determine the relationship between music and sacred ritual, especially in view of historical dynamics.

Choctaw Social Dance music provides a case in point. Choctaw religious traditions have never been well understood, in part because the available source materials are fragmented and contradictory. Furthermore, the discrete segments of Choctaw religion now operate independently of one another, exhibiting considerable variation from one community to the next. Thus, while scholars have long assumed that Choctaw Social Dance music is connected to sacred ritual, the nature of that relationship has not been fully comprehended. Some

---

community, united by ethnic, linguistic, religious, historical bonds, and sharing a worldview. Both the social function and the symbolic meaning of the festival are closely related to a series of overt values that the community recognizes as essential to its ideology and worldview, to its social identity, its historical continuity, and to its physical survival, which is ultimately what festival celebrates" (Falassi 1987, 2).

insight into this question may be gained by an exploration of the other segments of Choctaw religious thought, particularly myth and medicine. Prior to the twentieth century, Choctaw music, myth, and medicine were tightly integrated through the Ballgame ritual. Therefore, I begin with a summary of the Ballgame in Choctaw religious history.[2]

The Ballgame in Choctaw History

The Choctaw are descendents of the Mississippian people who flourished throughout most of the Southeast after 800 c.e. The Mississippians grew maize, beans, squash, and other crops but also depended heavily on hunting and gathering. Mississippian settlements featured large populations with centralized, stratified societies. They had rich and elaborate religious traditions; Mississippian sacred art depicts themes of agriculture, fertility, warfare, religious and medical specialists, and athletes, especially ball players (Howard 1968; Hudson 1976; Galloway 1989). A class of warrior-priests directed religious rituals. The head priests lived in houses built on earthen temple mounds with flattened tops. Temple mounds surrounded and faced a settlement's central plaza, which served as a ceremonial ground and Ballgame field (Hudson 1976, 78). The mounds were thus the focal point of significant religious ceremonies; a variety of seasonal, life cycle, and curing ceremonies were performed on the mounds and in the adjacent plaza. The Ballgame occupied a central role in Mississippian religious life, which is evident in the people's sacred art as well as in their method of structuring sacred space.

---

[2] The primary historical sources on the Choctaw Ballgame, religion, and musical culture are fully described and summarized by John Swanton (1928, 1931). Ethnographic and ethnomusicological sources include Bushnell (1909), Densmore (1943), Howard (1968), Peterson (1970), Hudson (1976), Draper (1980, 1983), Blanchard (1981), Galloway (1989), Howard and Levine (1990), Levine (1990, 1993), and Vennum (1994). My fieldwork among Choctaw communities in Oklahoma, Louisiana, and Mississippi was carried out in 1983 and 1985.

For a variety of societal and environmental reasons, Mississippian cultures were undergoing reorganization at the time of their first contact with Europeans in the sixteenth century (Johnson 1992, 18). After contact with Europeans, the heavy casualties inflicted by military aggression and disease epidemics hastened the reorganization. Those who survived the onslaught had to reconstruct their societies. In some cases, larger, more intact cultures assimilated the remnants of smaller groups with which they had prior economic or political alliances. In other cases, small, previously separate groups banded together to build informal confederacies; this is evidently how the Choctaw nation became established (Galloway 1992, 38).

By the early eighteenth century, the Choctaw people were a confederation of about fifty villages without a unified central government, located in the area that is now central and southern Mississippi, eastern Alabama, and southern Louisiana. Each village acted independently, although they were loosely organized into three districts (Wells 1992, 47). Villages were divided into two exogamous moieties with reciprocal ritual obligations. Village leadership was shared between a war chief and a peace chief, each of whom had assistants. Individual men progressed in status through four ranks, determined by war achievements and age. Choctaw religious traditions in the early eighteenth century included curing rituals, seasonal agricultural rituals, hunting rituals, funerary rites that involved the storage of ancestors' bones in ossuaries, war ceremonies such as an eight-day War Dance and an all-night Victory or Scalp Dance, and the Ballgame as well as other ritual games. At this time in Choctaw religious history, the Ballgame may have functioned in part as a moiety ritual, helping to maintain cosmic unity through ritual reciprocity.

The eighteenth century represents a watershed in Choctaw history. During the course of the century, the Ballgame gradually assumed greater importance and became more elaborate as other aspects of Choctaw culture and sacred life underwent radical change. Choctaw warfare declined and finally ceased in the second half of the century, and an integral venue for personal achievement and settling disputes disappeared. The Ballgame thus increased in significance as a means of enhancing individual status as well as conflict resolution on the intratribal and intertribal level; the role of the Ballgame as a surrogate for warfare has been examined thoroughly in an excellent recent study (Vennum 1994). Curing rites, communal rituals, and musical repertories previously associated with warfare were subsumed into the Ballgame. The Choctaw War Dance, performed as part of the ritual preparation for war expeditions, and the Victory Dance, performed upon the return of a war party, were probably absorbed by the Ballgame cycle, where they were reinterpreted as pre- and post-game ritual dances.

Choctaw funeral rituals also changed dramatically in the eighteenth century. In the early historic period, the Choctaw placed the bodies of the deceased on scaffolds, where they were allowed to decompose until the flesh could be removed from the bones. After the bones had been cleaned by a ritual specialist (*foni kashopa*, or bone-picker), they were packed in a deerskin bag for storage in an ossuary. Euramericans were simultaneously appalled and fascinated by this practice; increased contact, especially after the Revolutionary War, gradually forced the Choctaw to develop new funeral customs. By the 1820s, the Choctaw had replaced bone-picking with burial, accompanied by a mourning ritual known as the Cry. At about the same time, the release from mourning at the conclusion of the Cry began to be marked by a Ballgame.

Shamanism was central to Choctaw religious thought and medicine during the eighteenth century. European observers described the practices of various kinds of Choctaw ritual specialists: herb doctors who administered remedies made from plants and roots, medicine men who performed cupping to extract disease agents from the afflicted, prophets who could predict the future and influence weather conditions, and medicine men who used their powers to cause harm (Swanton 1918, 1931). Eighteenth-century authors were well aware of the role of prayer, trance, and communication with spirit beings among Choctaw ritual specialists. However, their own religious orientations led these authors to denounce such practices as devil worship (cf. Swanton 1918, 62).

The Choctaw evidently began to take protective measures to avoid increasing criticism, and by the early nineteenth century, they practiced traditional medicine and shamanism less openly, except in the context of the Ballgame.

In the early eighteenth century, the Choctaw probably continued to perform the Green Corn Ceremony, the most important seasonal observance for the Mississippians. The Green Corn Ceremony was an annual festival of world renewal; it combined agrarian fertility rites and ceremonies honoring game animals with a Ballgame performance. The ceremony focused on repairing and renewing relationships among members of the human community, between people and the spirits of animals and plants that provide human sustenance, and between complementary cosmic forces. In Mississippian times, buildings on top of sacred mounds were periodically destroyed and covered in a layer of earth as part of the ritual enactment of world renewal; sometimes entire mounds were destroyed and rebuilt. Southeastern peoples had stopped building large mounds in the early historic period, but other purification rituals, such as a renewal of the sacred fire, accompanied the Green Corn Ceremony in the eighteenth century. In addition, the Ballgame performed as part of this ceremony symbolized the destruction and recreation of the cosmos. The Choctaw discontinued the Green Corn Ceremony and other agricultural rites during the eighteenth century, perhaps because of economic changes. However, they continued to play the Ballgame as a reiteration of cosmic creation, particularly in small-scale, intracommunity games using only one goal post.

Thus, by the early nineteenth century, the Ballgame had become the focal point for Choctaw sacred life, compressing rituals previously associated with moieties, warfare, agriculture, funerals, medicine, and world renewal into one ceremonial cycle that could be altered and adapted to suit a specific occasion. As a sacred ritual, the Ballgame emphasized honoring and communicating with spiritual entities, restoring balance among the cosmic forces, and repairing and renewing relationships on several planes of existence. The Ballgame was not a religion in itself; rather, it became the primary mode of collective expression of Choctaw sacred ideology.

One reason for this development may have been the Euramerican perception of the Ballgame as mere sport, which enabled the Choctaw to conceal—and thereby preserve—its religious content.[3]

If the eighteenth century represents a watershed in Choctaw history, the nineteenth century represents a cataclysm. The Mississippi Territory was established in 1798, bringing a new influx of Euramerican settlers. In 1817, Mississippi became a state, and the following year the first Choctaw mission was established. Despite Choctaw efforts to accept and adapt to Euramerican culture, the settlers began to demand the removal of the Choctaw, which began in 1830. Within three years, most of the Choctaw had been sent west of the Mississippi River to the Indian Territory, where they established a sovereign nation. The Choctaw who remained in Mississippi lost all land rights; their economy shifted from large-scale agriculture and hunting to subsistence farming, and, after the Civil War, they became sharecroppers. In the 1890s, the United States dissolved land trusts in Indian Territory, made individual land allotments, and terminated tribal governments. More than one half of the remaining Mississippi Choctaw were then removed to Indian Territory, which became the state of Oklahoma in 1907.

The tragic disruption of Choctaw culture during the nineteenth century brought heightened significance to the Ballgame. As marginal subsistence farmers, the remaining Mississippi Choctaw lived in scattered, isolated communities. Ballgames became the most important means of social interaction among these communities, as

---

[3] Nineteenth-century Euramerican travelers among the Choctaw described the Ballgame as an athletic contest of Olympic proportions. Horatio Cushman, who grew up among the Mississippi Choctaw, wrote that "to any one of the present day, an ancient Choctaw ball-play would be an exhibition far more interesting, strange, wild and romantic, in all its features, than anything ever exhibited in a circus. . .excelling it in every particular of daring feats and wild recklessness" (Cushman 1962 [1899], 130). But Cushman and his contemporaries were puzzled by the apparent absence of Choctaw sacred ritual, and the idea that the Choctaw lacked religion has persisted until quite recently (cf. Debo 1961, 10). I believe that it is this sort of thinking on which the Choctaw capitalized in protecting their religious tradition.

well as the center of traditional religious life. They held highly ritualized matches, in which one community competed against another. The Choctaw who had been removed to Indian Territory also continued to perform the Ballgame, where matches became massive spectacles involving hundreds of players on each team, if accounts by nineteenth-century observers such as George Catlin can be believed (cf. Vennum 1994).

Choctaw Ballgames declined in scale and frequency in the late nineteenth century. Missionaries and government officials saw the Ballgame as an obstacle to Choctaw progress (Blanchard 1981, 41). In particular, they condemned the gambling that accompanied Ballgames, not understanding its ritual function in establishing reciprocity and demonstrating spiritual power. Ballgames had also become more violent, due in part to the introduction of alcohol and the intrusion of Euramerican spectators. Some players in Indian Territory had even begun to modify and use their ball sticks as weapons (Blanchard 1981, 42). By the early twentieth century, large match Ballgames had ceased. Small, localized Ballgames continued to be performed by members of conservative communities in the context of sacred festivals and Cries. In Mississippi, new contexts for the Ballgame also developed, such as wedding ceremonies, secular festivals at Choctaw community schools, and, by the late 1940s, the annual Choctaw Fair. The Mississippi Choctaw continue to play the Ballgame at the Choctaw Fair and in other exhibition matches. In Oklahoma, localized Ballgames continued among conservative Choctaw communities through the 1930s. The Ballgame is no longer played by the Oklahoma Choctaw, except in rare demonstrations, but the Social Dance music associated with the Ballgame is still performed in a few Oklahoma Choctaw communities (Levine 1993).

This brief history suggests that the Ballgame occupied a central role in Choctaw religious traditions for nearly four centuries, and, although its use and purpose changed, it maintained the primary sacred function of establishing and sustaining communication with the spirit world. It is easy to understand why Choctaw communal religious life coalesced around the Ballgame. The small, separate but related communities that banded together to form the Choctaw nation had different versions of the cosmogonic myth and somewhat different sacred beliefs and concepts. For these communities, the Ballgame provided a connection to the past, expressed a constellation of shared beliefs and values, and focused on world renewal and conflict resolution during a period of rapid social change. Most importantly, the Ballgame did not enact a particular form or version of the cosmogonic myth; thus it provided an ideologically inclusive arena for communal ritual, blending and uniting the various communities at a crucial juncture in Choctaw history. The religious beliefs and practices of the Ballgame may be further illuminated by an analysis of Choctaw myth and medicine, which also provides a basis for understanding the relationship between Choctaw music and religious traditions.

The Ballgame in Choctaw Myth and Medicine

The content of Choctaw sacred thought may be defined through myth and medicine, two of the most important segments of the Choctaw belief system. Each segment operates as a separate conceptual system with its own discrete qualities and functions. Choctaw myth, which addresses origins, sacred geography, and the conditions and meaning of human existence, provides a key for interpreting Choctaw religious concepts and symbols. Choctaw medicine, which focuses on curing and prevention of illness, sheds light on the distinctive worldview that underlies Choctaw religious function. Choctaw myth and medicine were united through the Ballgame, which integrated religious concepts, symbols, and function.

As a segment of Choctaw sacred thought, mythology constitutes a network of interrelated myths, legends, and tales that entertain as well as instruct. Within this body of sacred oral literature, there are two main forms of the Choctaw cosmogonic myth; one involves emergence, while the other involves migration. Each form of the origin story has been told in many variants (Swanton 1931, 5–35), all of which contribute to the understanding of Choctaw religious traditions. The longest, most detailed rendition of the Choctaw migration myth was collected by Giddeon Lincecum in the early nineteenth century.[4] Lincecum's version is important because it contains, to my knowledge, the only story of the origin of the Ballgame in Choctaw mythology. The passages in the Lincecum manuscript that relate to the Choctaw Ballgame may be summarized as follows.

> *Shilumbish Chito*, the supreme being, looked out from his home in the stars one day and saw a beautiful country, filled with game, water, and fruit. He and his wife decided to go there to live. They populated the country with their offspring and became known as *Inki* and *Ishki*, the father and mother of everyone. After instructing the people as to how they should live, *Inki* and *Ishki* returned to their home in the stars. An evil race of sorcerers, called *nahullo*,[5] appeared among the people, bringing disease and misfortune. The people fought the *nahullo* with the help of their *alekchi* (shaman), and the chief introduced a game to keep the men in fighting condition at all times; they called the game *Toli* (Ballgame). Along

---

[4] Giddeon Lincecum (1793–1874), a physician and naturalist, moved to Mississippi in 1818 and became fascinated with the earthen temple mounds he observed there. To research the history of these mounds, he learned the Choctaw language and then engaged an elder named Chahtaimmahtahah to dictate his version of the cosmogonic myth in a series of interviews that took place from 1822 until 1825. Lincecum recorded the myth in Choctaw; in 1861, having moved to Texas, he translated it into English. The original notes in Choctaw were subsequently lost. In 1889, Lincecum's daughter sent the manuscript, entitled "Traditional History of the Chahta Nation," to the Bureau of American Ethnology; a brief summary was later published. The manuscript is now preserved in the Eugene C. Barker Texas History Center of the University of Texas Library. A typescript copy was made in 1932 and is available at the Neshoba County Library in Philadelphia, Mississippi; the typescript contains over five hundred pages and is bound in two volumes.

[5] The word *nahullo* refers to shamans who use negative powers to cause illness or misfortune; in the version of the migration myth recorded by Lincecum, the first *nahullo* are described as a group of spirit beings with skin as pale as fish. In contemporary Choctaw slang, the word *nahullo* is a derogatory term for Euramericans.

with the Ballgame, the chief introduced dances, designed to strengthen the minds and character of the people. Despite their efforts, the people could not overcome the *nahullo*. The people decided to migrate to the east in search of a new home. The people were led on their journey by a white pole, which had been given to them by *Shilumbish Chito*, the supreme deity. The sacred pole was carried by the highest ranking shaman; each night, the shaman planted the pole upright in the ground near his bed. Each morning, the pole was discovered leaning toward the east, indicating the direction the people must take. When they finally arrived at the site of their sacred mound, *Nanih Waiya*, the pole remained upright, signifying that the people had reached their destination. The people built a small mound adjacent to *Nanih Waiya* as a permanent resting place for the sacred pole. When the pole was set into the ground, it jumped and danced vigorously before descending into the center of the mound (Lincecum 1932 [1861]).

This version of the Choctaw migration myth sanctions and institutionalizes the Ballgame, linking it directly to the origin of disease, warfare, medicine, and communal dance. Furthermore, Lincecum provides information on Choctaw concepts of sacred geography that illuminate the symbolism expressed through the Ballgame. According to Lincecum, the Choctaw, like other Southeastern Indians, described the shape of the sacred world as a circle, crosscut by the four cardinal directions. The circle represents wholeness and continuity, while the number four represents balance and order. *Nanih Waiya*, the Choctaw sacred mound, is located in the middle of the circle and thus represents the metaphorical center of the Choctaw world. It should be pointed out that while *Nanih Waiya* is the destination and point of distribution in Choctaw migration myths, it is the point of issue in Choctaw emergence myths.

The Choctaw sacred world is thought to exist on three levels: the world below, the world above, and the middle world. The world below is the source of fertility and life, as suggested by Choctaw emergence myths. At the same time, the world below is dangerous and represents unformed, uncontrollable chaos; in Choctaw legends and tales, the world below is inhabited by a variety of monsters and cannibals that can be harmful to humans. The world above represents order and stability; it is home to the more remote deities, including *Shilumbish Chito*, the supreme being and creator, who is symbolized by the sun and manifested on earth by fire. The world above and the world below exist in a complementary relationship. Humans, who occupy the middle world, must maintain balance between these complementary forces. Humans share the middle world with animals, plants, and a host of spirit beings, some helpful to humans, some harmful.

In some Southeastern religious traditions, the three levels of the sacred world are interconnected by four cords that suspend the middle world from the upper world or sky vault (Hudson 1976, 122). The four cords operate as cosmic pillars or *axes mundi*, supporting and defining the sacred universe while simultaneously providing a conduit for communication between the human and spirit worlds (Eliade 1959, 31–37). Similar concepts of cosmic pillars are found in many other Native American religious traditions (cf. Hultkrantz 1979). The migration myth suggests that, for the Choctaw, the cosmic pillar was represented by the sacred white pole, which guided the first people to *Nanih Waiya*.

Choctaw mythology ascribes various cosmological functions to the sacred pole. The sacred pole passes through all three levels of the Choctaw sacred world, defining the structure of the cosmos while providing a tangible connection between each plane of existence. The pole marks the center of the sacred world and consecrates sacred space, as demonstrated by the descent of the pole into the mound near *Nanih Waiya*. Thus the pole both delineates and articulates the sacred world for the Choctaw. At the same time, the pole represents a hierophany, a juncture at which the sacred reveals itself to humans (Eliade 1959, 36). Where the pole intersects the three levels of the sacred world, it opens a corridor between these worlds, facilitating communication among humans and spirit beings and enabling transformations from one plane of existence to another.

Because of its transformative power, the sacred pole has assumed several ritual guises in Choctaw religious history. According to

Lincecum, when the first people performed the Green Corn Ceremony, they erected a pole in the center of the dance ground and
decorated it with a perfect ear of green corn (Swanton 1931, 14).
Lincecum also describes a Scalp Dance in which scalps were
suspended from poles that had been set into the dance ground
(Lincecum 1932 [1861], 73). The sacred pole became an important
symbol of Choctaw funerary rituals during the nineteenth century.
When bone-picking was replaced by the Cry, the new burial ritual
included implanting a pole in the ground near the grave. The pole
was painted and decorated with a series of hoops that formed a spirit
ladder to assist the soul of the deceased in its ascent to the world
above. The end of the Cry was marked by taking down the pole in
a ritual called pole-pulling.

In addition to its other ritual manifestations, the Choctaw sacred
pole, or cosmic pillar, was symbolized by the Ballgame goal post.
This interpretation is suggested by historic practice as well as by
analogy with other Southeastern tribes. Historically, Ballgame goal
posts were set into small mounds, in what may have depicted the
relationship between the sacred pole and *Nanih Waiya*, the sacred
mound. Other Southeastern peoples have also conferred a direct
iconicity on the Ballgame goal post in recent decades. For example,
the Creek use a goal post surmounted with a carved fish, symbolic
of lower world powers, in Ballgames associated with performances
of the Green Corn Ceremony (Howard 1968, 63). But perhaps the
strongest indication that the Choctaw Ballgame goal post symbolized a cosmic pillar was the intensive native medicine practiced
within its sphere.

Traditional medicine, as a segment of Choctaw religious tradition, operates on the assumption that there is a profound and
palpable connection between human health, cosmic balance, and
reciprocal, respectful relations among all beings. Choctaw disease
etiology generally attributes illness and misfortune to an imbalance
between the complementary cosmic forces of the world above and
the world below. Other, more specific causes of disease include
animal spirits seeking revenge for disrespectful treatment by

humans; human ghosts who have remained in the middle world instead of passing to the world above; object intrusion inflicted by a *nahullo*; and soul loss, which occurs when the soul leaves the body during sleep and fails to return before the person awakens. Thus, in the Choctaw worldview, an essential aspect of medical practice is the restoration of balance between cosmic forces and the reconciliation of conflict between humans and other beings. The Choctaw religious specialists who have the ability to restore and maintain balance among the cosmic forces and to repair relationships among humans and non-humans are known as medicine men or doctors. In the past, the most potent vehicle for the public display of a doctor's knowledge, skill, and experience was the Ballgame.

Native American shamanism has been defined as "a social and religious institution in which a person with the aid of helping spirits attains a trance and communicates with the supernatural for the good of the community, often. . .for the purpose of curing disease" (Hultkrantz 1981, xxiii). In most Native American cultures, ritual specialists acquire their skills and abilities through an initial trance experience, in which they receive knowledge and gain access to metaphysical power from a spirit guardian or helper. The ritual specialist's use of trance to establish communication with spirit helpers has been well documented among the Choctaw since the eighteenth century (cf. Swanton 1918, 61). Choctaw ritual specialists prepare to enter trance through fasting and other purification techniques; they achieve trance by singing or reciting prayers (Swanton 1931). Certain kinds of Choctaw doctors acquire knowledge and assistance from spirit beings known as *kawanakasha* (Bushnell 1909, 30–31) or *bohpoli* (Blanchard 1981, 145). In addition, Choctaw ritual specialists maintain continual communication with spirit beings through dreams and omens.

Native American ritual specialists assume a variety of interrelated roles, including healer, religious practitioner, prophet, weather controller, teacher, repository of community knowledge and history, political leader, and public spokesman. Various Choctaw ritual specialists undertake each of these roles, depending upon their specific circumstances, and may be either men or women. There are three main categories of Choctaw ritual specialists, differentiated by abilities, kinds of knowledge, and levels of expertise. The *hopayi* is a person of inborn spiritual power who is clairvoyant, able to predict the future and to find lost things, and capable of influencing the weather. The *alekchi* is a medical specialist or herb doctor, usually trained and guided by a *kawanakasha* and able to employ a broad spectrum of methods, depending upon individual skill and experience. Traditional Choctaw curing methods include herbal remedies ingested or applied externally, cupping or sucking to extract a foreign object, sweat baths, use of smoke, scratching (scarification), and prayer. The *nahullo* or *hoshkona* is a doctor who inflicts disease or misfortune on others through the negative use of spiritual power; the *nahullo* can fly through the air and is able to transform himself or herself into a floating light, an animal, or a bird. The negative use of spiritual power is, in most cases, unacceptable in Choctaw tradition, and in earlier times anyone identified as a practicing *nahullo* was killed (Swanton 1931, 239).

Ritual specialists of all three categories engaged in ritual activities throughout the performance of the Choctaw Ballgame. Prior to the Ballgame, some doctors purified and strengthened the players by administering special medicines, while others ritually prepared the rackets, balls, and other equipment used in the Ballgame. *Hopayi* worked to predict and influence the outcome of the game, sometimes manipulating weather conditions to produce the desired result (Blanchard 1981, 40). Doctors could also invoke negative powers to weaken the opposing players and their equipment. Indeed, the Ballgame was the only context in which negative medicine was acceptable—within certain limits—because it was necessary in order to counteract the doctors working on behalf of the rival team.

During the Ballgame, ritual specialists continued to work to benefit their team. Doctors stood by to administer medicines and medicinal techniques to the players, such as scratching the legs of the players to prevent cramps (Blanchard 1981, 36). Practitioners walked up and down the field during the game, praying, drumming, and playing a medicine flute to counteract the negative medicine of the rival doctors. One nineteenth-century observer reported that each practitioner carried a small mirror, which he used to deflect sunlight onto his players; this infused the players with the power of the sun, the source of all life and the physical representation of *Shilumbish Chito* (Swanton 1931, 149).

Choctaw ritual specialists had the ability to gain access to spiritual power from beings of either the world above or the world below; they were able to invoke such assistance because of their personal relationships with spirit beings, established through the initial ecstatic experience and cultivated through subsequent trances, dreams, and omens. The process of engaging spirit beings involved entering an elevated state of consciousness, which permitted the practitioner to achieve the superhuman sensory perception necessary for communication with other-than-humans. This process was facilitated as well as manifested in the Ballgame by the goal post, which, as a symbol of the sacred pole, provided an open channel between the sacred and human realms. In addition, Choctaw ritual specialists employed several genres of music to engage spirit beings.

Music in the Choctaw Ballgame

Music is strongly associated with Choctaw religious experience, in which it provides the tangible link between humans and the spirit world (Draper 1983, 291). The origin of Choctaw music is attributed to *Shilumbish Chito*, who is said to have given the first people their traditional songs and dances during the mythic migration. Beyond the cosmogonic myths, other Choctaw legends associate singing with supernatural encounters of various kinds (cf. Bushnell 1909). In these stories, people sing in order to summon a spiritual presence, and sometimes contact is validated when the spirit joins the people in song. Choctaw family folklore contains stories of visitations by spirit beings, who are sometimes heard singing at an old dance ground. Thus, as a segment of Choctaw religious tradition, music is an expressive medium that unites people with the spiritual powers of the sacred realms.[6] This function may be demonstrated by an analysis of music in the Ballgame.

The musical repertory that accompanied the Ballgame included at least four discrete genres: doctors' music performed before and during the Ballgame; personal songs performed privately by ball players; music for the Ballplay Dance performed prior to the game; and music for the communal night dances performed after the game. These genres were clearly differentiated from one another by musical style and form, song texts, performance practice, and instrumental accompaniment. Each genre had a specific sacred function and accompanied a certain part of the Ballgame ritual, helping to achieve an explicit objective while helping to define and articulate the structure of the event as a whole. The only genre that has survived into the present is music for the communal night dances performed after the game. However, some insight into the nature of doctors' music, ball players' personal songs, and Ballplay Dance songs may be gleaned from historical and ethnographic sources.

Historical accounts suggest that Choctaw doctors of all categories—seers, weather controllers, and herb doctors—used music in a variety of ways before, during, and after the Ballgame. The doctors' Ballgame repertory included conjuring or medicine songs, flute music, and drumming. No detailed descriptions, musical notations, or audio recordings of Choctaw medicine songs have been published; most ritual specialists prohibit the publication of recordings or transcriptions of medicine songs in order to maintain their potency and to ensure proper use, although doctors occa-

---

[6] Michelene Pesantubbee, a religious studies scholar, points out that thought is the generative power among the Choctaw and other Native Americans from the southeast. She explains that since thought can be expressed either silently *or* aloud through speech, prayer, and song, music is not necessarily required in Choctaw sacred rituals but may serve a specific purpose in enhancing the power of thought. It is not the music itself that is active in engaging spirit beings; rather, music is a medium that helps convey human thought into the spiritual realm (Michelene Pesantubbee, personal communication, 1996). It is to be hoped that this concept can be explored more fully in future research on Choctaw music and religious traditions.

sionally discuss or demonstrate the genre (cf. Densmore 1943, 111; Draper 1980, 148). By analogy with related Southeastern tribes, it may be inferred that each Choctaw doctor had his own secret repertory of medicine songs for the Ballgame, obtained through direct contact with spirit helpers or learned from another ritual specialist. These songs were probably very short and iterative, often featuring a level melodic contour and natural speech rhythms derived from the song text. Medicine songs were performed solo by the doctor in a barely audible voice.

Emphasis in the medicine songs was placed on the song text. The texts invoked the name of the spirit being summoned and thus the words of the songs had a compulsive, creative power. Some medicine songs summoned animal or bird spirits that could enhance the ball players' skills—speed, agility, endurance, intelligence, sharp sight, and so forth. These kinds of songs were generally performed privately at the request of an individual ball player prior to the game, after the player had undergone ritual purification. Other medicine songs were performed immediately before and during the game; these included songs to control the weather, thereby influencing the outcome of the game, medicine songs for the ritual preparation of the ball and Ballgame sticks, and songs to weaken the opposite team, a kind of negative medicine condoned only in the context of the Ballgame and within well-defined limits. It is possible that medicine songs were also performed after the game, to restore the players to their everyday condition, but no information exists on these songs in the historical or ethnographic literature.

In addition to various medicine songs, each Choctaw doctor had two or three cane flutes or whistles (*o'skula*), which could be played before and during the Ballgame to bring success to their team (Densmore 1943, 128) and to counteract the negative medicine of the opponents' doctors (Vennum 1994, 43). According to Frances Densmore, Choctaw Ballgame flutes were decorated with such ritual symbols as a snake or an animal's face or with the doctor's personal mark (Densmore 1943, 129–30). Densmore recorded several performances on Ballgame flutes and notated three of these melodies (shown in Figure 1). The asymmetrical phrasing and frequent

FIGURE 1

"Whistle Melody" performed by Robert Henry (Densmore1943,130)

changes of meter are features that are typical of Choctaw music in general. What distinguishes the style of these pieces from any other genre of Choctaw music is their rhapsodic, improvisational quality; they feature intricate, irregular rhythms and widely undulating melodies without any formal repetitions. Exactly how the Ballgame flute functioned in Choctaw ritual may never be known, but the use of the flute in certain kinds of medicine is widespread in native North America.

The Choctaw have used several kinds of drums in different communities at various periods in their history, including water drums (Swanton 1918, 69), cylinder drums (Bushnell 1909, 22), hand drums (Densmore 1943, 117), and instruments inspired by the European snare drum (Howard and Levine 1990, 24–27). Choctaw drums are played with one or two sticks by one man at a time. The Choctaw strongly associated drums with sacred rituals, especially those surrounding the Ballgame (Draper 1980, 150). The kind of drum doctors played during the Ballgame was evidently a small hand drum. Densmore reported that each doctor had his own drum, which he played while walking up and down the sidelines while the Ballgame was in progress (Densmore 1943, 128). In recent decades, a respected elder, not necessarily a ritual specialist, often served as the drummer. The Ballgame drum was played with two sticks in alternating single strokes that increased in tempo and volume in response to action on the playing field (Levine 1990, 112). During the twentieth century, drumming during ball play has served primarily to generate enthusiasm among the players and spectators and to signal the game's progress (Blanchard 1981, 36). It is possible that in an earlier era, the Ballgame drum had a role in doctoring, perhaps in helping the practitioner sustain the trance state necessary for communication with spirit beings.

Ball players' personal songs were performed privately by the players before they arrived on the Ballgame field. As with the doctors' secret medicine songs, no recordings or transcriptions of ball players' personal songs have been published. This genre may have been similar in musical style and textual content to other Choctaw medicine songs, but would have focused specifically on enhancing an individual player's skills, strength, and endurance by invoking the name of a particular animal or bird spirit. It is possible that some ball players received their personal songs directly from spirit helpers through dreams, while others may have inherited songs or obtained them from ritual specialists. Since a man's status and prestige in the community increased through successful perform-ance in the Ballgame, a powerful personal song was a valuable possession.

Somewhat greater information is available on the Ballplay Dance, which was performed by the ball players and their female relatives at various intervals during the night before the game and again during the daytime, immediately prior to the game. The primary purpose of the Ballplay Dance was to imbue the rackets or ball sticks with spiritual power, so that the ball sticks themselves would attract the ball (Vennum 1994, 41). Before the performance of the Ballplay Dance, the sticks were ritually prepared by the team's doctors through prayer and the application of medicines, feathers, pieces of animal skins, or painted designs. The members of each team then performed the Ballplay Dance separately, dancing in a tight circle around their respective goal posts. The players held a ball stick in each hand with the arms extended directly outward from the chest; they moved the sticks up and down alternately while singing and dancing counterclockwise around the pole (Levine 1990, 112). The women danced in a separate line behind the ball players and may have had their own set of songs, which perhaps were directed at weakening the power of the opposing team and its shamans (cf. Herndon 1971, 343).

No published recordings of the Choctaw Ballplay Dance (*Toli Hihla*) are available, although Densmore published musical tran-scriptions for two versions of the song, one of which appears in Figure 2 (Densmore 1943, 131). Densmore's notation represents the song as a simple, four-measure melody that is repeated twice. She describes this song as "almost an incantation" (Densmore 1943, 131), but the subtle descent in the melodic line would have distinguished the style of this song from medicine songs, which tended to have level contours. In addition, the song was sung in

FIGURE 2
"Song for Success in the Ball Game" performed by Gus Willis
(Densmore 1943,131)

Voice ♩ = 60
Striking Sticks ♩ = 60
See rhythm of striking sticks below

Rhythm of striking sticks: ♪♪♪♪♪♪

unison by the ball players; it would have been repeated as many
times as necessary for each player to complete one full circuit
around the pole. Densmore does not provide a textual underlay for
her transcription. The text of a Ballplay Dance song performed for
me consisted primarily of vocables, with a final phrase translated
as "This is what I'll do, and then I'll make a killing." The word
"killing" refers to scoring a point by striking the goal post with the
ball.

The largest and best known musical genre associated with the
Choctaw Ballgame is Social Dance music, which accompanied the
communal dances that were performed throughout the night after a
Ballgame. This repertory, which is also sometimes called Night
Dance or Stomp Dance music, is now performed in abbreviated
formats, usually during the daytime, in secular contexts unconnected
to the Ballgame. Until the middle of the twentieth century, the Night
Dance part of the Ballgame cycle began at dusk and was loosely

divided into four segments, each with its own internal sequence of distinctive dances and songs. The Night Dance concluded at sunrise with the performance of the Snake Dance.[7]

Social Dance music differs markedly in style and form from all of the other genres associated with the Choctaw Ballgame. Choctaw Social Dance songs generally employ anhemitonic scales with four to six notes; the melodies range from a fourth to a tenth. Various tempos and rhythmic patterns are used, depending upon the particular dance, and the meter changes frequently in most songs. Melodic rhythms tend to be strongly accented through the use of vocal pulsations or sforzandos. The Choctaw employ a moderately relaxed, slightly nasal vocal quality. Most Social Dance song texts consist of vocable patterns, but roughly one-fifth of the songs include some lines of meaningful text. Social Dance songs conclude with a formulaic call of indefinite pitch. Unlike other Ballgame musical genres, which have short, iterative forms (medicine songs, Ballplay Dance song) or rhapsodic, through-composed forms (flute melodies), Social Dance songs use a variety of sectional and strophic forms and feature variations improvised by the song leader. Perhaps the greatest contrast between this musical genre and the other genres associated with the Choctaw Ballgame is that most Social Dance songs employ antiphony or call and response; a song leader sings the call and is answered by the dancers in unison. In most cases women double the men's melodic line at the octave, but certain songs are sung only by the men. A few Social Dance songs are sung as solos by the song leader. Finally, this is the only musical genre associated with the Choctaw Ballgame that involves instrumental accompaniment; most Social Dance songs are accompanied by a pair of striking sticks (Mississippi) or a double-headed hand drum (Oklahoma).

---

[7] The structure of Choctaw Night Dance events and the order in which dances were performed has been a gaping lacuna in the ethnomusicology of the Choctaw. I proposed the four-part structure mentioned here on the basis of oral histories collected through fieldwork, ethnographic sources, musical analysis, and analogy with closely related tribes. The details of my argument and supporting data are presented elsewhere (Levine 1990; Levine 1993).

Aside from these general stylistic observations, the Social Dance genre is further subdivided into four main categories of songs, following the structure of the Night Dance event: Jump or Stomp Dances (*Tolobli Hihla*), Walk or Tick Dances (*Shotoni Hihla*), Drunk or Corn Dances (*Ishko Hihla*), and War or Drum Dances (*Shinka Boli Hihla*). Each of these subgenres includes a number of discrete songs identified by the generic title and used to accompany one standard choreography. In addition, each category includes special songs with individual titles used to accompany a variant of the main choreographic style or related, optional dances. For example, the Jump Dance category includes the Starting Dance and the Double-Header Dance (*Hihla Falama*); the War Dance category includes several variants (eg., Criss-Cross Dance, or *Itiopatami Hihla*) as well as several animal dances. The Snake Dance (*Sinti Hihla*), which concludes the Social Dance event, stands on its own, musically and conceptually, and constitutes a fifth category.

Each category of Social Dance music has distinctive characteristics of style, form, and textual content, which have been fully described elsewhere (Howard and Levine 1990; Levine 1990). For the sake of comparison with the other Ballgame musical genres illustrated here, Figure 3 provides a typical example of one category of Social Dance, the Jump Dance. Many other musical transcriptions of Choctaw Social Dance songs are available in published sources (Bushnell 1909; Densmore 1943; Draper 1980, 1983; Howard and Levine 1990).

The musical repertory associated with the Choctaw Ballgame was extraordinarily rich and diverse. Songs performed during the Ballgame were prayers, heard on the spiritual plane as well as in the human world; therefore, music was performed almost continually throughout the Ballgame cycle, in both public and private spheres. In the private sphere of ritual specialists, several genres of music were used to accompany a diverse spectrum of medicine rituals. Medicine songs mediated between the human and spiritual realms, inviting and engaging sacred entities whose active participation in the Ballgame was necessary to effect world renewal. In the public sphere of communal dances, music for the Ballplay Dance

FIGURE 3: "Jump Dance Song" performed by Adam Sampson
(Howard and Levine 1990, 89)

as well as for the Night Dances defined the structure of the event as a whole while reiterating and enacting religious concepts and symbols. Most importantly, the juxtaposition of the Ballgame, which symbolized cosmic destruction and primordial chaos, against the night-long Social Dances, which symbolized the restoration of order and the realignment of cosmic forces, actualized world renewal for the participants and afforded them a direct, personal experience of spiritual power.

Conclusions

Religious traditions and sacred music tend to be conservative domains of culture, and the depth of historical continuity in these aspects of Native American life is truly impressive. At the same time, American Indian religious traditions and sacred musics are vibrant, dynamic, and subject to continual change or reinterpretation. This study suggests that, for the Choctaw, ritual is the most adaptive element and its ability to change has helped to preserve a more stable core of beliefs and values, as expressed through myth, medicine, and music. Today, the Choctaw play the Ballgame and perform its Social Dance music apart from one another in diverse secular contexts. The Ballplay Dance and medicine songs associated with this ritual cycle are remembered by few people, although similar doctor's songs continue to play a role in traditional medicine. However, the Social Dance songs have become the most significant repertory of traditional Choctaw music; as an emblem of ethnic identity, Social Dance music is second in importance only to the Choctaw language. I believe that it is because of its origin as a segment of Choctaw sacred tradition that Social Dance music has acquired such power as an expression of ethnicity and continues to inspire religious feeling among its practitioners.

Sources Cited

Blanchard, Kendall
  1981   *The Mississippi Choctaw at Play: The Serious Side of Leisure*. Urbana: University of Illinois Press.
Bushnell, David I., Jr.
  1909   *The Choctaw of Bayou Lacomb, St. Tammany Parish, Louisiana*. Bureau of American Ethnology Bulletin, 48. Washington, D.C.: Government Printing Office.
Campbell, T. N.
  1959   "Choctaw Subsistence: Ethnographic Notes from the Lincecum Manuscript." *The Florida Anthropologist* 12(1):9–24.
Cushman, Horatio Bardwell
  1962 [1899] *History of the Choctaw, Chickasaw and Natchez Indians*. Ed. Angie Debo. New York: Russell and Russell.
Debo, Angie
  1961   *The Rise and Fall of the Choctaw Republic*. 2nd ed. Norman: University of Oklahoma Press.
Densmore, Frances
  1933   Unpublished field notes.
  1943   *Choctaw Music*. Bureau of American Ethnology Bulletin, 136. Washington, D.C.: Government Printing Office.
Draper, David E.
  1980   "Occasions for the Performance of Native Choctaw Music." *Selected Reports in Ethnomusicology* 3:147–73.
  1983   "Breath in Music: Concept and Practice among the Choctaw Indians." *Selected Reports in Ethnomusicology* 4:285–300.
Eliade, Mircea
  1959   *The Sacred and the Profane: The Nature of Religion*. Trans. Willard R. Trask. New York: Harcourt Brace Jovanovich.
  1963   *Myth and Reality*. Trans. Willard R. Trask. New York: Harper Torchbooks.
Falassi, Alessandro
  1987   "Festival: Definition and Morphology." In Alessandro Falassi, ed., *Time Out of Time: Essays on the Festival*, pp. 1–10. Albuquerque: University of New Mexico Press.

Fogelson, Raymond D.
1971   "The Cherokee Ballgame Cycle: An Ethnographer's
            View." *Ethnomusicology* 15:327–38.
Galloway, Patricia, ed.
1989   *The Southeastern Ceremonial Complex: Artifacts and
            Analysis*. Lincoln: University of Nebraska Press.
1992   "The Emergence of Historic Indian Tribes in the South-
            east." In Barbara Carpenter, ed., *Ethnic Heritage in
            Mississippi*, pp. 21–44. Jackson: The University Press of
            Mississippi.
Herndon, Marcia
1971   "The Cherokee Ballgame Cycle: An Ethnomusicologist's
            View." *Ethnomusicology* 15:339–52.
Howard, James H.
1968   *The Southeastern Ceremonial Complex and Its Interpre-
            tation*. Memoir of the Missouri Archaeological Society,
            no. 6. Columbia: Missouri Archaeological Society.
1978   "Oklahoma Choctaw Revive Native Dances." *Actes du
            XLIIᵉ Congrès International des Americanistes* 5:315–23.
Howard, James H. and Victoria Lindsay Levine
1990   *Choctaw Music and Dance*. Norman: University of
            Oklahoma Press.
Hudson, Charles
1976   *The Southeastern Indians*. Knoxville: The University of
            Tennessee Press.
Hultkrantz, Åke
1979   "Ritual in Native North American Religion." In Earle H.
            Waugh and K. Dad Prithipaul, eds., *Native Religious
            Traditions*, pp. 135–47. The Proceedings of the Joint
            International Symposium of Elders and Scholars, 1977.
            Waterloo, Ontario: Wilfred Laurier University.
1981   *Belief and Worship in Native North America*. Ed.
            Christopher Vecsey. Syracuse: Syracuse University Press.
1984   "An Ideological Dichotomy: Myths and Folk Beliefs
            among the Shoshoni." In Alan Dundes, ed., *Sacred
            Narrative: Readings in the Theory of Myth*, pp. 152–65.
            Berkeley: University of California Press.
1987   *Native Religions of North America: The Power of Visions
            and Fertility*. New York: Harper Collins Publishers.

Johnson, Jay K.
  1992   "Prehistoric Mississippi." In Barbara Carpenter, ed.,
                    Ethnic Heritage in Mississippi, pp. 9–20. Jackson: The
                    University Press of Mississippi.
Levine, Victoria Lindsay
  1990   "Choctaw Indian Musical Cultures in the Twentieth
                    Century." Ph.D. diss., University of Illinois at Urbana-
                    Champaign.
  1993   "Musical Revitalization among the Choctaw." *American
                    Music* 11(4):391–411.
Lincecum, Giddeon
  1932 [1861] "Traditional History of the Chahta Nation." Typescript.
Peterson, John
  1970   "The Mississippi Band of Choctaw Indians: Their Recent
                    History and Current Social Relations." Ph.D. diss.,
                    University of Georgia at Athens.
Swanton, John R.
  1918   "An Early Account of the Choctaw Indians." *Memoirs of
                    the American Anthropological Association* 5:53–72.
  1928   "Aboriginal Culture of the Southeast." *Forty-Second
                    Annual Report of the Bureau of American Ethnology*,
                    pp. 673–726. Washington, D.C.: Government Printing
                    Office.
  1931   *Source Material for the Social and Ceremonial Life of
                    the Choctaw Indians*. Bureau of American Ethnology
                    Bulletin, 103. Washington, D.C.: Government Printing
                    Office.
Vennum, Thomas, Jr.
  1994   *American Indian Lacrosse: Little Brother of War*.
                    Washington, D.C.: Smithsonian Institution Press.
Wells, Samuel J.
  1992   "Trail of Treaties: The Choctaws from the American
                    Revolution to Removal." In Barbara Carpenter, ed.,
                    Ethnic Heritage in Mississippi, pp. 45–56. Jackson: The
                    University Press of Mississippi.

Islam and Music:
The Legal and the Spiritual Dimensions[*]

Seyyed Hossein Nasr

> Inanimate wood, inanimate string, inanimate skin[1]
> from where cometh, then, this song of the Friend?
> —*attributed to Jalāl al-Dīn Rūmī*

One could say that it is in answer to the rhetorical question posed by the greatest troubadour of spirituality in Islam, Jalāl al-Dīn Rūmī—who combined music and spirituality with religion and poetry—that Islamic civilization has delved into the significance of music: in a deeper sense, music is the sound of the Friend. The fact that music can be produced through these few inanimate materials— wood, string, skin—joined together is one of the greatest miracles of existence, if one truly understands what music is and how it touches the deepest layers of the soul. At the same time, of course, music has a more external function. It affects the souls of men and of women outwardly, and influences the social structure which brings human beings together. From the very beginning of Islamic history, therefore, the question of music and its legal status has been surrounded by an aura of ambiguity, which, in fact, has been a positive rather than a negative aspect of Islamic Law.

[*] This text comprises the edited transcription of the author's lecture given at the Harvard University Center for the Study of World Religions.
[1] Describing the Persian *tār*, or *sitār*.

The Legal Status of Music in Islam

There have been many authorities throughout Islamic history who have considered it a blessing that there is no specific legal injunction against music—and that the *'ulamā'*, the religious scholars, have themselves had differences over the centuries as to whether music is acceptable, that is, legitimate, licit (*ḥalāl*), or illicit (*ḥarām*) according to the *Sharī'ah*, the Divine Law of Islam. Music is, therefore, dealt with in a variety of ways. One of the causes of this ambiguity lies with the very usage of the word "music."

When we say "Islam and music," there is an ambivalence in this terminology that needs to be elucidated. What do we mean by music? The word "music," translated from the Greek into Arabic as "*mūsīqā*" and into Persian as "*mūsīqī,*" for the most part means the same thing as it does in English: Brahms's Third Symphony would be called *mūsīqā* (*mūsīqī* in Persian), or music. There are, however, sounds and patterns which to the ear would appear musical and which would be considered "music" according to the Western definition of the term "music" but which are not called *mūsīqā* in Arabic—hence the juridical difficulty present from the very beginning in defining this term. To explain further: for example, should someone who knows no Arabic and has had no acquaintance with Islam whatsoever hear the chanting of the Qur'an for the first time, that person would hear "music." But the chanting of the Qur'an would never be called *mūsīqā* in Arabic; this would be considered blasphemy. Therefore, the word "music" has been used in a more limited sense in the Arabic language and other Islamic languages than it has in non-Islamic languages. There are expressions in the Islamic world that are music but which would not be called "music."

The debate in which the *'ulamā'* have been engaged has always involved precisely those elements which are called music in Islamic languages. There has never been any doubt concerning those types of expression which are musical without being called music and which have to do with the sacred elements of Islamic revelation. Not even the strictest Wahhābī *'ālim* in Saudi Arabia would ban the chanting of the *adhān, the call to prayer*. The *adhān* is always chanted, as anyone who has made the pilgrimmage to Mecca or Medina will confirm. There is no debate over that. This ambiguity in the usage of the term "music" is, therefore, one of the confusing issues in the Islamic world which has continued over the centuries and which needs clarification.

According to the *Sharī'ah, the Divine Law of Islam*, there are different categories of human actions and corresponding categories of music, which are accepted or rejected legally. First, there is the category of music that is *ḥalāl, legitimate or allowed*, from the point of view of religious law. Second, there is the category of music that is *mubāh. Types of music in this category are allowed, but they are not looked upon with great favor and are perhaps somewhat* circumspect; they may be performed, but they are not *ḥalāl* and therefore are in a lower category. There are then those kinds of music, called *makrūh, which are improper, which are disapproved of by religion, but which are not totally forbidden by Islamic Law*. Finally, there is that which is *ḥarām, forbidden or illicit*. It is important to reiterate that these rulings are not unanimous and there are differences of interpretation among various religious scholars as to where the distinctions between categories lie. The divisions drawn on the right of the chart in Figure 1 are not, therefore, absolute. On the left, however, a crucial distinction is drawn between music which is non-*mūsīqā*, which is not called "music" in Arabic and other Islamic languages, and music which is called "music."

Of those genres which are "non-music," non-*mūsīqā*, first is the chanting *(qirā'ah)* of the sacred text, which, according to the Qur'an itself, should be chanted with a strong, clear voice. There are sciences of chanting of the Qur'an which go back, according to Islamic tradition, to the prophet David and which have continued unabated to this day. *The chanting is revealed and of sacred origin; it is not a human creation but divinely inspired.*

The *adhān*, the call to prayer, is also—again going back to the time of the Prophet—always chanted. There is no part of the Islamic world, no different school of law, Sunni or Shi'ite, according to

Figure 1
Hierarchy of *Handasat al-Ṣawt* Genres
(The Status of Music in the Islamic World)[2]

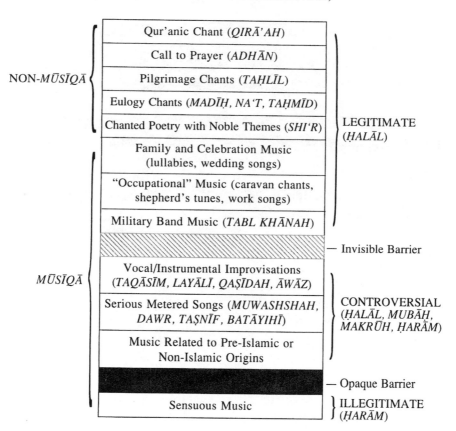

NON-*MŪSĪQĀ*	Qur'anic Chant (*QIRĀ'AH*)
	Call to Prayer (*ADHĀN*)
	Pilgrimage Chants (*TAḤLĪL*)
	Eulogy Chants (*MADĪḤ, NA'T, TAḤMĪD*)
	Chanted Poetry with Noble Themes (*SHI'R*)

LEGITIMATE
(*ḤALĀL*)

Family and Celebration Music
(lullabies, wedding songs)

"Occupational" Music (caravan chants,
shepherd's tunes, work songs)

Military Band Music (*TABL KHĀNAH*)

— Invisible Barrier

MŪSĪQĀ

Vocal/Instrumental Improvisations
(*TAQĀSĪM, LAYĀLĪ, QAṢĪDAH, ĀWĀZ*)

Serious Metered Songs (*MUWASHSHAH,
DAWR, TAṢNĪF, BATĀYIHĪ*)

Music Related to Pre-Islamic or
Non-Islamic Origins

CONTROVERSIAL
(*ḤALĀL, MUBĀḤ,
MAKRŪH, ḤARĀM*)

— Opaque Barrier

Sensuous Music

ILLEGITIMATE
(*ḤARĀM*)

[2] From Lois al-Fārūqī, *Islam and Art* (Islamabad, 1985), 179.

which the *adhān* is simply uttered. It is *always* chanted, and it is always chanted in a clear, strong voice. Certain syllables in the *adhān* are always elongated according to the *Sunnah* of the Prophet, with a certain inner effect that they have upon the soul.

Next, there are all the chants, called *tahlīl*, which have to do with the Hajj, the great pilgrimage to Mecca, as well as with other, lesser, pilgrimages. *Tahlīl* are like caravan songs, which are themselves extremely beautiful. The *tahlīl*, the singing and chanting, is one of the exquisite art forms that surrounded the often months-long pilgrimage journeys from different parts of the Islamic world to Mecca.

Following this category are the various eulogies, usually called *madīh* in Arabic, but including also the *na't*, *tahmīd*, and other eulogies on the life of the Prophet. The great songs that mark religious rites, such as the birth of the Prophet, and ceremonies are always chanted. For example, in Alexandria, every Friday after prayers, at the tomb of Būsīrī, which is in the center of the city, the *Burdah*, the famous song about the Prophet, is always chanted in its entirety; it is also usually repeated on the radio during the time of the commemoration of his birth. And, in the Shi'ite world, of course, the *ta'ziyah*—literally, "consolation"—the passion play commemorating (in a spiritual sense) the tragedy of Karbalā' and its aftermath, is always "sung," or recited. This, too, then, is a religious category which would never be called *mūsīqī* or *mūsīqā*; to do so would be blasphemy. This kind of chanting or recitation would, nevertheless, in the non-Islamic world be called music.

Finally, we have what used to be traditional in the Islamic world: the recitation of poetry. Arabic poetry deals at once with words and phrases *and* music (for example, the *Kitāb al-aghānī* in fact means "The Book of Songs"). Likewise, of course, many Persian and Turkish poems were usually sung. This is the reason so much of the poetry of the Islamic peoples is very musical and, vice versa, why Islamic music always has a poetic dimension to it.

As outlined in Figure 1, all of these types are non-*mūsīqā* and are excluded from the category of music in the Islamic world; and yet they are music. The *'ulamā'* have had very little disagreement about the legal status of this type of "music." There is, to be perfectly honest, one exception to this. Certain Wahhābī and Ḥanbalī *'ulamā'* are opposed to the celebration of the birth of the Prophet, which may appear strange but which marks a point of difference within the Sunni world. The elaborate chants and musical performances commemorating the birth of the Prophet and his life are usually decried by them. This is why in Medina, the city of the Prophet, you will not see performed or hear chanted in public this category of eulogy or *madīḥ* poems concerning the Prophet.

Farther down on the chart there are categories called music or *mūsīqā* in Arabic which have to do with certain features of life or with certain professions. The Prophet, we know, not only accepted but encouraged music at the time of weddings, a practice that exists in every civilization and among all peoples. Therefore, wedding music and music dealing with various family celebrations such as the circumcision of boys, singing a child to sleep with lullabies— what might be called music for family occasions—was also accepted throughout the Islamic world. There are very few people, even the staunchest opponents of music, who have objected vehemently to this category of music.

Next there is what the late Lois al-Fārūqī called "occupational music," music that relates to one's work or labor, linking economic activity to the psychological and spiritual dimensions of the inner life. For example, anyone who has seen a traditional builder in the Islamic world will know that, as the stones or the bricks are thrown up to him one by one, he is singing. And the person who is throwing up the bricks is also singing. Or, in Syria, where stone architecture is common, stone chiselers will do the same—they will sing. This practice of course also existed in medieval Europe and in other traditional societies; it is not unique to Islam. Music universally is combined with architecture in the very act of building. The same holds true with harvesting and other traditional activities in which music was included and accepted.

Finally, there is the type of music which people in the West do not usually identify with the Islamic world—though its origins, as far as the West is concerned, are Islamic—and this is what we know as military music. All civilizations, of course, from the old Roman empire and the Persian empire, had some kind of military music. In Islam as well this was allowed. In fact, as long as it was not lascivious or sensuous, as long as it helped to increase courage and fortitude in battle, this kind of music was not only accepted but encouraged. It is on the basis of that early tradition that the later military band was developed, leading finally to the band of the Janissaries, which itself was the origin of the Western military band as we know it. We have only to think of the "Turkish March" of Mozart to know that it is no accident that it sounds like a military march. Much of the seventeenth- and eighteenth-century Austrian world was very much interested in the elaborate military music of the Janissaries, a very beautiful form of military music that goes back to this early Medinan example of the Prophet.

We now come to those realms of music that are controversial in a legal sense. And here, various views have been given by the *'ulamā'* on the level of the law. First, there are the different kinds of vocal and instrumental music which are the classical traditions of the Islamic world. Much of the music of the Islamic peoples that one hears in the West today belongs to this category, which would correspond to Western classical music. The music of the Islamic people encompasses several major classical traditions. One of these is Andalusian music—*mūsīqā-al-andalūs*—of Morocco which originated in Spain and migrated with the expulsion of the Muslims in 1492 to Morocco. *Mūsīqā-al-andalūs* still survives, distinct from Eastern Arabic music, which had its major center in Cairo, where classical Arabic music also began to wane after the introduction of Western music, epitomized by the Cairo opera for whose inauguration Verdi composed his "Aïda."

Eastern Arabic classical music also had a great deal of exchange with classical Persian music—as the presence of classical Persian musical names, like *Nahāwand* and *Chahārḡah* indicates. Classical Persian music itself has a historical continuity that goes back, as far as we know, to the Achaemenian period. Following the Persian conquest of Egypt, ancient Egyptian musical forms were also integrated into classical Persian music, which reached its peak in the Sassanid period. This music was enjoyed at the court of the caliphs and was made popular as well by the great Persian musician

Zaryāb, who also influenced the music of Spain and the Umayyad court of Cordova. The Turkish classical tradition is in some ways close to the Persian and yet is quite distinct. As for North Indian music, it displays elements of Persian music but also has elements taken by Muslims from Hindu sources. For many centuries this tradition has been a very important vehicle for the expression of Sufism in India. Many people in the West do not associate North Indian music with Islam at all, and they think it accidental that most of the masters of North Indian music have names like Ali Akbar Khan. Even Ravi Shankar's teacher, Riḍā Qulī Khan, was a very famous Muslim teacher from Rampur. Here you have, as a vehicle of expression, a tradition which is both Hindu and Islamic and into which sentiments of two different religions have poured.

Other traditions, not perhaps as well known in the West, are also a part of the Islamic musical tradition. The Sundanese music of Java, an incredible tradition of music, is very rich and is specifically Islamic. The music of the Muslims of China, the Hui and those of the Uighur area of Western China, are also very close to ancient Persian music. This music in China has its own local variation; it does not sound identical to, let us say, classical Persian music from Tehran, but, nevertheless, there is a family resemblance. All this, then, constitutes the classical music of the Islamic people, which is combined, usually, with various types of songs, such as those which were developed in Andalusia by Muslim poets.

Another category of music is that surviving from the pre-Islamic period which Muslims accepted—as long as it was not passionate—but did not integrate into their own musical vocabulary. For example, in Java and Sumatra, the rich musical tradition of the gamelan goes back to the Buddhist and Hindu period in that area of the world; Muslims accepted this tradition but did not incorporate it. Likewise, gamelan music on the island of Bali has not been Muslimized; it is pure, classical, and is played by Hindus in Bali. This, then, is a separate category that continues to exist within the Islamic world. Another example is the presence of Armenian music among the people of Azerbaijan. It is in this category that some have tried to include Western classical music.

The categorization of the types of music outlined here has been, as I stated, the subject of a great legal debate in which there has never been total agreement. The categorization of one type of music, however, has been completely unanimous. All music which is lascivious, which may arouse the lower passions, has been banned by the *'ulamā* . Within the Islamic world, it is more or less clear to people what types of music have been banned—at least it was clear before the onslaught of modernism. The arrival of any new form of music from outside the Islamic world has at first caused a great deal of debate—a debate that dies down only with the arrival of yet another new form. Fifty years ago, some folk songs from Naples and other parts of Italy came to the Eastern Mediterranean and to the Arab and Persian worlds. This Italian music was popular among the more modernized Arabs. The *'ulamā'*, however, debated the categorization of this type and were rather opposed to it, until the next new wave of music came, a very loud and jarring type of music which developed in the Western world in the decades following the Second World War. The categorization of these new forms of Western music then became plain to everybody: I have never heard of any *'ulamā'* who has categorized "rock and roll," "hard rock," or "metallic rock"—which, admittedly, are not very conducive to the remembrance of God (at least not in the Islamic context)—as anything other than belonging to the last category, to that which is *harām*, illegitimate.

There is, therefore, a very wide spectrum as far as religious attitudes toward music are concerned, in contrast to what one might suppose. If someone says, "I am a good Muslim; I know music is *harām* in Islam," this person does not really know what he or she is talking about. The relationship of music to Islam is much more complicated. This ambivalence and ambiguity, as I have said, has played a very important role in the survival and cultivation of music in the Islamic world, from Ismaili songs in India to prayers in Morocco and everything in between. If there had been a categorical definition of what is licit and what is illicit, it would have made a great deal of difference in the creative processes of the art.

Many people, especially modernized Muslims, think that the

great music of the Islamic people developed *despite* Islam. This, however, is impossible; great art cannot develop despite the world view within which it is cultivated, although it can always protest against something within that world view. Perhaps this misconception is due to the fact that whenever any segment of Islamic society has been under great duress, enduring economic, political or military upheavals, it has usually tried to distance itself from "music" in the Arabic sense—though not from those first categories that are permanent within Islamic civilization and that Islam associates with the delights of paradise, of happiness, and of joy. One of the most remarkable instances of this process occurred in recent years in Iran.

Iran has always been one of the great centers of classical music. Persian classical music has been preserved over the centuries by two patrons—the court and the Sufi orders. Moreover, performers at court were often also great Sufis. During the Qājār period (1779–1923), when many other aspects of Persian culture were decaying, due to foreign invasions, with half of Iran lost to the Russians in 1837, there was a remarkable revival of Persian music. Great masters appeared, one after another, right up to the Pahlavi period—masters such as Darwīsh Khān and ʿAbdallāh Khān, some of whose students are still alive, now in their eighties—the last surviving musicians from the very early period of the Pahlavi dynasty. The end of the Qājār period (from the time of Nāṣir al-Dīn Shah [1848]) to the beginning of the Pahlavi period marks the flowering of classical Persian music.

The modern movement, which began with the Qājār period, flourished and spread in the Pahlavi period, and the two patrons of classical music, the court and the Sufi orders, receded into the background. As soon as the aristocracy learned a few words of French or English, it was no longer interested in classical Persian music. The Sufi orders also withdrew from the great cities, and that Sufi music which was to survive in Iran did so in Sanandaj in Kurdistān, in Balūchīstan, in parts of Khurāsān in the northeast, but was not to be found in the major cities. One could no longer hear Sufi music performed in Tehran. In fact, when Sufi music was performed for the first time on the birthday of ʿAlī, about thirty years ago in Tehran, it was a major event in that city. Classical

Persian music had, therefore, begun to wane until a movement began in the 1960s to revive it. The renewed popularity of classical music led, however, as time went on, to a form of decadence, in which the great income and showy lifestyle of many artists created an ambience of immorality in which classical music was being performed, causing many pious Muslims to turn against this music. Then came the revolution, and the first thing to be banned was music. The great masters of Iranian music disappeared from the scene; many of them taught music in the basements of their houses, and there was no sign of music in public—music, that is, in the sense we have defined, not the chanting of the Qur'an, of course, or the eulogies, the *madīḥ*. The first time this taboo was broken, interestingly enough, was when Beethoven's *Eroica* was played on the radio. One would not, as a matter of course, think of music for Oriental dancing girls and a Beethoven symphony in the same category of things illicit; hence, classical Western music gradually began to be performed.

Possibly the most important legal injunction on music ever given by a religious scholar was that of the late Ayatollah Khomeini, just before his death. Although we do not often identify the image of the Ayatollah Khomeini, who symbolized revolutionary Islam, with music, he in fact loved music very much as a young man. When the head of the Iranian national radio and television, an important governmental instrument, asked in a *fatwā*, a religious edict, whether music was *ḥalāl* or *ḥarām*, the Ayatollah pronounced, quite incredibly, that music, as long as it did not incite the passions and except for women singing to men, was *ḥalāl*. Within a few days, this one *fatwā*, which took only ten minutes to pronounce, changed the entire musical scene. During all those years when music was not a public event and performers were not being paid thousands of dollars to chant for five minutes, true musicians dedicated to their art had continued to study underground. Following the Ayatollah's *fatwā*, they reappeared. 'Abd al-Wahhāb Shāhīdī, one of the finest voices of Iran, and one of the greatest masters of music, survived imprisonment and hunger and began teaching students publicly again. When one of the great teachers of voice, Shajarian, visited me recently in Washington, I asked him whether he had any students. He said, "I have so many that I cannot accept any students for the next two years; they have to wait in line." Today, after all the ups and downs of various *fatwā*s given over the centuries, the opinion of the most powerful legal authority of the land—an authority who would never be identified with leniency, one might say, toward the "feminine arts," of which music, an art which melts the soul, is the supreme example—has caused us to witness a remarkable revival of classical Persian music.

The legality of music in Islam still remains and will always remain ambiguous as divinely willed. This ambiguity serves a useful purpose in that it accepts varying modes and forms of music without permitting that music which separates the listener from religion and is an obstacle to the remembrance of God. It is that music which Islam has always shunned and has never developed. There is *no* music in the Islamic world which does not remind one of God. Even music to which people dance at weddings carries with it a reminiscence of the classical modes, which themselves are related to inner states combined with the yearning of the soul for God.

The Spiritual Significance of Music

Music has a tremendous impact upon the soul and its sonorousness reverberates within us and thus creates a sense of intimacy.

Music, as a means of enlivening the soul and bringing it to a realization of its inner nature and its reunion with God, has remained an extremely important element in the history of Islam, primarily through Sufism. Sufism, the esoteric inner dimension of Islam, corresponds roughly, but only roughly, to what we identify as Christian mysticism; it is not exactly the same thing, but there are certain parallels. The power of music upon the soul was realized from the very beginning of the development of Islamic culture. Two groups of people wrote about it: the Sufis and the Islamic philosophers. I want, first, to quote a text from the tenth- and eleventh-century Muslim writers called the Ikhwān al-Ṣafā', the Brethren of Purity. What they defined as the highest form of music falls under the category of "non-*mūsīqā*":

Tradition teaches that the sweetest melody which the inhabitants of paradise have at their disposal and the most beautiful song they hear is the discourse of God—great be His praise. It is thus that the Word of God Most High states, "The greeting which [will welcome them], there will be peace!" (Quran X, 10–11) [that is, coming from the Qur'an, 'salām']. And the end of the invocation will be: "Praise to Allāh, Lord of the worlds." It is said that Moses—peace be upon him—upon hearing the words of his Lord, was overcome with joy, with happiness and with rapture to the point of being unable to contain himself. He was overwhelmed by emotion, transported while listening to this serene melody and from that point on regarded all rhythms, all melodies, and all songs as insignificant.[3]

Moses had heard the most supreme form of music, which is the music of divine revelation itself. The Ikhwān al-Ṣafā' defend music on this highest level. They speak also of the impact of music upon the soul: its effects, imprinted by the rhythms and melodies of musicians on the souls of listeners, are of different types:

In the same way, the pleasure which souls draw from these rhythms and melodies and the manner in which they enjoy them are variable and diverse. All that depends on the degree which each soul occupies in the domain of gnosis (*al-ma'arif*) and on the nature of the good actions which make up the permanent object of his love. Therefore, each soul, while listening to descriptions which correspond to the object of his desires and to melodies which are in accord with the object of his delight, rejoices, is exalted and delights in the image that music makes of his beloved.[4]

It is this tradition which entered into Islamic learning, and, in the old days, any truly learned person was well-versed in theoretical music: a solid knowledge of classical Arabic or Persian music, even if one did not play an instrument or sing, was part of education.

---

[3] Quoted in Jean-Louis Michon, "Sacred Music and Dance in Islam," in S. H. Nasr, ed., *Islamic Spirituality: Manifestations,* World Spirituality: An Encyclopedic History of the Religious Quest, 20 (New York: Crossroad, 1991), 474.

[4] Michon, 474.

Therefore, this philosophical explanation of the inner meaning of music was important throughout the history of Islamic thought.

It is the Sufis, however, who not only wrote about the significance of music but also used it in their practices. The Sufi practice of music is called *samā'* in Arabic—from the word "to hear," *samī'a*—meaning "audition" or "hearing." The *samā'* is not performed by all Sufi orders, but it is performed by many, and in some Sufi orders, *samā'* occupies the primary position (as far as techniques for spiritual realization are concerned) after the invocation, which is itself the supreme technique. Other orders, such as the Naqshbandīs, have usually not had much recourse to music. Music in the Sufi context varies from simple beating of drums, which is what most Sufi orders use, to very elaborate orchestras. In the range from simplicity to complexity, different Sufi orders use either pure rhythm or pure melody or a combination of both, often together with the chanting of verses. The blending of the chanting of verses, of certain poems either by the founder of the order or by another great Sufi, with music—which usually occurs after the canonical prayers and litanies drawn from the Qur'an and *Ḥadīth*—prepares the soul for the final invocation and integration into the Divine Presence.

The Sufis have written very extensively on why music is significant for the soul. Abū Ḥāmid al-Ghazzālī, one of the greatest of all Islamic thinkers—and an authority on legal, juridical and ethical questions—is also one of our best sources on the significance of music. He writes:

> Hearts and inmost thoughts, are treasuries of secrets and mines of jewels. Infolded in them are their jewels like as fire is infolded in iron and stone, and concealed as water is concealed under dust and loam. There is no way to the extracting of their hidden things save by the flint and steel of listening to music and singing, and there is no entrance to the heart save by the ante-chamber of the ears. So musical tones, measure them pleasing, bring forth what is in it and make evident its beauties and defects. For when the heart is moved there is made evident that only which it contains like as a vessel drips only what is in it. And listening to music and singing is for the heart a true touchstone and a speaking standard; whenever the

soul of the music and singing reaches the heart, then there stirs in the heart that which in it preponderates.[5]

This statement of al-Ghazzālī's alludes to a very important principle—the Sufi belief that for a person whose soul is ready to move in the direction of the Divine, that is, for one for whom there is already this attraction for the Divine, music has the power of accelerating this attraction and, in a sense, helping the person achieve what is very difficult to do otherwise. Music for such a person becomes a vehicle for the journey of the soul to God, whereas for a person who does not have that inclination, music simply increases the passions. There is a very famous saying in Persian that music causes whatever is within the soul to become more intense. If the soul has an inclination to sink like a rock, it will sink faster, toward the world of passions; but if it has the inclination to fly like a bird, music will strengthen the soul's wings.

Let me allude to one more quotation from the patron saint of Shiraz, again one of the great masters of the exposition of music and himself a noted troubador, Rūzbihān Baqlī, a poet, musician, and commentator of the Qur'an. He says that:

> Spiritual music is the key to the treasury of Divine Verities. The gnostics are divided: some listen with the help of the stations *(maqāmāt)*; some with the help of the states *(ḥālāt)*; some with the help of spiritual unveiling *(mukāshifāt)*; some with the help of vision *(mushāhidāt)*. When they listen according to the stations, they are in reproach. When they listen according to the states, they are in a state of return. When they listen according to spiritual unveiling, they are in union *(wiṣāl)*; when they listen according to vision, they are immersed in the Divine Beauty.[6]

This includes all those who seek the knowledge of God. People listen with the different faculties given to human beings; the highest of these faculties is the *sirr*, the inner center of one's being, where

---

[5] From the eighth book of the section of al-Ghazzālī's *Iḥyā' 'ulūm al-dīn*, trans. Duncan B. Macdonald, *Journal of the Royal Asiatic Society*, April 1901, 199.

[6] From Baqlī's *Risālat al-quds*, in S. H. Nasr, trans., *Islamic Art and Spirituality* (Albany, N.Y.: SUNY Press, 1987), 157.

in fact one hears what Plato calls 'silent music.' It must be remembered that Plato identified two kinds of music: music which is audible and is for everyone, and silent music, which is for the sages.[7]

Music finally, in a sense, flows into silence. Silence is the origin of all spiritual music and is always present in that music—through the use of rhythm, which integrates one level of reality to another, and through melody (the feminine element in music as rhythm is the masculine), which melts the soul and creates the reminiscence for one's own origin.

As I mentioned at the start, in Islamic civilization, by and large, music was very much wed to poetry. Poetry is the favorite art form of the Islamic world, a direct result of the poetic structure of the Qur'anic revelation. There are no Islamic peoples who do not have a very elaborate poetic tradition. In Islam, as the various poetic traditions developed, the poems were often chanted and music played to the accompaniment of poetry. Some of the greatest poets in the Islamic world have also been master musicians, thus creating a poetry which is highly musical. Ḥāfiẓ is the greatest musical poet of the Persian language—and, therefore, the most difficult of poets to translate. The *Dīwān* of Ḥāfiẓ is both a *Dīwān* of poetry and a book of music. If one reads Ḥāfiẓ correctly, one is truly performing music, not only reading poetry. Let me conclude, then, with one of his poems which both speaks about music and is itself extremely musical.

> O cup-bearer, brighten our goblets with the light of wine!
> O minstrel, tell how the world has succumbed to our desires!
> We have seen in the cup the reflection of the face of the Friend,
> O you who know nothing of the joy of our eternal wine-drinking!
> He whose heart has been made living by love never dies;
> Our permanence is recorded within the pages of the cosmic text.[8]

---

[7] The idea of silent music is associated with Plato although not explicitly mentioned by him. The idea is, however, fully implied in the *Republic*, Book VII, 531, as well as in some of his other writings.

[8] Nasr, *Islamic Art and Spirituality*, 173–74.

Selected Bibliography

al-Fārūqī, Lois.
    1985   *Islam and Art*. Islamabad: National Hijra Council.

Caron, Nelly, and Dariouch Safvate.
    1972   *Iran. Les Traditions musicale*, vol. 2. Paris: Buchet-Chastel.

During, Jean.
    1988   *Musique et extase: L'audition mystique dans la tradition soufie*. Collection "Spiritualités vivantes." Paris: Albin Michel.

Erlanger, Rodolphe d'.
    1930–59 *La Musiqe arabe*. 6 vols. Paris: P. Geuthner.

Farmer, Henry G.
    1973   *A History of Arabian Music to the XIIIth Century*. London: Luzac.

Michon, Jean-Louis.
    1991   "Sacred Music and Dance in Islam." In S. H. Nasr, ed., *Islamic Spirituality: Manifestations*, pp. 469–505. World Spirituality: An Encyclopedic History of the Religious Quest, 20. New York: Crossroad.

Nasr, Seyyed Hossein.
    1987   *Islamic Art and Spirituality*. Albany: State University of New York Press.

Nurbakhsh, Javad.
    1976   *Samā' in Sufism*. New York: Khanaqah-i Nimat Allahi.

Shiloah, Amnon.
    1965, 1967
        "L'Epître sur la musique des Ikhwān al-Ṣafā'." *Revue des Etudes Islamiques*, 1965, pp. 125–62; 1967, pp. 159–93.

Music and the
Confucian Sacrificial Ceremony*

Rulan Chao Pian

At the beginning of the twentieth century, when China was still
under the rule of the Manchu government of the Ching dynasty
(1644–1911), the Sacrificial Ceremony to Confucius was held
regularly. The ceremony continued on and off after 1911, when
China became a republic. When the Nationalist government moved
to Taiwan in 1949, it was discovered that the Confucian ceremonial
tradition had continued in Taiwan even during the Japanese
occupation.

In 1968 the late President Chiang Kai-shek issued an order to
reform the routine of the Confucian sacrificial rites in Taiwan. The
committee assigned to this project consisted of several government
officials, the music scholar, Juang Been-lih, and Koong Der-cherng,
the seventy-seventh descendant of Confucius.

The committee published a preliminary report[1] on the reform of
the Sacrificial Ceremony to Confucius in 1970. Musically, rather
than keeping the set of melodies used during the Ching dynasty, the
reform called for the adoption of a different set of melodies from a
Ming dynasty (1368–1644) source. There was also to be an increase

---

* In this article, the tonal spelling system of Chinese is used, except in the
cases of established, familiar forms such as dynastic names.

[1] *Jih Koong Lii Yueh Jy Gae Jinn* (Reform of the Confucian Sacrificial
Ceremony and Music) (Taiwan: Jih Koong Lii Yueh Gong Tzuoh Woei Yuan Huey
[The Committee on the Confucian Sacrificial Ceremony and Music], 1970).

in the number of musical instruments used for the performance. Much of the reform was done after consulting various treatises from earlier periods. In addition to the changes in the music, there were also reforms in the dances, the costumes of the celebrants, and the number of dancers and musicians. The report also stated that for practical reasons, to meet the demands of modern times, the total duration of the ceremony was to be reduced, with the aim of shortening the ceremony to one hour.

In 1972 a documentary film was made of an actual Confucian Sacrificial Ceremony which took place in Taiwan. The following is a translation of the film's narration describing the event, which represents the official viewpoint regarding the ceremony.

Sound Track of *A Confucian Ceremony* (Taiwan, 1972)

The architecture of this Confucian temple is adorned with carved beams and painted rafters, creating an atmosphere of antique splendor. Confucius not only passed down to us the cultural heritage of several thousand years ago, he also established the foundation of a Chinese culture which will last forever and ever. Therefore, he is revered as the most perfect teacher of all. Each year on the twenty-eighth day of the ninth month, the whole nation holds an impressive ceremony to commemorate this great sage.

From the ceremonial music, the ritual acts, and the display we can easily see the social beliefs and the political structure of the time of Confucius. Ritual and music embody the basic spirit of education in ancient China. That is to say, ritual represents order, while music harmonizes the spirits. They are used to discipline the people's temperament, to lead their hearts in the right direction, thus enabling the people to benefit from the legacy of the ancients and to raise the standard of morals.

From the Han (206 B.C.E.–C.E. 220) and Tang (618–906) dynasties to the Ming (1368–1644) and Ching (1644–1911) dynasties, the Confucian ceremony has been used time and again as a national ceremony. The form of the rites is splendid and dignified.

From ancient times our nation has had music and dance, which were especially emphasized in the Chou dynasty (1122–249 B.C.E.). However, it is only since the time of Confucius that the king of a nation has made use of the Eight-Row Dance, which had sixty-four dancers. The dukes had what was called the Six-Row Dance, which had thirty-six dancers. There are two kinds of dance: the civil and the military. Today the civil dancers hold in their hands feathers and a flute. The dances occur during the first, second, and third offerings and are accompanied by music and ceremonial acts. Each dance routine is accompanied by a separate stanza of the song. The meanings of the gestures are indeed profound.

From these rites, we can imagine the grandeur of the ceremony and music of ancient times. This enables us to appreciate even more the spirit behind Chinese ceremony and Chinese music, both of which have long traditions. . . . Much of this ceremony and music can be traced back 2,800 years to the ceremonial music of the time of Duke Chou. The instruments are numerous and the music is noble and elegant. It occupies a unique position in the music of the world.

In the ceremony for Confucius, an entire program has a total of thirty-four steps. The whole ceremony is splendid and dignified, arousing in the listeners a sense of respect. In such a ceremony, which has persisted from dynasty to dynasty, we see that each detail suggests the importance of ceremonial behavior. The spirit of the government of the ancient sages is demonstrated all the more vividly by the ceremony. All the guests who participated in this ceremony hope that following generations will clearly understand this and will look toward the principles of Confucius.

The documentary also records that the temple where the ceremony takes place has an altar on which are displayed many spirit tablets, or wooden plaques, each bearing the name of a sage. The spirit tablet of Confucius, which is the largest, is placed in the center of the altar. Arranged in rows on either side are tablets with the names of the Lesser Sages.[2] The offerings on the altar include incense, food, wine, and a bolt of silk. On the temple grounds the offerings of the carcasses of an ox, a sheep, and a pig are also on display.

As noted by the narrator in the film, the ceremony consists of a sequence of actions arranged in thirty-four steps. Each step has a title, such as "The Beginning of the Sacrificial Ceremony," "First

---

[2] The four so-called major Lesser Sages are: Yan Tzyy, Tzyy-sy Tzyy, Tzeng Tzyy, and Menq Tzyy (Mencius).

Session of Drumming," "Opening of the Gate," or "Bowing." Each title is written in large characters on a sheet of paper and displayed conspicuously, one after another, as the ceremony progresses. At the same time, the Master of Ceremonies loudly calls out each step. The order of the thirty-four steps, with brief descriptions of the actions of the celebrants, is as follows.

The Annual Confucian Sacrificial Ceremony
(as observed since the 1969 reform)

1. "The Beginning of the Sacrificial Ceremony."
2. "The First Session of Drumming": All the incense and candles are lit.
3. "The Second Session of Drumming": The musicians, dancers, and attendants stand along the sides of the temple courtyard.
4. "The Third Session of Drumming": The Master of Ceremonies leads the celebrants into the courtyard.
5. "All Attendants Assume Their Posts": While doing this, the attendants keep time with the drum beat.
6. "The Musicians and Dancers Assume Their Posts": They follow the banner carriers to their posts, keeping time with the drum beat.
7. "The Supervising Officer Assumes His Post": He follows the Master of Ceremonies.
8. "The Secondary Celebrant Assumes His Post."
9. "The Associate Celebrant Assumes His Post": He follows the Master of Ceremonies.
10. "The Chief Celebrant Assumes His Post": He follows the Master of Ceremonies.
11. "The Opening of the Gate."
12. "Burying the Sacrificial Blood": The attendant carries a tray with the vessel of [animal] blood to the burying place.
13. "Welcoming the Approaching Spirits": The Music Master intones, "Perform 'The Song of Unity'!" (Song I; see the music score in Appendix 1). As the spirits are supposedly ushered in, the Master of Ceremonies intones, "The congregation will rise!"

14. "Bowing": The Master of Ceremonies says, "Bow again! Bow a third time!"
15. "Setting of the Food Vessels": The attendants carry in the sacrificial caldron.
16. "Presentation of the Incense": The Music Master intones, "Perform 'The Song of Peace'!" (Song II). The Chief Celebrant washes his hands and, following behind the Master of Ceremonies, approaches the incense table with his incense, offers it, and bows three times. If the president of the republic himself, or his deputy, makes the presentation of the incense, this act is performed just before step 25.
17. "The First Offering": The Music Master intones, "Perform 'The Song of Tranquility'!" (Song III). The attendants then signal with their banners for the dancers to begin performing. At the same time, the Chief Celebrant, following the Master of Ceremonies, approaches the spirit tablet of Confucius and makes his offering of the bolt of silk and the wine cup. He then bows three times.
18. "The First Offering by the Associate Celebrant": He makes the offering for the Lesser Sages after being led in by the Master of Ceremonies.
19. "Respectfully Reading the Text of Invocation": The Music Master intones, "The end of music!" The Master of Ceremonies intones, "The Congregation will rise!"
20. "Bowing": The Master of Ceremonies continues with, "Bow again! Bow a third time!"
21. "The Second Offering": The Music Master intones, "Perform 'The Song of Brilliance'!" (Song IV). The attendants signal with their banners for the dancers to perform. At the same time, the Chief Celebrant, following the Master of Ceremonies, approaches the spirit tablet of Confucius and makes his offering of the wine cup again. He bows three times.
22. "The Second Offering by the Associate Celebrant": He makes the offering for the Lesser Sages after being led in by the Master of Ceremonies.
23. "The Final Offering": The actions described in step 21 are repeated.

24. "The Final Offering by the Associate Celebrant": Step 22 is repeated.
25. "Partaking of the Sacrificial Wine and Flesh": The Chief Celebrant approaches the altar behind the Master of Ceremonies and performs [symbolically?]. He bows three times.
26. "Withdrawing of the Offerings": This is performed by the attendants while the Music Master intones, "Perform 'The Song of Unity'!" (Song V. This song's melody differs from that of Song I, sung as part of step 13.)
27. "Escorting the Spirits Back": The Music Master repeats, "Perform 'The Song of Unity'!" (Song VI. The melody differs from both that of Song I in step 13 and Song V in step 26), while the Master of Ceremonies intones, "The congregation will all rise!"
28. "Bowing": The Master of Ceremonies continues with, "Bow again! Bow a third time!"
29. "Carrying the Text of Invocation and the Sacrificial Silk to the Burning Ground": The celebrants who read the Invocation and made the offering of silk carry the objects to the burning ground.
30. "Watching the Burning": The Music Master intones, "Perform 'The Song of Unity'!" as the bells and drums are struck. The Master of Ceremonies leads the Chief Celebrant to the burning ground. Which melody is played here is not clear.
31. "The Celebrants Return to Their Positions": The Chief Celebrant returns with the Master of Ceremonies, after which the music stops.
32. "The Closing of the Gate."
33. "Procession Leaving the Temple Grounds": The musicians, dancers, and the attendants process in time to the drum beat.
34. "The End of the Ceremony."

The description of the thirty-four steps of the ceremony offers a glimpse of the stately atmosphere of the event. The ceremonial songs, as recorded on the film, are sung in a very slow tempo by an all-male chorus. During the ceremony the actions are preceded or followed by the playing of various kinds of percussive instruments—the deep drum or smaller drums, the rattle, the wooden trough, the gong. These instruments are either played in flourishes or with a steady beat. Most intriguing of all is the presence of a small carved wooden tiger among the instruments. At the end of the melodic section, the performer would tap the head of the tiger with a small bundle of sticks and then scrape the tiger's serrated back a few times, creating a rasping noise. The juxtaposition of the percussive instruments and the melodic singing of the choir in long sustained notes, together with the occasional intoning of the Master of Ceremonies, forms an interesting combination of tonal texture.

The six songs which are specifically used in praise of Confucius all have the same basic structure (see the music score,[3] the Chinese text, and the English translation of the six songs in Appendix 1). Each song contains eight melodic phrases with four notes to a phrase, which fits the four-syllable phrases of the song text. The tempo marking given on the score is fairly close to the tempo of the recorded song—that is, each note is a little more than four seconds long. During the performance there are also long pauses between the phrases. This style of music is purportedly influenced by the Confucian concept of proper music. The slow and even-paced melody, with a syllabic setting of the text, is stylistically unlike most other kinds of Chinese music.

On the other hand, textually, the four-syllable phrasing, which is one of the most common textual structures of this type of sacrificial song, can be traced back to the four-syllable poetic lines in the *Classic of Poetry* (*Shy Jing*), which is a collection of folk song texts traditionally said to be compiled and edited by Confucius himself.

The six songs, which, according to Juang Been-lih, are based on a Ming dynasty source, are all built upon the same pentatonic scale: d-e-g-a-b and the octave note d'. And, as mentioned earlier,

---

[3] In the report published by the reform committee, Juang Been-lih indicates that the transcription of the score is based on a Ming dynasty music score, without further specification. It is possible that it is based upon a work by the Ming scholar Lii Jy-tzao (see also fn. 8) because he is mentioned in the report, although in a different context.

the melodic phrases are all equal lengths of four whole notes. Thus, the likelihood of similar or identical melodic phrases recurring is high. Indeed, we find many identical phrases (which might also be referred to as a melodic motif) reappearing again and again, here and there, among the six songs.

While these repeated motifs often occur at corresponding locations in the different songs, they also often appear at different locations among the songs. In Appendix 1 I have identified and labeled the motifs that appear at least twice in the six songs. The songs are numbered I through VI on the score. Each song contains eight phrases and each phrase is one measure long. The repeated motifs, all exactly one measure, are identified by the capital letters A, B, C, D, etc. Thus, motif D appears twice in song I, in measures 4 and 8, and once in song III, in measure 6.

Although the six songs have a total of forty-eight measures, there are altogether only twenty different melodic motifs. The most frequent one is motif C, which appears eight times. Motif G appears seven times, motifs A, D, H, I, L each appear three times, and motifs B, E, F, J, and K each appear twice. Only eight motifs (not labeled on the music score) appear just once.

If we take smaller segments, for example, phrases of two notes each, we find even more recurrences of the same two-note units. The immediate repetition of one- or two-note units between the end of one measure and the beginning of the next measure (see especially songs III and IV) is worth noting. The two-note units are also sometimes repeated in mirror image, as with the e-g and g-e units in measures 3 and 4 of song V. Joseph S. C. Lam, in his very detailed analysis of a much larger body of Ming dynasty state sacrificial songs,[4] discusses formulism and shows that such melodic characteristics as the recurrence of melodic motifs, long or short, as well as the immediate cross measure repetitions, e.g., of single notes, or two-note segments, actually contribute to a general sense

---

[4] See Joseph Sui Ching Lam, "Creativity within Bounds: State Sacrificial Songs from the Ming Dynasty 1368-1644 A.D." (Ph.D. diss., Harvard University, 1987), for Ming dynasty source materials on ceremonial songs.

of continuity and unity, while each song still has its own individuality.

The Sacrificial Ceremony to Confucius, as we know it today, took shape gradually over a long period of time. The following chronological outline is based primarily upon an account by Juang Been-lih, with some additional information from other sources.[5]

The official dates for Confucius are 551–479 B.C.E. It is said that one year after his death a temple had already been erected in his honor. In 195 B.C.E. Emperor Gau Tzuu of the Former Han dynasty initiated the offering of three sacrificial animals—an ox, a sheep, and a pig—to Confucius. By C.E. 72 Emperor Ming Dih of the Late Han dynasty included sacrifices to all seventy-two disciples of Confucius. In C.E. 76 Emperor Jang Dih of the Han dynasty introduced the use of music at the Sacrificial Ceremony. The first visible symbol, a statue of Confucius, was introduced in C.E. 178. (However, in 1469, during the Ming dynasty, the statue was replaced by the spirit tablet on the altar.) The sacrificial dance was introduced as part of the ceremony in C.E. 485 under Emperor Wuu of the State of Chyi. The singing of sacrificial songs at such ceremonies began under Emperor Wen of the Sui dynasty in C.E. 609.

Although the Tang dynasty (618–960) is known for the flourishing of secular music, the performance of ceremonial music was also conscientiously observed in the court. It was during the Kaiyuan period (eighth century) that the semiannual schedule of the Confucian Sacrificial Ceremony was established. The two ceremonies, held once in the spring (the second month) and once in the fall (the eighth month), were called the Ding Sacrifices because they were always held on the fourth cyclical day—called the Ding Day—

[5] Juang Been-lih, "Jong Gwo Jih Koong Lii Yueh Jyi Yih Wuu" (The Music and Dance of the Chinese Confucian Sacrificial Ceremony), lecture delivered in Taiwan, 1984. Other sources of information are: C. L. Arlington, "Some Remarks on the Worship Offered Confucius in the Confucian Temple," *The Peiping Chronicle*, January 1935; and Shiue Tzong-ming, *Jong Way In Yueh Dah Shyh Nian Beau* (A chronology of the Major Musical Events in China and in the World) (Taiwan: The Commercial Press, 1990).

of the month. This tradition was continued until the early part of the twentieth century, when China became a republic. The ceremony was then held only once a year, on the official birthday of Confucius. (Currently, the day is also celebrated as Teacher's Day.) The semiannual observance of the Sacrificial Ceremony continued in Taiwan for a much longer time, and it is still followed in Korea today.

During the Sung dynasty (960–1279) the government as well as many individual scholars continued to be interested in improving the sacrificial rites. New songs were commissioned, and more musical instruments, such as the elaborate sets of bell chimes and stone chimes, were constructed by imperial order. Scholarly treatises, including works on ceremonial music, written during the Sung dynasty greatly influenced later periods.[6] During the Yuan dynasty (1264–1368), when China was under Mongolian rule, the Mongols continued the Sung dynasty tradition of ceremonial music. According to Juang Been-lih, a new set of ceremonial melodies were composed at that time; they were, however, never actually used.[7]

By the Ming dynasty (1368–1644), China was again under the rule of the Han Chinese. Numerous treatises and collections of state sacrificial music from this period are still extant today. These writings provide evidence that, in addition to Confucius and his disciples, many other spirits were worshipped at the Sacrificial Ceremonies. For example, the 1476 treatise, *Tay Charng Tzoong Laan* (General record of the court of imperial sacrifices), lists Songs for the Sacrifice to Heaven and Earth, the Imperial Ancestors, Confucius, the Deities of Soil and Grain, the Heavenly and Earthly Deities, the Meritorious Sovereigns of Past Dynasties, and the Progenitor of Agriculture.

During the early part of the Ming dynasty, the founding emperor Tay Tzuu suggested that the ceremonial songs should have simpler,

---

[6] See R. C. Pian, *Sonq Dynasty Musical Sources and Their Interpretation*, Harvard-Yenching Institute Monograph Series, 16 (Cambridge, Mass.: Harvard University Press, 1967).

[7] Mentioned by Juang in his 1984 lecture (see fn. 5 above).

pentatonic melodies, though the texts, which were from Sung dynasty sources, could continue to be used.

For his study of Ming dynasty ceremonial songs, Joseph Lam was able to gather, from several hitherto little-known Ming dynasty sources, no less than two hundred eighty different ceremonial songs used for various purposes. This collection shows that, although many of the songs do have longer phrase lengths and although some pieces are based upon the heptatonic rather than the pentatonic scale, they are on the whole stylistically quite similar to the six sacrificial songs discussed above.

These six songs, still used in Taiwan today, can be found as a set in at least three Ming dynasty works, of which the earliest is the *General Record of the Court of Imperial Sacrifices* of 1476, mentioned above.[8] At least the first of the six pieces may be traced back to a song in a still earlier work, the *Seh Puu*, a collection of songs to be accompanied by the *seh*, a twenty-five-stringed zither, which was compiled by the scholar Shyong Perng-lai (1246–1323) toward the end of the Sung dynasty.[9] A comparison of the two songs (see Appendices 1 and 2) shows that the melodies are in certain ways similar to each other and the texts practically identical.[10] According to Robert C. Provine, the Ming dynasty melody is actually the pentatonic version of the same melody in Shyong Perng-lai's collection, which is in the original heptatonic style[11] (see further discussion of the two collections below). Of course, all these songs must have been influenced by the set of twelve songs collected by the Neo-Confucian scholar, Ju Shi (1130–1200), which

---

[8] The other two are *Tay Charng Kao* (Monograph on the court of imperial sacrifices), dated some time after 1530, and *Pann Gong Lii Yueh Shu* (Memorial on ceremonial music in the Confucian temple) by Lii Jy-tzao, 1616.

[9] Pian, *Sonq Dynasty Musical Sources,* 10–11 and 221.

[10] Twelve of the thirty-two notes in the two melodies are identical and twenty-eight of the thirty-two characters of the text are the same.

[11] Robert C. Provine, "Tracing the Ta-Sheng Yueh-P'u, a Progenitor of Korean Aak," in *Essays on Sino-Korean Musicology: The Early Sources for Korean Ritual Music,* 139–40, Traditional Korean Music Series, no. 2 (Seoul: Il Ji Sa Publishing Co., 1988).

are the earliest known notated examples of this type of ceremonial song.[12]

In considering the limitations of the musical materials and the restrictions in style placed upon these sacrificial songs, Lam points out that, given the large quantity of songs composed, there was still room for what he calls "creativity within bounds." It is not clear, however, how many of these songs had actually been performed at the ceremonies. Lam argues that the slow-moving melodies are better suited as accompaniment for the stately, solemn acts of the ceremony, such as making offerings, and, as mentioned above, the inevitable formulism in the music actually serves to create an overall sense of continuity and unity.[13] He concludes that such a style of music appropriately helps to suggest a legacy from the past. Furthermore, the state sacrifices and proper music afforded a public means for the Ming sovereign and the bureaucracy to demonstrate their desire for an ideal Confucian society.[14] Such motivations as these undoubtedly explain the use of similar styles of ceremonial music in other periods of Chinese history.

During the Ching dynasty (1644–1911), when China was under Manchu rule, the government was very much concerned with continuing the tradition of the Confucian Sacrificial Ceremonies.[15] As in several past dynasties in Chinese history, the previous dynasty's sacrificial music was at first adopted. Gradually, new songs, or new melodies set to old texts, then replaced the old songs. By imperial decree, bureaus were established for the training in and managing of the Sacrificial Ceremonies. New musical treatises were written and additional ceremonial musical instruments, such as the drums and the elaborate bell chimes, were made. It is interesting

---

[12] Pian, *Sonq Dynasty Musical Sources,* 10 and 157–73. According to Ju Shi, these songs were not in style in his time but were cited indirectly from a source that dated the songs further back, to the Kai Yuan (eighth century) period.

[13] Lam, "Creativity within Bounds," chap. 9, sec. H, p. 439.

[14] Lam, "Creativity within Bounds," chap. 10, passim.

[15] See Shiue Tzong-ming, *Chronology* (fn. 5 above). Keith Pratt, in his article, "Change and Continuity in Qing Court Music" (*Chime*, 1993, no. 7:90–103), provides a general survey.

that during the Ching period there were numerous efforts to establish and improve the Confucian ceremony in Tainan, the southern part of Taiwan, where a· large Confucian temple was built.

In the late nineteenth century several Western scholars published studies of the Confucian Sacrificial Ceremony. J. A. van Aalst[16] in 1884, for example, not only described the routine of the ceremony in great detail but also provided the musical notation of the ceremonial songs. He noted that, according to a 1743 decree, this was the only set of songs to be used in honoring Confucius. This set of ceremonial songs, also six in number, differs, however, from the Ming dynasty version both in music and in the text. Nevertheless, stylistically—the very slow, four-note setting of the four-syllable lines of the text—they are quite similar.

A very detailed description of the Confucian ceremony, including the movements of the dancers, was written by Bishop G. E. Moule, who witnessed the ritual in Hangchow in 1891[17] and again in 1898. The music and the texts he cites from a Chinese score indicate that his version is identical to the version presented by van Aalst. On the other hand, in 1874, J. Edkins in his report "A Visit to the City of Confucius"[18] quoted the text of the Confucian Sacrificial songs in English translation (see Appendix 3). Although Edkins provides no supplemental information about the music, the translation clearly shows that his are not the same songs heard by either van Aalst or Moule. Rather, they strongly suggest the six songs from the Ming period. Since Edkins observed the ceremony in Chiu Fuu, the home of Confucius, rather than in the capital, it could be that in some areas the Ming dynasty version of the ceremonial songs was used.

As noted at the beginning of this essay, during the early part of the Republican period (since 1911), the Sacrificial Ceremony to

[16] J. A. van Aalst, *Chinese Music* (Shanghai and London, 1884; reprint, New York: Paragon Book Reprint Corp., 1964), 25–35, section on "Ritual Music."

[17] G. F. Moule, "Notes on the Ting Chi, or Half-yearly Sacrifice to Confucius" *Journal of the North-China Branch of the Royal Asiatic Society* (Shanghai) 33 (1888–1900):120–56.

[18] J. Edkins, "A Visit to the City of Confucius," *Journal of the North-China Branch of the Royal Asiatic Society,* n.s., 8 (1874):83–91 (chap. 2.18.12).

Confucius continued to be observed and the Ching dynasty version
of the ceremonial songs were, for a time, still used. It was generally
assumed that from 1949 all Confucian ceremonies had ceased.
However, as late as 1956, the musicologist Yang Yinn-liou witnessed
a Confucian Sacrificial ceremony in the city of Liou Yang, Hunan
Province.[19]

The practice of the Confucian Ceremony was not and still is not
limited to areas within China. It has been adopted by the
neighboring countries of Korea and Vietnam. It is also interesting
that, while the large-scale Confucian Ceremony was not known to
have been held in Japan,[20] the Japanese government did encourage
the worship of Confucius in Northeast China and in Taiwan, when
these areas were under Japanese occupation.

Today in Korea the Sacrificial Ceremony in honor of Confucius
is still held semiannually, which is the more traditional arrangement.
The sequence of steps of the program is, on the whole, very similar
to that observed in Taiwan today, although it is somewhat more
elaborate than the Taiwan version. As far back as the Sung period,
there had been efforts to introduce Confucian ceremonial music and
instruments to Korea.[21] Later, Korean scholars studied the ceremony

[19] Yang Yinn-liou, "Koong Miaw Ding Jih In Yueh De Chu Buh Yan Jiou" (A
preliminary study of the spring and autumn sacrificial music in the Confucian
temple), *In Yueh Yan Jiou* (Journal of music) 1, no. 1 (1958):54–69.

[20] In the O-Cha-no-Mizu district of Tokyo, there is a Confucian temple in
which the shrine still displays a miniature statue of Confucius. It is said that on
certain occasions the wind instrument players from the court *gagaku* orchestra
perform at the temple.

In Japan the so-called *gagaku* (the same term in Chinese, *yea yueh*, means
Confucian ceremonial music) that we hear today is not Confucian ceremonial
music but borrowings of the Chinese court entertainment music of the Tang period.
Today, *gagaku* and its subsequently developed forms in Japan are used on a variety
of occasions in the Japanese royal court.

[21] See Song Kyong-rin, "Ritual Music: The Confucius Temple Music," chap.
5, sec. 1 in *Survey of Korean Arts: Traditional Music* (Seoul: National Academy
of Arts, 1973). See also Robert C. Provine, "The Treatise on Ceremonial Music
(1430) in the Annals of the Korean King Sejong," *Ethnomusicology* 18, no. 1
(1974):1–29.

by examining Chinese documents and sources and reconstructed what they considered an even more authentic version of the ceremony. Robert Provine has written a detailed study[22] of the history of some Confucian ceremonial songs introduced to Korea by the Chinese scholar Lin Yu in 1349; he has been able to trace the origin of these songs to the time of the emperor Hui Tzong (early twelfth century) of the Sung dynasty. As in the series of ceremonial songs in *Seh Puu* compiled by Shyong Perng-lai, the Lin Yu collection also has as the initial piece, "The Song for Welcoming the Spirits," which is identical in text and melody to the *Seh Puu* version and is similarly related to the version used in Taiwan today. In addition, the Lin Yu series also contains the texts of the remaining five of the six songs, although they are set to different melodies.

The actual performance practices can be a very important factor in comparing different musical cultures. Our only sources, however, are the available recordings of performances produced in recent history and the occasional report of a witness who attempts to describe the actual sound. In Korea Confucian ceremonial music is now all instrumental. One uniquely Korean feature of the playing technique is the ending of each note with a quick and short upward glide, which is not found in Chinese performance technique. In Taiwan great emphasis is placed on singing the songs during the ceremony. Here, one can discern the influence of Western vocal technique.

Confucianism has also influenced music in Vietnam from fairly early times.[23] In the fifteenth century a court official was sent to China specifically to study the Ming court ceremonial music, the outcome of which was the Dai Viet court music and dance, used for various ritual purposes in the court. The practice lasted well into the middle of the twentieth century.

The question of whether Confucianism is a religion continues to be a topic of debate. In a recent issue of the *Journal of Asian Studies*

[22] Provine, "Tracing the Ta-Sheng Yueh-P'u, a Progenitor of Korean Aak."

[23] R. C. Pian, "Diversity and Interrelationships of the Musics of East Asia" (published in Japanese), in *Music Traditions of Japan, Asia and Oceania*, vol. 3 (Tokyo: Iwanami Shoten, 1988), 145–58.

(1995, no. 2), a series of articles summarizes recent studies of Asian religious traditions still alive today. Included under Chinese religions are: Taoism, Confucianism, Buddhism, Islam, and popular religion. In the introduction to the section on Confucianism, the authors Rodney L. Taylor and Gary Arbuckle, who had surveyed numerous articles on the topic, noted that, "Approaching Confucianism as a lived and living faith rather than a philosophy or an ethic is still uncommon, but it is no longer as lonely a path to take as it once was."[24] As early as 1961, C. K. Yang pointed out several features, such as belief in heaven and fate, sacrificial and ancestor worhip, divination practices, and the theory of yin and yang and the five elements, which speak strongly of the religious nature of Confucianism.[25] In the Confucian Sacrificial Ceremony, we see that communication with the supernatural spirits is a very important part of the ritual, for it is a way to show respect to Confucius and other outstanding historical Confucian personalities.

There is a great self-consciousness behind the practice and reform of the Confucian ceremony. Every detail is planned, down to each single stroke of drum and bell. There is a constant searching for historical justification. The Confucian ceremony and its ideals have resulted in a unique style of music. Confucianism is of course one of the main areas of study for the traditional Chinese scholar. These scholars also contemplated music theory—including the philosophical, cosmological, as well as the practical and technical issues of music. It is interesting that their concern for the Confucian ceremony is not merely that of purely antiquarian interest: constant efforts to reform the details of the ceremony so that the practice is effective and meaningful to the contemporary public make their scholarly interest a practical concern.

[24] Rodney L. Taylor and Gary Arbuckle, "Confucianism," *Journal of Asian Studies* 54, no. 2 (May 1995), Issue on Chinese Religions: The State of the Field, pt. 2:347–54.

[25] C. K. Yang, "Religious Aspects of Confucianism in Its Doctrine and Practice," chap. 10 in *Religion in Chinese Society: A Study of Contemporary Social Functions of Religion and Some of Their Historical Factors* (Berkeley: University of California Press, 1970).

The Confucian ceremony offers a powerful means for recon-firming the status of the celebrants.[26] This holds true as far back as the Han dynasty and through all the subsequent periods in Chinese history. The Confucian ceremony promotes a sense of loyalty to the government and a desire for peace and social order. This is one reason that during each new regime the government concerns itself with reinstating the Confucian ceremony, correcting it or reforming it if necessary. This was equally true under Mongolian rule during the Yuan dynasty as under Manchurian rule during the Ching dynasty.

Belief in the power of music and in music's relation to rituals has been finely expressed in the classics, familiar to all traditional Chinese scholars. The earliest work on the subject still extant today is the *Yueh Jih* (The Book of Music), which dates back to the second century B.C.E. It is part of *Lii Jih* (The Book of Rites, chap. 19). I shall conclude with a passage from the *Yueh Jih* as translated by Lin Yu-tang:[27]

> Music unites, while rituals differentiate. Through union the people come to be friendly toward one another, and through differentiation the people come to learn respect for one another. If music pre-dominates, the social structure becomes too amorphous, and if rituals predominate, social life becomes too cold. To bring the people's inner feelings and their external conduct into balance is the work of rituals and music. The establishment of rituals gives a well defined sense of order and discipline, while the general spread

[26] Both Joseph Lam (see fn. 4) and Keith Pratt (fn. 15) have emphasized this.

[27] Lin Yu-tang, ed. and trans., *The Wisdom of Confucius* (New York: The Modern Library, 1943), chap. 10, sec. 2, 234. A more recent translation with annotation, by Scott Cook, of *The Record of Music* appears in *Asian Music* 26, no. 2 (1995).

For a thorough study of ancient music theory and the relevant classical works in China, see Kenneth J. DeWoskin, *A Song for One or Two, Music and the Concept of Art in Early China*, Michigan Papers in Chinese Studies, no. 42 (Ann Arbor: The University of Michigan Center for Chinese Studies, 1982).

of music and song establishes the general atmosphere of peace in the people. . . .

Music comes from the inside, while rituals come from the outside. Because music comes from the inside, it is characterized by quiet and calm. And because rituals come from the outside, they are characterized by formalism. Truly great music is always simple in movement, and truly great rituals are always simple in form. When good music prevails there is no feeling of dissatisfaction and when proper rituals prevail, there is no strife and struggle. When we say that by mere bowing in salute the king can rule the world, we mean thereby the influence of ritual and music.

Appendix 1
The Six Songs for the Confucian Sacrificial Ceremony

Chinese Text of the Songs

大成樂章

I。迎神　大哉孔聖　道德尊榮　舉持王化　斯民是宗
　　　　　典祀有常　精純並隆　神其來格　於昭聖埋

II。奠帛　自生民來　誰底其盛　惟師神明　度越前聖
　　　　　粢帛具成　禮容斯稱　黍稷非馨　惟神之聽

III。初獻　大哉聖師　實天生德　作樂以崇　時祀無斁
　　　　　清酤惟馨　嘉牲孔碩　薦羞神明　庶幾昭格

IV。亞獻　百王宗師　生民物歸　瞻之洋洋　神其寧止
　　終獻　酌彼金罍　惟清其旨　登獻惟三　於嘻成禮

V。徹饌　犧象在前　豆籩在列　以享以薦　既芬既潔
　　　　　禮成樂備　人和神悅　祭則受福　率遵無越

VI。送神　有嚴學宮　四方淶崇　恪恭祀事　威儀雝雝
　　　　　歆茲惟馨　神馭還復　明煙斯畢　咸膺百福

Titles of the Melodies[*]

I. "Shyan Her Jy Cheu" (The Song of Unity):   咸和之曲
   Welcoming the approaching spirits

II. "Ning Her Jy Cheu" (The Song of Peace):   寧和之曲
    Presentation of the incense or silk

III. "An Her Jy Cheu" (The Song of Tranquility):   安和之曲
     The first offering

IV. "Jiing Her Jy Cheu" (The Song of Brilliance):   景和之曲
    The second and third offerings

V. "Shyan Her Jy Cheu" (The Song of Unity):   咸和之曲
   Withdrawing of the offerings

VI. "Shyan Her Jy Cheu" (The Song of Unity):   咸和之曲
    Escorting the spirits back

[*] The score shows that the melodies of Song I, V, and VI are different, although for some reason all three songs bear the same title.

The Melodies (adapted from Juang Been-lih's transcription)

Appendix 2
"Song for Welcoming the Spirits,"
from Shyong Perng-lai's *Seh Puu*
(R. C. Pian, *Sonq Dynasty Musical Sources and Their Interpretation*, p. 221)

迎 神 凝 安 之 曲

Appendix 3
*Odes to Confucius**

I. Great is Confucius—the Sage.
    His virtue and teaching are exalted.
    The people reverence him, having felt the renovating effect of his
       exhortations.
    Thy sacrifices are constantly offered
    They are pure and without defect;
    They are plentifully provided.
    The spirit comes.
    There is light beaming from the sacred countenance of the Sage.

II. From the beginning of the human race,
     Who can fully imagine his abundance of goodness and wisdom?
     He only can be called the divine and enlightened teacher,
     Passing all former sages in excellence.
     The offerings of grain and of silk are complete,
     And suitable,
     While there is a lack of the fruits of the earth.
     The spirit of the Sage listens.

III. Great is the wise teacher,
      Who truly from heaven has derived his virtue.
      We perform music in honor of him.
      We present sacrifices without cessation.
      Our wine is fragrant,
      Our animal offerings are of the best.
      While we offer them to the spirits,
      Surely it may be said that the spirits manifestly appear.

IV.   Honoured teacher of a hundred kings,
      Ruler of living beings and things,
      See how vast and various are his activities,
      How marvellous his repose!

---

* Translated by J. Edkins, in "A Visit to the City of Confucius," *Journal of
the North-China Branch of the Royal Asiatic Society*, n.s., 8 (1874):83–91. I have
modified a few lines to match more closely the Chinese text.

And pour out from the golden cup,
The pure and well tasted wine.
This is our Third Presentation,
Thus we complete the ceremonies as they are appointed.

V.   The sacrificial animals are here,
     With the baskets and bowls,
     In orderly arrangement.
     They are fragrant; they are pure.
     The offerings and the music being complete,
     Men are in harmony and the spirits rejoice.
     We receive blessing through sacrificing,
     And obey the rules without fault.

VI.   To the grand old hall of learning,
     Scholars from the four quarters of the horizon come to show
       respect.
     Reverentially they perform the ceremonies of the sacrifice,
     With all the solemn show required by the ritual.
     The spirit having enjoyed the fragrant odours of the gifts
     Returns to its place.
     The presentation of the offerings is finished.
     All who have shared in the ceremony enjoy great variety of
       happiness.

Glossary of Chinese Terms

Chiu Fuu	曲阜
Chou (Duke) or Chou Gong	周公
Ding Sacrifices (or Ting Chi)	丁祭
Gagaku (*see* Yea Yueh)	
Gau Tzuu (Emperor) of Han	漢高祖
Hui Tzong (Emperor) of Sung	宋徽宗
In Yueh Yan Jiou	音樂研究
Jang Dih (Emperor) of Han	漢章帝
Jih Koong Lii Yueh Gong Tzuoh Woei Yuan Huey	祭孔禮樂工作委員會
Jih Koong Lii Yueh Jy Gae Jinn	祭孔禮樂之改進
Jong Gwo Jih Koong Lii Yueh Jyi Yih Wuu	中國祭孔禮樂及佾舞
Jong Way In Yueh Dah Shyh Nian Beau	中外音樂大事年表
Ju Shi	朱熹
Juang Been-lih	莊本立
Kai Yuan	開元
Koong Der-cherng	孔德成
Koong Miaw Ding Jih In Yueh De Chu Buh Yan Jiou	孔廟丁祭音樂的初步研究
Lam, Joseph S. C.	林萃青
Lii Jih	禮記
Lii Jy-tzao	李之藻
Lii Yueh	禮樂
Lin Yu	林宇
Lin Yu-tang	林語堂
Liou Yang	瀏陽

Ming Dih (Emperor) of Han	漢明帝
Menq Tzyy	孟子
Pann Gong Lii Yueh Shu	判宮禮樂疏
Seh Puu	瑟譜
Shiue Tzong-ming	薛宗明
Shyong Perng-lai	熊朋來
Shy Jing	詩經
Ta-sheng Yueh-p'u (Dah Shenq Yueh Puu)	大晟樂譜
Tay Charng Kao	太常考
Tay Charng Tzoong Laan	太常總覽
Tay Tzuu (Emperor) of Ming	明太祖
Ting Chi (or Ding Jih)	丁祭
Tzeng Tzyy	曾子
Tzyy-Sy Tzyy	子思子
Wuu (Emperor) of Chyi	齊武帝
Wen (Emperor) of Sui	隋文帝
Yan Tzyy	顏子
Yang Yinn-liou	楊蔭瀏
Yea Yueh	雅樂
Yueh Jih	樂記

Sounding the Word:
Music in the Life of Islam[*]

Regula Burckhardt Qureshi

This essay is about music in the life of Islam as created by Muslims. Music is a theologically controversial concept in Islam. Nonetheless, musical sound plays a highly significant role in articulating the singularly verbal message of Islam, both in its universal Qur'anic form and in the form of local traditions.

To explore this reality, I have drawn upon my intellectual studies as well as my life among urban, middle-class, Urdu-speaking South Asian Muslims, in India (Lucknow and Delhi), in Pakistan (Karachi), and in Canada (Edmonton and Calgary). Today, South Asian Muslims make up a transnational community, solidly situated conceptually in a history of transnationality anchored in the universalist foundation of Islam and the political history of trans-ethnic/transnational Muslim polities that formed the first "world system" in the thirteenth century (Abu-Lughod 1989).

Musical life, however, is always local and particular. In sharing what is eminently shareable, Muslims have taught me that to learn about music in the life of their Islam means learning how music works in the lives of believers. My agenda, then, is first to offer a vignette of traditional sonic religious practices among Urdu-speaking Muslims, as I experienced, recorded, and researched them twenty-five years ago in Karachi, their largest center of concentration. The second goal is to examine this musical life among

[*] Special thanks go to Amera Raza and Saleem Qureshi, Aqil and Ansa Athar, Yasmeen Nizam, and Atiya Siddiqui.

migrants to North America, as part of an ongoing process involving
the "organization of the current situation in the terms of a past"
(Sahlins 1985, 155), and to relate it to issues of Muslim transnationality and identity in the North American diaspora.

Music in Islam: Rules and Effects

Muslims, like Jews and Christians, consider themselves people of
the Book, and their religion is based on the ontology of the divine
Word. Though preserved in written form, the Word lives as a verbal
message emanating from God to human beings, hence its "abiding
intrinsic orality" (Graham 1987). The appropriately sounded Word
is, therefore, central to Islamic ritual observance; hence, an
exclusive and exquisite melodic-rhythmic system has been developed to sound the divine Word and articulate its distinct uniqueness,
different from any other words or music. This distinct musical form
of religious recitation stands in conceptual opposition to all non-
religious musical sounds, both vocal and, especially, instrumental.
Indeed, a theological debate continues over what is religiously
acceptable musical sound, fueled in particular by the spiritual use
of musical sounds by Islamic mystics. A copious literature on the
subject testifies to the relevance of the issue.[1]

The Greek-derived gloss, "music," is therefore religiously
inappropriate for religiously used musical sound, as is the secular
term "song/singing." The term in use since the Prophet himself is
"reading" (Arabic, *qirā'a;* Urdu, *parhna*), which also means
"reciting" or "chanting." Significantly, Muslim linguistic use does
not distinguish an oral/aural version of reading from a visual one:
to read means at the same time to articulate sound and to apprehend
meaning.[2]

---

[1] For an extensive review see Roychaudhury 1957; also see Nelson 1985 and
Seyyed Hussein Nasr's article in this volume.

[2] For a comprehensive and culturally appropriate discussion of this issue, see
Nelson 1985; see also al Faruqi 1981.

My title, then, should properly read "Chant, or Recitation, in the Life of Islam." There is clearly a conceptual contradiction between Muslim concepts and the discourse of ethnomusicologists interested in the properties, uses, and effects of musical sound wherever it is present. Equally clearly, at the level of experience and perception, Muslims respond to and culturally manage musical sound by using the religious rule system in highly complex and creative ways— ways that transcend the simple yardstick of the normative and reveal deep sensitivity for and interest in the "significant effects" of musical sound, especially in relation to the primary verbal communication. The very persistence of intense disputations about music testifies to this, as docs the central place accorded to the musical arts by the patrons and creators of Muslim high culture from Spain to Indonesia.

Whether called music or recitation, what are the significant effects of musical sound? Unlike verbal sound, musical sonority both prefigures signification and envelops it. With its powerful evocative capacity, its immediacy, and its reach, the very sound of music inexorably calls forth sensation and emotion—a response that is both physiological and affective. The aural/physical sensation of music not only activates feeling, it also activates links with others who feel. In an instant, musical sound creates bonds that are as deep and intimate as they are broad and universal. Since the ephemeral bond of sound does not commit spatially, experiencing music together leaves the personal, individual, and interior domain unviolated. Yet, at the same time, the experience becomes public, shared and exterior. Such a reification of one's feeling and sensation, in turn, endows musical sound with a social existence that we code as identity ("our" music) and with shared associations and connotations that we code as aesthetics ("art"). Underrated in musical scholarship, the social nature of musical experience is thus deeply and significantly intertwined with its personal, individual character.

An Ethnographic Approach to Islamic "Music"

If Islamic "music" is a socially as well as aesthetically grounded process, it needs to be explored as a practice, as behavior among those who create and receive it, as meaning articulated and shared, as religious life, not just religious rule. To adopt such a perspective is also to address a crucial contemporary question arising from a widely proclaimed self-definition that has penetrated public consciousness, identifying Islam as a highly universalist, global movement of assertion and conformity. This identity is projected by religious-political constituencies that identify closely with fundamental tenets of orthodox Islam, an Islam deliberately purged of place- and time-specific manifestations. Today, any discourse on Muslims inevitably comes up against such questions, raised both within and outside the Muslim milieu: What does this "fundamentalist" movement represent in the life of Islam? To what extent does it represent Muslims in actual communities? What is the status of universalist vis-à-vis local practices and, conversely, how are local differences sustained, or not sustained, in the face of an assertively global Islamist paradigm? How do Muslims live this dialectic?

Music is a deeply involving, inclusive, and non-coercive process in religious practice. Can the musical domain, so central as a focus for the fusing of emotion with cognition and of individual with shared experience, teach us about the way difference coexists with universality in the practice of Islam? And, in a more activist vein, can these qualities of music be mobilized to offer access to understanding from outside while also maintaining the integrity of those within? This capsule ethnography attempts to offer a lived instance within the complex web of cultural and ideational strands that Aziz al-Azmeh deconstructs in his masterly interpretation of contemporary Islam (al-Azmeh 1993).

To gain a sense of the concrete, let us move our focus to Pakistan, in the "ethnographic present" of 1969, where I spent one year participating in and documenting Islamic recitation.[3] Karachi, Pakistan's largest city and home to the large Urdu-speaking migrant community from India, had by then become the collective center of North Indian Muslim culture and Islamic practice.

The Word of God: Arabic Liturgical Texts

A rich and diverse soundscape of religious texts and reciting traditions forms part of the South Asian Muslim religious experience. Supreme and universal is the recitation of the Qur'an and related liturgical texts in Arabic, foremost the call to prayer (*azān/ adhān*) and prayer itself (*namāz/salāt*),[4] as well as salutations to the Prophet of God.

Example 1 is the call to prayer from a neighborhood mosque in the P.E.C.H.S. residential area of Karachi, as heard by residents over the mosque's public address system.[5] A Middle Eastern model is clearly discernible in the melodic outline and syllabic distribution of this and the myriad similar *azān* recitations.

As the chanting of sacred text in which God himself addresses believers, this tradition adheres quite closely to Arabic standards imparted at theological schools, though untrained reciters often reveal more of a South Asian tonal idiom. Qur'anic cantillation (*qir'at*) is the Islamic vocal idiom par excellence; it frames religious rituals and is performed formally in the mosque as well as informally in the home by professional reciters (*qārī*), religious functionaries, and Muslim laymen and women. The first message that reaches the ear of a newborn infant is the recitation of the Islamic creed (*kalmā*). In homes, older family members recite from the Qur'an at night or after *fajr*, the early morning prayer. But the real season of Qur'an recitation is Ramadan, the month when

[3] The financial support of the Canada Council for research conducted during 1968–69 is gratefully acknowledged.

[4] Liturgical terms are given according to Farsi-derived Pakistani usage, followed by their standard Arabic equivalents, where different.

[5] All examples are drawn from my own recordings unless otherwise indicated. The generosity of the reciters is gratefully acknowledged.

Example 1: *Azān/Adhān* (Call to Prayer)
(Karachi, P.E.C.H.S. Mosque, February 1969)

Text

Allāhu akbar (4x)
Ashhadū an lā ilāha illa 'llah (2x)
Ashhadū anna Muhammadan rasūl Allāh (2x)
Hayya 'ala 'l salāt (2x)
Hayya 'ala 'l falah (2x)
Allāhu akbar (2x)
Lā ilāha illa 'llah (2x)

Translation

God is most great
I testify that there is no god but God
I testify that Muhammad is the Messenger of God
Come to prayer
God is most great
There is no god but God
Come to salvation

Transcription

Example 1: Transcription, continued

Ashhadū an- na Muhammad- an rasūl Al- lāh ———

Hay- ya 'ala'l sa- lāt

Hay- ya 'ala'l sa- lāt

Hay- ya 'al- a'l fa- lah

Hay- ya 'al- a'l fa- lah ————————

Al- lā- hu ak- bar Al- la —————————— hu ak- bar

Ashadū an lā i- lā- ha il- la 'llah ——————

Muhammad's revelation was completed. Mosques resound with
qi'rat throughout the night as the entire Qur'an is recited as many
times as possible. Men assemble there to say the day's last prayer
(*ishā*) and take part in this continuous recitation (*tarāwīh*).

The Qur'an in its written form is, of course, present in every
Muslim's life, most commonly in the form of the Book itself and
also in the form of selected calligraphic representations. What
should be stressed is that, for Muslims, neither the Qur'anic message
nor its written representation is a locus of contemplation; these are
meant to initiate articulation and action. Engaging in such articulation and action forms the basis of individual Muslim identity;
sharing that engagement links Muslims into a community. Rituals
provide such sharing, and they make it both audible and visible to
those who partake in it, whether as participants or as observers.
Prayer, the primary ritual, is performed congregationally in the
mosque by men, but it is as much an individual observance of
recitation as a public, shared endeavor.

An ubiquitous form of individual *qir'at* is the reading of chosen
passages from the Qur'an following prayers or at any other suitable
time. Normally done silently, such recitation may also be chanted,
depending on the reciter's inclination and vocal skill. What is
essential is that uttering God's word in the Qur'an and, by extension,
in other religious texts, is an oral/aural activity, with its full
implication of internal and external participation. Words are not a
transparent conduit of meaning; their sound is deeply implicated in
the experience of their meaning. Hence, the sound of the words is
also set apart in recitation by making the words sonically appealing
(*khushilhan*, literally "well-sounding"). Recitation means making
the words one's own and making them live by actually saying them,
whether aloud or silently to oneself.

Example 2 is a Qur'anic chant by Zahir Qasmi, one of Pakistan's
best-known reciters, whose training reveals distinct Egyptian
influence. Melodious and deliberately "affecting in its beauty," this
recitation represents the performative reciting style of professional
*qārī*s. For years, Zahir Qasmi's regular early morning broadcasts of
qir'at made his recitation a daily presence in most Karachi homes.

Example 2: *Qir'at* (*Qirā'a*), Qur'anic Chant,
elaborated style (sura 96:6–10)
(early morning broadcast, Radio Pakistan, by Zahir Qasmi,
professional *qārī,* Karachi, December 1968)

Text (Arabic)

Kalla inn al insāna ley atagha
Anrā' aus taghna
Inna ilā rabbi karrujā
Ara 'ayt allazī inhā
Aba dann 'iza sallā

Translation

Nay, man is surely inordinate,
Because he looks upon himself as self-sufficient
Surely to thy Lord is the return.
Hast thou seen him who forbids
A servant when he prays?

Transcription

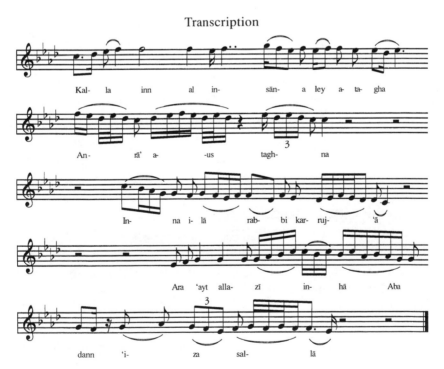

In contrast, example 3 represents an unadorned "simple" style of *qir'at* used by lay persons and also by trained reciters when reciting extended portions of the Qur'an, as during Ramadan, when this recording was made outside a Karachi mosque.

Both simple and elaborated *qir'at* styles are based on the same rules of phonetic representation of the Qur'anic text (*tajwīd*) but differ in their sonic character and function. The two styles correspond to the two contrasting recitational styles identified in Arabic usage by the public, deliberately aesthetic *mujawwad* and the private, devotional *murattal* (Nelson 1985, xxvii, xxiv), though these terms are not in use in South Asia.

Vernacular, Non-Canonical Texts

Based on the Qur'anic word and reinforced by the Persian Sufi tradition since the thirteenth century, this ideology of the sounded word also extends to vernacular religious hymns. Their principal language is Urdu and they are musically South Asian.[6] These hymns can be recited by anyone anywhere, but they are usually performed during devotional assemblies centering on principal religious figures of Islam. A lead reciter, usually with a supporting group, presents a series of hymns to an audience of devotees who respond in specific ways to the religious listening experience. The performance style of each assembly is directly linked to the function of enhancing the religious poem and of expressing the spiritual-emotional experience it evokes in the listener.

In the tradition of urban Urdu speakers, there are three distinct types of such ritual-musical events ("a formal procedure in a religious observance"): *mīlād, majlis, and samā'*. Each type is associated with a specific religious function and also with a core constituency of devotees. Each of the three is built on a repertoire of appropriate hymns with a distinct musical style that gives articulation to the identity of the ritual. At the same time, a

---

[6] Vernacular hymns exist in other Muslim regions and traditions and represent a recognized category of recitation (*talḥīn*; see Farmer 1965).

Example 3: *Qir'at (Qirā'a)*, Qur'anic Chant, simple style
(sura 18:75–77) (nightly recitation, Karachi, Ramadan 1968)

Text

Qāla alam 'aqul laka 'innaka lan tastatīa ma'iya sabrā?
Qāla 'in sa'al tuka an shain b'ad'hā falā tusa hibnī qad balaghta
   min ladunni uzrā
Fantalaqā hattā idhā 'atayā 'ahla qaryat-in'nistatama 'ahlahā. . . .

Translation

He said (to Moses): Did I not say to thee that thou couldst not
   have patience with me?
He said: If I ask thee about anything after this, keep not company with me: Then wouldst Thou have received (full) excuse
   from my side.
So they went on, until, when they came to the people of a town. . . .

Transcription

universalizing aspect in all the assemblies is their permeation with scriptural phrases and passages in Arabic, especially at the beginning and the end.

Mīlād: Assembly Celebrating the Prophet and his Birth

Most universally practised is the *mīlād*, the assembly celebrating the birth of the Prophet Muhammad. Its primary season is the month of Rabi-ul-Awwal, and the most auspicious date is the twelfth of the month, the Prophet's actual birthday. Muslims will also hold a *mīlād* to mark an auspicious event (such as moving into a new house—note figure 2), a practice held especially by the Sunni majority, although the *mīlād* is associated with all Muslims. Families host *mīlād*s in their homes. The *mīlād* is particularly a women's event; in common parlance people even call it the "womens' *qawwālī*," suggesting a parallel to the all-male assembly of Sufi hymns (see below). Among Sunnis especially, everyone is familiar with many well-known *na't* hymns and anyone can join in the *salām* or *durūd* if they feel like it. For most Muslim girls and women, such recitation is the only approved way of expressing musicality and regaling an audience with musical beauty. In fact, in Pakistan schools and colleges have a tradition of presenting impressive *mīlād*s.

The *mīlād* has a clearly delineated performance structure and sequence of sound events. A lead reciter and a small supporting group present a series of *na't,* or hymns, in praise of the Prophet. The hymns are chanted in unison, alternating with spoken prose passages that relate to the life and divine verbal mesage of the Prophet. The transition between the two is marked by a brief Arabic praise litany for the Prophet. Like all religious events the *mīlād* begins in the name of God, with a *ḥamd*, a hymn in His praise, and is sometimes preceded by a passage recited from the Qur'an. It ends with an intercessary prayer (*du'a*), followed by a silent recitation of the qur'anic *sūra-al-fatehā*. The audience listens quietly until the

Example 4: *Mīlād*: *Salām* (concluding hymn of salutation)
(private women's *mīlād* by professional reciter and group,
Karachi, Rabi-ul-Awwal 1969)

Text (Arabic)

Ya nabī salām alaikā
Ya rasūl salām alaikā
Ya habīb salām alaikā
Salawāt-ullah alaikā

Translation

O Prophet, peace be upon you
O Messenger of God, peace be upon you
O Lover of God, peace be upon you
May the blessings of God be upon you.

Transcription

final hymn, the *salām* to the Prophet, when everyone rises to a respectful standing position and joins in reciting the Arabic refrain that frames the Urdu verses.

Example 4 shows how this musically simple congregational participation in the set refrain alternates with the embellished solo version of the same melody chanted by the leader to highlight each new verse.

Musically, *mīlād* hymns evoke feelings of both devotion and exultation through their melodic simplicity and upward surge; participation in a *mīlād* conveys an experience of veneration and submission before the most exalted personage in Islam and evokes a deep affection for his humanity. The spoken narrative (*riwāyāt* or *bayān*) also embodies these sentiments when traditional reciters use a chanted delivery to set off the hallowed events surrounding the Prophet from ordinary narrative.

Example 5 offers an excerpt by one of Karachi's most valued reciters at the time; significantly, she did recitation both as a religious service and as a quasi-professional engagement. The featured episode is itself a telling instance of the overarching importance of Islam's textual Message. *Riwāyāt* recitation is usually drawn from a written compilation of prose episode and hymns,[7] but competent reciters are free to create their own texts appropriate to the occasion since, in the absence of ordained priestly authority, religious practice is validated by tradition and consensus.

Majlis: Assembly Commemorating Imam Husain and the Martyrs of Karbala

Based on the same fundamental concept and performance structure, the *majlis* is the recitational assembly to commemorate the martyrdom of Imam Husain and the tragedy of Karbala. At the heart of religious practice for Shi'a Muslims, it is performed in homes and,

---

[7] Best known and favorite among these is the *Mīlād-e-Akbar*, compiled by Khwaja Muhammad Akbar Warsi (Akbar Warsi n.d.).

Example 5: *Mīlād*: *Riwāyāt* (chanted narrative): Excerpt
(family *mīlād* by professional reciter and group, Karachi,
Rabi-ul-Awwal 1969)

Text (Urdu)

Ek martaba Hazrat Āyesha ne irshād farmāyā: Ai Madīne ke tājdār āp ko
tamām umr meṅ sab se zyāda kab taklīf pahoṅchī. . . . Yeh sun kar āp
ābdīda hogaye. Irshād farmāyā: Āyesha, tamām 'umr men mujhe ek
martaba sab se zyāda taklīf pahoṅchī. Woh is līe keh maiṅ kalām-e-Ilāhī
parh parh kar logoṅ ko sunātā thā. To ai Āyesha, ek martaba maiṅ Araboṅ
ke bāzāroṅ se guzar rahā thā. To tamām mard o aurteṅ aur bachche mil
kar mujh par pattharoṅ kī bārish parne lage. . . .

Translation

Once Hazrat Ayesha (wife of the Prophet) said: "Oh Ruler of Madina, what
has hurt you the most in your entire life?". . . . When he heard this, tears
came to his eyes and he spoke: "Ayesha, this is when I was hurt most of
all: Once I was reciting the Word of God to the people in the bazaars of
Arabia. Then, oh Ayesha, all the men, women, and children started
throwing stones at me." . . .

Example 5: Transcription

Ek martaba haz- rat e Āyesha ne irshād farmā- yā

Ai Madīne ke tājdār, āp ko tamām umar men sab se zyāda

kab tak- līf pahonchī Yeh sun kar āp āb- dī- da ho- ga-

ye Irshād farmā- yā Āyesha tamām umar men mujhe ek

mart- tā- ba sab se zyā- da taklīf pahonchi Woh is liye keh main

kalām- e- Ilā- hi parh parh kar logon ko su- nā- tā thā

To ai Āyesha ek mar- ta- ba main A- ra- bon ke baza- ron

se guzar rahā thā To tamām mard- o- aurten aur

bachche mil kar mujh par patt haron kī bārish parhe lage ———

more prominently, in *imāmbārā*s,[8] buildings that serve as Shi'a religious centers. *Majlis* assemblies constitute the primary religious observance during the month of Muharram, marking especially each of the first ten days that culminate in Husain's martyrdom on the tenth of Muharram (*āshūra*). *Majlis* are also performed on other significant days throughout the year and for personal spiritual benefit.

Diverse hymns that express all spiritual and emotional facets of mourning, devotion, and remembrance are gathered together in a sequence that takes the listener from hymns expressing introspective personal grief, through dramatic narrative poetry and a sermon, to fervent communal mourning which is marked by intense participation through *mātam*, the beating of the chest in mourning. Musically, *majlis* hymns range widely from ornate, raga-based solo hymns chanted by trained performers to simple folk hymns recited responsorially to the pulse of breast-beating.

The event opens with *soz* and *salām*, the art genres of *majlis* hymns. These short, intensely focused poems with an expressively ornate melody have traditionally been the domain of *sozkhwān*, *soz* reciters with training in raga music. The accompanists support the solo melody with a vocal drone that is clearly an acceptable substitute for the drone instrument of raga music.

Example 6 is a moving elegy rendered by one of Karachi's favorite professional reciters of *majlis* who may also be heard on the radio during Muharram. A simple text is set to an expressively rendered melody drawn from raga *khamāj*.

Following the *soz* are the more narrative hymns' *salām* and *marsiya*. These precede a dramatic sermon which recreates the tragic drama of Karbala. Next, the chanting of simple *nauha* laments brings the articulation of grief directly to the audience, as the music emulates weeping. At last, the reciters intone the final *mātam* hymns, and all stand up to participate in the breast-beating that punctuates the recitation and culminates in fervent calls to the martyrs.

---

[8] Also termed *imāmbārgah*.

Example 6: *Majlis*: *Soz* (elegy based on raga *khamāj*, with drone)
(private men's *majlis*/broadcast, Radio Pakistan, by Akhtar Vasi Ali,
professional *sozkhwān*, Karachi, Muharram 1969)

Text (Urdu)

Kahtī thīṅ Bano: Asghar jānī kab tum ghar men āoge?
Daryā par se pī kar pānī, kab tum ghar men āoge?
Apnī dikhāne shakl-e-nūranī, kab tum ghar men āoge?
Ran se mere Yūsuf-e-sānī, kab tum ghar meṅ āoge?
Sog men tere ham ne pyāre pahni kālī kafnī hai
Bhūre bāloṅwāle ājā, jhūlā tera khālī hai
Kahtī thīṅ Bano

Translation

Said Bano (Husain's wife) "Darling Asghar, when will you come home?
You went to drink water from the river, when will you come home?
To show me your radiant face, when will you come home?
From the war, my second Joseph,[9] when will you come home?
In my grief for you, dearest, I have put on black clothes of mourning;
Come, my fair-haired one, your cradle is empty,"
Said Bano.

[9] To Muslims, the Joseph of the Old Testament was renowned for his beauty.

Example 6: Transcription

Kahtī   thin Ba-   no   As- ghar pya ———

——————————— re   kab tum   ghar

men   ā ——————————— o- ge

Daryā   par se   pī   kar pā ——————————————

— nī   kab   tum   ghar   men

ā ——————————— o- ge

Ap- ni ————————— dikhā-   ne   shakl- e-

nū- ra-   nī   kab tum

Example 7 shows a well-known *mātam* hymn sung responsorially between the leader and accompanists of the reciting group. All participants accompany the chanting with rhythmic breast-beating which continues during the subsequent calls to Husain and to Hazrat Ali, the Prophet's son-in-law and father of Husain.

Like the *mīlād*, the *majlis* ends with a salutation, this time in Arabic and recited as a solo. It is followed by a qur'anic passage, while all participants remain standing in reverence.

Majlis music, in reinforcing the strongly emotional message of the text, creates for listeners a deep involvement in suffering that is both universal and deeply personal. It also, through the coordinated movement of breast-beating, creates a participatory bond among Shi'as which other Muslims who attend may not share. That bond is publicly articulated in *mātam* processions during Muharram. In the broadest sense, *majlis* hymns constitute a repository of Shi'a heritage, interpretation, and sentiment which their recitation brings to life for the community.

Samā' Associated with Sufi Practice

Expressly designated an "assembly for listening," *samā'* (Arabic, listening), or *qawwālī*, employs mystical poetry set to music as an essential means of reaching a state of ecstatic communion with God. For this purpose musical delivery of Sufi poems is improvisational, responding to the listeners' spiritual needs of the moment. A strong rhythm of drum beats and clapping articulates the incessant repetition of God's name in *zikr*. But the use of instrumental accompaniment (*dholak*, or drum, and harmonium) and an unorthodox emphasis on cultivating emotion have always rendered *qawwālī* hymns religiously controversial, even among some Sufi orders. Performers are highly skilled hereditary professionals, related to classical musicians.

Samā' is an intimate, spiritual experience among a brotherly circle of Sufi disciples; it is also the most public and institutionalized of the recitational assemblies. *Qawwālī* events are held

Example 7: *Majlis*: *Mātam* (hymn of mourning with breast-beating)
(*majlis* at P.E.C.H.S. Women's *imāmbārā* by amateur reciters
and congregation, Karachi, Muharram 1969)

Text (Urdu)

Lāj dulārā Zahrā kā zakhmī hai aur pyāsā hai
Būnd nahīn' hai pānī kā, khūn ka daryā bahtā hai
Getī ūnchī hotī hai, girne na degī ghore se, hae
Apnī god men lelegī, kis kī god men pālā hai

Responsorial Calls:

Husain Husain
Alī Maulā, Hyder Maulā

Translation

(Husain), the most beloved son of Zehra (Fatima) is mortally
    wounded and thirsty
There is not a drop of water, but a river of blood is flowing
The earth rises, she will not let let him fall from his horse
She will receive him in her arms; after all, in whose (exalted)
    arms has he been raised?

Example 7: Transcription

throughout the year, both among exclusive spiritual groups in any location and at shrines before large public audiences. The principal occasions are the anniversaries of the numerous Sufi saints, especially of the great *Chishtī* and *Qādrī* founders of Indic Sufism. A succession of powerful and moving hymns are drawn from a diverse repertoire that includes venerable foundational poetry in classical Persian and Hindi and also in contemporary Urdu. *Qawwālī* texts emphasize and evoke mystical love; they also extol the hierarchy of Sufi spiritual personages from sheikh and saints to Hazrat Ali and the Prophet Muhammad.

Example 8 is a well-known *qawwālī* hymn extolling the Prophet Muhammad. Skillfully wrought to include Arabic epithets of the Prophet, the Urdu verses are effectively set to a rhythmically intense realization of the poetic meter. This rendition was widely disseminated on the Sabri Brothers' first and most famous LP record; it reflects their recitation of this song across Sufi assemblies of Karachi.

A men's event, *qawwālī* is widely attended by non-Muslim Sufis and even by non-Sufis. At the same time *qawwālī*, along with participation in Sufism itself, is quite marginal in the religious life of the vast majority of urban South Asian Muslims. Today, the music is developing into a secular concert genre in Pakistan, somewhat akin to concerts of religious compositions in the West. What is remarkable is that, even on the stage, essentially traditional Sufi musicians, like the Sabri Brothers and now Nusrat Fateh Ali, retain their spiritual repertoire and performance style.

An Islamic Soundscape

Recitation offers a diverse set of contexts and genres as well as a varied annual calendar for experiencing religious words. Recitational assemblies in particular also offer a choice for the audience to join in without actively participating; this allows the assemblies to be open to participants from anywhere within the faith and even from outside it. By their attendance, outsiders show their respect

Example 8: *Samā': Qawwālī*
('*urs* [anniversary] of Gudri Shah, by Ghulam Farid Sabri and group,
Karachi, April 1969; also his first LP, 1968: LKCA 2000)

Text (Urdu)

Sar-e-lāmakāṅ se talab huī
Sūe muntahā woh chale nabī
Koi had hai un ke urūj kī
[Arabic] Balaghal ulā ba kamālehī

Translation

A call came from the threshold of the Almighty,
And the Prophet rose toward the Infinite
Is there any limit to his exaltation?
He attained the height of eminence by his perfection

Transcription

Example 8: Transcription, continued

for and support of other traditions; pluralism thereby becomes institutionalized. This is most strongly so in the case of the publicly held Sufi *qawwālī,* through which Muslims in South Asia have been sharing the Word with their neighbors and co-citizens of other religions.

The recitational soundscape of recitational assemblies also articulates community of language and social group, and it makes room for individual voices. Floating above all these voices, yet inseparably joined with them, is the universal sound of scriptural recitation. Through the call to prayer and *qir'at* from mosques within each neighborhood, the canonical grid of prayers and of time-determined duties—such as fasting during Ramadan—is inserted into daily Muslim experience intertwined with the uniquely scheduled sound events of *mīlād, majlis,* and *qawwālī.*

This multiple soundscape of South Asian Islam is echoed back and further amplified by media technology, but not without being filtered, aesthetically as well as politically. For decades the state radio has reinforced the sonic experience of religious recitation, starting with early morning *qir'at,* Friday *qawwālī,* and appropriate hymns for Rabi-ul-Awwal and Muharram—exclusively so in Pakistan and sharing broadcast time with other religions in India. In Pakistan, first radio and now television patronage—including daily televised calls to prayer—have significantly contributed to the fame of artist reciters, amplified incrementally by the incredible proliferation of religious cassette recordings in both India and Pakistan. To exemplify this dimension, recording technology is represented here by the examples of two radio broadcasts (examples 2 and 6) and an LP (example 8).

Altogether, the sound of recited Islamic words envelops the individual and punctuates daily life, creating a sonic identity for those who share this tradition. It is a highly portable identity, rooted not in Islamic institutions or buildings but in the Muslim participants themselves.

The Canadian Diaspora: Assemblies Sounded and Silent

What happens to this sonic identity in the North American environment? Moving away from the "ethnographic present" to the actual present a quarter of a century later, we find a growing community of Urdu-speaking Muslims in Canadian cities like Edmonton and Calgary (and in cities in the United States). The recitational traditions that the members of this community have brought with them have become an important focus in the task of situating private lives, defining community, and negotiating interaction with the Western public domain.

South Asian Muslims have been creating their community from the inside out. Family, ties among women and among men, generational ties between adults, their children, and their parents, ties of friendship between families from the same home region—all these add up to a family's "circle." The life of the many such personal networks from South Asia revolves around weekend socializing in each other's homes over a meal, usually dinner.

Recitational assemblies are embedded within this social pattern of family and personal interaction carried out through hospitality. While they follow the format of the devotional assembly of the homeland, in Canada they always conclude with a shared meal and with informal socializing. *Mīlād* and *majlis* assemblies have been held from the outset and are now well established as standard religious practice in Canada. Both are family based and are organized by women. Reciters are drawn from one's personal circle—anyone who is competent and confident and willing to contribute—since experts who offer recitation as a service are not often found in the immigrant community. Figure 1 shows such a reciting group led by the hostess of the *mīlād,* while figure 2 shows a *mīlād* audience of women from several families.

Of the three types of assemblies, the all-male *qawwālī* does not fit into the Canadian pattern of Muslim living, nor does much Sufi patronage exist among individuals. Above all, there are no per-

Figure 1: *Mīlād* Reciting group of hostess and her friends
(*mīlād* for circle of family/friends, Edmonton, Canada,
Rabi-ul-Awwal 1987)

Figure 2: *Mīlād* Audience of family groups
(first *mīlād* in a new home, Edmonton, Canada,
Rabi-ul-Awwal 1992)

forming groups with the special competence to present Sufi hymns. Some committed Sufis do hold assemblies for the common recitation of *zikr*, but they do so with some circumspection as to participants, since a majority of the middle-class South Asian Muslims do not really approve of this emotionally charged practice.

In recent years, two other recitational assemblies have become widely practiced. Both are based on qur'anic words. More significantly, neither assembly involves a voiced performance of those words. Instead, everyone present shares equally and individually in a major task of recitation: the complete text of the Qur'an at the *qur'ānkhwānī* (Qur'an recital) and 125,000 utterances of a specified qur'anic verse at the *āyat-e-karīmā* (Verse of Mercy). Both recitational events are convened to invoke blessings and benefice. Most important is *qur'ānkhwānī*, which is also traditionally recited upon the death of a family member. In both assemblies, the total text is divided up between individual participants who recite individually, silently, and simultaneously until the task is complete. Then, as in the *mīlād* or *majlis,* a time of socializing follows.

These recitational assemblies, whether performative and musical or participational and silent, add a dimension of manifest mutual support within the strongly family-based social world of immigrant South Asian Muslims. By invoking shared ways of articulating religious words, they also invoke shared means of coping with present-day life situations.

From Home to Mosque: Muslim Self-Definition in the Public Sphere

What strikes one in considering this shared religious life among immigrants is its essentially private, personal, and deeply conservative nature. Recitational practice, as we have seen, is deeply intertwined with the intensification and grounding of the domestic sphere. But the Muslim sense of community and, even more so, the sense of religious identity have increasingly been extending beyond the home. Today, the mosque is also the place where South Asian

Muslims are negotiating a communal identity.[10] This development is, of course, predicated on the presence of a South Asian community mosque. Within the last fifteen years, an increasing number of mosques has been built across North America through community effort and supported by funds from Muslim countries, mainly Saudi Arabia, Egypt, and Libya.

As in the South Asian experience, the mosque is primarily the locus of canonical prayer and Qur'an recitation: congregational prayers are held on Friday and also on Sunday, since it is the universally available holiday; *qir'at* recitation is carried out principally during Ramadan, when men repair to the mosque for *tarawih* recitation after breaking the fast at sunset. There are, however, obvious limits to creating a public Islamic soundscape in the West. When the Edmonton South Asian mosque was built, the imam initiated calling for prayer outside, but neighborhood complaints soon caused him to discontinue this public *adhān*.

There is another, uniquely North American, level of involvement in mosque activity: the participation of women in religious events at the mosque. The significance of this trend becomes obvious if one considers comparatively such centers of minority Muslim worship as the South Asian Shi'a *imāmbārā* (or *imāmbārgah*) or, even more so, the Isma'ili *jama'tkhāna* where women, and with them children, participate in complementary roles as fully as do men; for these Muslims, their centers have become truly community spaces.

Like *majlis* recitation in the *imāmbārā* among Shi'as, the Sunni trend today is toward holding recitational assemblies in the mosque as the locus of Muslim community activity. Most obvious are *qur'ānkhwānī* and *āyat-e-karīmā*, for, as recitation of the divine Word, they may be held in the mosque proper. Men recite in the main prayer area, whereas women do so upstairs in an enclosed balcony assigned exclusively to them. The non-canonical, vernacular

---

[10] In Edmonton, as elsewhere in Canada and the United States, such support includes mosque construction and supplying a trained imam as mosque functionary.

mīlād, on the other hand, can only be held in the basement of the mosque.

What stands out is that women are involved in managing all these assemblies, even those held in the mosque, because they invariably include a shared meal that requires organization and collaboration. Thus, even the mosque assemblies become social events linked to personal circles of linked friends and families. The mosque, however, is also the primary locus of control in the name of Islamic fundamentals: imams and mosque committees enforce strict segregation of the sexes even in the basement, do not grant permission for certain secular activities, and certainly allow no instrumental music.

It appears, then, that the North American mosque is becoming the site where recitational assemblies serve to contribute to an expanded sense of local community while also becoming a touchstone of universalist orthodox ideology. At the same time, recitational practice appears to be shifting away from the traditions particular to that community. What is the multiple dynamic behind the movement toward the increased prevalence of the participatory, soundless, leaderless gathering of Arabic recitation over the nearly three decades of the community's existence in Canada? Is it the silencing of a particularistic, "local" Muslim voice—what Derek Sayer evocatively terms the "violence of abstraction" (1987)?

That there is a growing preference for *qur'ānkhwānī* not only in North America but also in Pakistan probably does reflect the impact of the pan-Islamic movement. There are other factors, however. An occasional obstacle to holding a *mīlād* is the lack of performance resources resulting from the truncated social group of middle- and upper-class South Asian immigrants from which traditional service professions are conspicuously absent.

More salient is the fact that the assembly of collaborative recitation reflects the North American reality of a voluntary association between individuals who share a bond of religion and community but otherwise live autonomously; this bond, therefore, is activated solely by mutual goodwill, leaving behind the ties of dominance and dependence which characterized social relationships

in the South Asian homelands. The *qur'ānkhwānī* accurately
represents this reality, where each voice speaks independently and
no one voice predominates. This contrasts clearly with the *mīlād*
model which projects dominance and submission between reciters
and listeners and among reciters as well; its ordered recitational
sequence also projects a temporal-spatial coordination within the
group.

Faisal Ali Devji has argued for nineteenth-century India that the
public domain ceased to be Muslim under British rule (Devji 1991);
hence, a shift took place toward making the home the locus of
Islamic life, and women, rather than men, became the repository
of Islamic identity. Along with a thrust toward women's religious
education, the traditional predominance of women in creating the
life of religious assemblies in India and Pakistan offers clear
evidence of practice for this interpretation. Extending that premise
to the public sphere in North America, the first generation's response
has been to activate the same pattern of focusing religious life in
the home.

Today, after a generation of residence in America, Muslims are
beginning to engage more specifically with their particular reality
in North American public space. The issue of public self-representation thus assumes greater priority. Islamicists, especially through
the organs of the Islamic Society of North America,[11] offer a model
of self-representation that is adapted to existing within and also
challenging the Western world order, but it is an exclusive model
that requires conformity. Many South Asian Muslims are moving
toward an exclusive Islamic universalism, both publicly and
privately. At the same time, others continue to build identity by
creating an inclusive sound world of recitation that allows pluralism
while solidly grounding their expression of identity in the Word of
Islam. Yet others patronize recitational events in South Asia or invite
reciters to North America as part of a transnational lifestyle that is
fairly common among prosperous professional immigrants today.

[11] The ISNA, formerly the Muslim Students Association, has long been strongly
supported by Saudi Arabia and still directs most of its energy toward students
and especially to university campuses.

For a religious self-articulation based on sounding the word, the issue does arise of how Muslims situate themselves within the Western public domain where the soundscape is not only secular but filled with ubiquitous background sounds that do not mean to represent anyone or to engage the listener. Using the traditional means of public self-representation by sounding the word in public is impossible. This became drastically obvious when the first imam of the Pakistani mosque in Edmonton recited the call for prayer and neighbors complained to the police.

One general representational trend fostered by the Islamist movement, and clearly adapted to the visually oriented public sphere of the West, is to choose visual ways of making Islam present, above all through "Islamic" head covering for women but also through the display of Islamic words via their written representation. Among urban South Asian Muslims in Canada, and to an extent also in South Asia, Islamic words in their visual form are playing an increasing part in articulating Islamic identity, though less so in the public than in the personal and domestic spheres. Pendants with Islamic inscriptions have become common, especially among second-generation Muslims, as personal statements, independent of clothing style. But most prominent in this development are visible displays of qur'anic words in Muslim homes. Verses, phrases, and divine names are displayed in both decorative and didactic forms, serving not only to articulate but also to teach Islamic words to the children of the house. Figures 3 and 4, both in a Calgary home, exemplify the two forms: the first is an artistically painted *sūra-al-rahmān* in a living room; the second is the *kalmā* (creed) affixed to the refrigerator.

Words in writing, words recited without sound—is the voice of recitation about to be silenced? Not likely, because traditional "musical" recitation continues to be practiced side by side with silent recitation. The devotional assembly, a uniquely South Asian tradition of Muslim recitation, offers a highly effective model for sharing a sound message that has been generically termed "cultural performance" (Singer 1974). Not only in homes but even on the world stage, Muslim religious texts continue today to be heard

Figure 3: Qur'anic Word in the home
(*sūra-al-rahmān*, painting in family room, Calgary, Canada, 1992)

Figure 4: Qur'anic Word in the home
(*kalmā* on refrigerator transfer, kitchen, Calgary, Canada, 1992)

through this model. One need but point to the unadulterated *qawwālī* hymns that have been spread internationally by the great Pakistani *qawwāl,* Nusrat Fateh Ali.

Finally, even silent recitation is an oral articulation of words, set within that same context of the devotional assembly. It remains to be seen how the second generation, further removed from South Asian models and language skills, will deal with their particular recitational heritage; but given the emotional and spiritual and social power of the recitational world of their families, "sounding the word" is, and will continue to be, meaningful to their experience of Islam. Responding to particular conditions, Muslims in both Canada and South Asia will continue to create their religious experience through the words of the Islamic message, retaining the richness and challenge of a culturally particular, yet universally framed and connected religious practice.

References

Abu-Lughod, J.
  1989   *Before European Hegemony: The World System A.D. 1250–1350*. New York: Oxford University Press.
Akbar Warsi, Khwaja Muhammad
  n.d.   *Milad-e-Akbar*. Delhi: Ratan and Co.
al-Azmeh, Aziz
  1993   *Islams and Modernities*. London: Verso.
Devji, Faisal Fatehali
  1991   "Gender and the Politics of Space: The Movement for Women's Reform in Muslim India 1857–1900." In *Aspects of the Public in Colonial South Asia*, ed. Sandria Freitag. *South Asia* (n. s.) 24(1):141–54.
Farmer, Henry George
  1965   "Ghina." In *Encyclopedia of Islam*, ed. B. Lewis, Ch. Pellat, and J. Schacht, vol. 2, pp. 1072–75, 2nd ed. Leiden: Brill.
al Faruqi, Lois Ibsen
  1981   *An Annotated Glossary of Arabic Musical Terms*. Westport, Conn.: Greenwood Press.
Graham, William A.
  1987   *Beyond the Written Word: Oral Aspects of Scripture in the History of Religion*. Cambridge: Cambridge University Press.
Nelson, Kristina
  1985   *The Art of Reciting the Qur'an*. Austin: University of Texas Press.
Roychaudhury, M. L.
  1957   "Music in Islam." *Journal of the Asiatic Society of Bengal: Letters* 13:43–102.
Sahlins, Marshall
  1985   *Islands of History*. Chicago: Chicago University Press.
Sayer, Derek
  1987   *The Violence of Abstraction: The Analytic Foundations of Historical Materialism*. Oxford: Blackwell.
Singer, Milton
  1974   *When a Great Tradition Modernizes*. Chicago: Chicago University Press.

Mythologies and Realities
in the Study of Jewish Music

Kay Kaufman Shelemay

Jewish music, like all topics having to do with Jewish history and culture, is virtually without boundaries in time or space. In time, Jewish music spans a period from biblical days to the present. In terms of space, it stretches from the Middle East in its broadest sense to Europe, the Americas, and parts of Asia and Africa as well. What is remarkable in the face of this extraordinary historical and geographical spread is that a critical core of Jewish literary output, philosophy, and ritual has survived universally and has throughout history been transmitted relatively intact wherever Jews have lived. But can one really anticipate musical continuity as well? Why would one expect that there be a "Jewish music," given the varied history of different communities in the Jewish Diaspora?

Needless to say, I am not the first to stress the wide range of musical practices among Jewish communities. Virtually everyone who has studied Jewish music has been struck by its diversity. First and foremost among these observers was the "father of Jewish music research" (Adler, Bayer, and Schleifer 1986, 11), Abraham Zvi Idelsohn, who was born into an observant Jewish family in Latvia in 1882.[1] Idelsohn was both a cantor and a scholar trained at music conservatories in Berlin and Leipzig. Preoccupied with the idea of

---

[1] Biographical information about Idelsohn presented here has been taken from Idelsohn's autobiographical article 1986 (1935) and Schleifer 1986. I will not here dwell on inconsistencies in dating, raised by Schleifer, op cit.

studying "Jewish song," Idelsohn went to Jerusalem in 1906 to study Jewish music and was immediately struck by the diversity he encountered: "In Jerusalem I found about 300 synagogues. . . . The various synagogues were conducted according to the customs of the respective countries, and their traditional song varied greatly from one another" (Idelsohn 1986 [1935], 21).

Yet, despite his description of differences in liturgical music among Jewish communities of his period, and his acknowledgment that Jewish song incorporates non-Jewish elements (Idelsohn 1986 [1935], 21), Idelsohn insisted that ". . .the Jewish elements are found in all traditions, and only these are of interest to the scholars" (Idelsohn 1986 [1935], 21). Idelsohn sought to demonstrate, through recordings, transcription, and analysis, that an essential continuity was present.

I begin with the example of Idelsohn and his work because I believe that it demonstrates a central paradox in the understanding of Jewish music initially established by scholars and perpetuated in popular imagination. While Idelsohn perceived and acknowledged diversity as the reality in Jewish musical practice, he spent his entire career seeking to document commonalities that he believed existed within divergent musical traditions.

This paradox or contradiction between mythologies[2] and realities arises first and foremost, it appears, because of the history of scholarship in Jewish studies and, secondarily, because of the background of the individuals who have studied Jewish tradition. Modern studies of all aspects of Jewish religious and cultural tradition date to the 1820s in Berlin, where a group of intellectuals launched a movement called the "science of Judaism" (*Wissenschaft*

---

[2] I use the term mythology in a manner similar to that of historian William McNeill, who writes that mythology and history are "close kin inasmuch as both explain how things got to be the way they are by telling some sort of story" (1986, 3). In this context, mythologies refer to shared truths that grow out of social experience and that have been transmitted over time. I am furthermore interested in the relationship between mythology and reality, that is, in exploring the interaction between what McNeill has called "myth making" and "myth breaking."

des Judentums), a field concerned with the analysis of written texts.[3] Scholars were concerned with applying modern research methods and with editing critically the biblical and rabbinic literature (Hoffman 1979, 1).

In addition to their concern with texts, these early scholars of Judaica were united by a shared characteristic: they were almost without exception Jews. Most were first trained in traditional settings in their own communities and then later exposed to academic studies in German universities. Therefore, out of the nineteenth century came an academic study of Judaism which was, on the one hand, explicitly interested in documenting surviving texts in relation to prior tradition, and, on the other, carried out by individuals emotionally committed to that study.[4] Thus, scholarly goals were combined with a strong personal commitment to the tradition studied and a desire to establish beyond all doubt its authenticity and antiquity

These same perspectives are reflected in Idelsohn's work, as well as in many scholarly publications on Jewish music written before the last decade.[5] For example, one writer asserts that "Jewish musical life. . .yields a composite picture of convincing force, showing an unbroken chain" (Sendrey 1970, 23), concluding in a later passage that "just as most of the religious and secular institutions of the Hebrews were of foreign origin, adjusted to suit their own national needs, so their music, though greatly influenced by that of the environment, preserved obvious Jewish traits" (Sendrey 1970, 420).

---

[3] For further information on the history of this movement, see "Wissenschaft" 1972.

[4] With a few notable exceptions, the study of Jewish music has continued to be largely an "insider" enterprise, a factor that certainly contributed to the maintenance of the mythology of continuity into scholarship of the mid-twentieth century.

[5] See Adler 1982 and Shiloah 1992, 21–26 for critical discussions of the issues surrounding the preoccupation with a "common source" for Jewish music. Shiloah suggests that Idelsohn's perspective was shaped by the scholarship of Christian researchers "searching for the roots of ancient Christian music" (Shiloah 1992, 26).

These attitudes have resonated outside the academy, resulting in a well-established mythology of a Jewish music tradition made of whole cloth, rather than the patchwork one actually encounters. Thus, the modern ethnomusicologist studying aspects of Jewish musical traditions encounters the same dilemma sketched by historian Yosef Yerushalmi, who describes "a Jewish historiography divorced from Jewish collective memory, and in crucial respects, thoroughly at odds with it" (Yerushalmi 1989 [1982], 93). The historian is expected to "act under a moral pressure to restore a nation's memory. . . ," while in reality memory and modern historiography stand in "radically different relations to the past" (Yerushalmi 1989 [1982], 93–94). The same situation pertains in relation to attitudes toward music in Jewish religious life and practice, where myths of continuity are necessarily disputed by scholarly scrutiny of the reality of change.

Issues in Jewish Music Scholarship: Borrowings and Authenticity

If any characteristic of Jewish secular and liturgical music repertories challenges the myth of continuity in Jewish music, it is the widespread presence of contrafacta, pre-existent melodies borrowed from outside the Jewish cultural orbit.[6] One particularly striking example is that provided by Hasidic tradition, where performance of a song is believed to be one of the most effective vehicles for achieving what is termed *devekuth* (literally, "adhesion" [of the soul to God]), an ecstatic experience through which one receives divine knowledge. The singing of wordless melodies (*nigunim*) is an integral part of Hasidic religious experience: the songs are sung during prayer, at meals, at weddings, gatherings, and holidays. Most of the melodies are borrowed from preexisting songs, since a melody

---

[6] Borrowings also took place between repertories *within* Jewish tradition, for example, the appropriation of Judeo-Spanish song melodies to set statutory prayers in the liturgy. See Avenary 1960 and Seroussi and Weich-Shahak 1990–91.

of any origin can be borrowed and used, sacralizing it in the process (Koskoff 1978, 157).

In her study of the Lubavitcher Hasidic movement in Brooklyn, New York, ethnomusicologist Ellen Koskoff has documented the usage of a number of colorful contrafacta, including use of a commercial ditty of the Pepsi-Cola Company, "There's a Whole New Way of Livin' " (Koskoff 1978, 173). This Lubavitcher *nigun* provides a fine example of this most common process in the music history of all Jewish communities—borrowing both the general musical styles and even specific melodies of peoples among whom they live. Secondly, it shows how materials that are borrowed can become "traditional" over time and set styles for subsequent generations. In fact, individuals today composing in the Brooklyn Lubavitcher community generally do one of two things: they may compose original melodies which in some way resemble "old" Lubavitcher tradition, or they may borrow melodies or certain stylistic features from current musical traditions of their "host" society (Koskoff 1978, 158). The Lubavitcher example therefore demonstrates the manner in which a Jewish community intentionally draws upon the broader musical world surrounding it and how that music, originally borrowed, can itself become an "authentic" part of Jewish tradition for years to come.

One can look at the music of virtually any Jewish community and find similar examples of borrowing and adaptation of local musical style. To take an example from the Sephardic orbit, Syrian Jews living in Israel and the Americas borrow popular Arabic melodies to set newly composed Hebrew texts for songs (*pizmonim*) sung on a variety of liturgical, paraliturgical, and social occasions (Shelemay and Weiss 1985). The Syrian case tells a story similar to that of the Lubavitcher Hasidic tradition: first, music is borrowed from the environment in which Jews live,[7] reflecting changing influences over time; and second, borrowed music becomes a traditional and fully accepted part of Jewish religious and social life.

---

[7] Sound recordings also provide a venue through which music can continue to be borrowed from locales in which a community lived in the past. Syrian Jews

Jewish Musical Studies: Some Methodological Considerations

To return to the comparison of the study of Jewish texts with those of Jewish music, the search for authenticity and antiquity was far easier to accomplish with the textual study of Jewish liturgy and literature. The task has been complicated for scholars of Jewish music, who, while working within an intellectual framework and emotional environment that sought to document continuity, were constantly confronting evidence of diversity and change. To explore more fully the methodological implication of this position, it is useful to survey the scholarly study of the Judeo-Spanish ballad.

When the Jews were expelled from Spain in 1492, they left the Iberian peninsula in many directions and established new communities elsewhere in Europe, throughout the Mediterranean, and the Americas. They took very little with them in the way of material possessions. Luckily, song is carried in the memory, not an incidental factor in the powerful survival of song traditions among Sephardic Jews.

In order to discuss the Sephardic musical tradition and its survival in the various countries of relocation, it has generally been the practice to start at the beginning, to recount the departure from Spain in the late fifteenth and early sixteenth centuries and to trace the course of a song's history from that point in the past until the present. However, in fact the data suggest the need to do just the opposite: to begin with the present and make excursions backward in time. This approach is necessary both to gain insight into the nature of the musical materials and to correct some of the myths surrounding them.

Although it is certain that ballads were actively sung and

---

in the Americas, for example, have depended almost exclusively upon recordings of Arabic music to "refresh" their musical repertories since their departure from Syria in the first decades of the twentieth century. Scholarly recordings, including those preserved in archives and published in the last quarter century, have served as sources for repertory performed and re-recorded by professionals.

transmitted within Sephardic families over the course of centuries, little documentary evidence exists concerning their content and performance prior to or following the departure from Spain. Most of the Sephardic song texts and virtually all of their melodies were carried exclusively in the oral tradition; there was little internal motivation or outside interest in committing the songs to writing until the current century.[8] Thus, documentary evidence from the past is painfully thin. What we are able to recount of the history of Sephardic music must be reconstructed almost exclusively from the surviving songs and from the networks of tradition surrounding their transmission by twentieth-century descendants of the Spanish-Jewish exiles.

By the early twentieth century, Spanish literary scholars had become aware that songs no longer extant on the Iberian peninsula itself were perpetuated abroad in the oral traditions of Sephardic Jews.[9] Of particular interest were the narrative ballads, called *romances*, still sung in Judeo-Spanish dialects by Sephardic Jews in the scattered locales in which they lived. Comparisons of these orally transmitted ballad texts with those found in early written Spanish sources show striking degrees of correspondence between the two repertories after more than four hundred years of separation.[10] Thus the initial interest in Sephardic songs was primarily

[8] The situation was somewhat different in relation to sacred song texts in Hebrew, which were written down, sometimes with indications of popular melodies to which they were to be sung. The most notable early example was Israel Najara's "*Zemiroth Yisrael*," a songster first printed in Safed in 1587 (see Seroussi 1990, Yahalom 1982). Judeo-Spanish song tests were not included in such sources, although some of their melodies were borrowed to set the Hebrew hymns (*piyyutim*). In 1922 Yacob Abraham Yona, a Sephardic Jew who lived for most of his life in Salonika, Greece, distributed chapbooks containing texts of popular Judeo-Spanish ballads along with his own original compositions. Yona's ballad collections have been edited and published in Armistead and Silverman 1971.

[9] The major early research in this area was carried out by Ramón Menéndez Pidal, discussed in Katz (1972, 21–24, 31–34).

[10] The broader issue of concordances between modern orally transmitted ballad texts and medieval Spanish models is a complex one and is discussed at length in Armistead and Silverman 1986.

focused on the texts of the ballads and their relationship to medieval song repertories no longer extant in Spain itself.

These studies raised considerable interest in what had been, before that point, simply an obscure ethnic song tradition little known outside the Sephardic community itself. However, early scholars approached the songs almost exclusively as a residue of the past, largely ignoring the impact of cultural traditions from the countries of relocation as well as the active roles of these songs in everyday life. Secondly, scholarly fascination with the ballad, given the possibility of comparing it with extant Spanish written sources, led to the neglect of other equally important Sephardic song repertories, both in Judeo-Spanish dialects and in Hebrew. But most problematically for our discussion here, it was assumed that the strong Spanish concordances with ballad texts also extended to their melodies. Thus, as early scholars documented the Sephardic song tradition, their work resulted in the popular perception of the Sephardic song tradition as a conservative one, consisting primarily of ballads perpetuating texts and tunes that had changed little since the fifteenth century.

In fact, the scholarly study of Sephardic song during the second half of the twentieth century has gained momentum and has sought to dispel many of the above preconceptions.[11] The availability of portable sound recording equipment provided many new insights, for it made it possible to record systematically the complete song repertories of individual Sephardic Jews where they lived. Editions of Sephardic songs multiplied,[12] serving to document surviving songs and to make possible comparative studies of multiple versions. An unanticipated consequence was the role of the editions in reinvigorating transmission of the songs both within and outside of Sephardic communities, a factor that served to embed mythol-

---

[11] See, for example, Shiloah and Cohen 1983 and Seroussi 1993.

[12] The first publication of a Sephardic ballad with musical notation dates from the end of the nineteenth century. For a detailed, critical discussion of the numerous editions of Sephardic ballads containing transcriptions from the oral tradition, see Katz 1972, 20–124.

ogies of continuity among both audiences and performers. This issue will be discussed further below.

Other factors, too, shaped reception of the Judeo-Spanish ballad repertories outside of scholarly circles. By the late 1960s, both recording and publication activities had become extremely urgent. European and Balkan Sephardic communities had been largely destroyed during the Holocaust, and their survivors had been forced to relocate yet again, primarily to Israel and to different urban centers in the Americas. The study of Sephardic music in the late twentieth century became in many cases an attempt to document songs whose longtime transmission had been abruptly halted along with the life of whole communities by whom they had been sung. Additionally, Sephardic communities which had for centuries existed in the Arab world had, by the 1960s, been for nearly two decades resettled in Israel, where many different regional Sephardic styles were beginning to meld into a larger, distinctive pan-Sephardic song tradition.

An appreciation of the surviving Sephardic song repertories allows us to understand the extraordinary amount of diversity that actually constituted Sephardic music over the centuries. Were we simply to move outward from fifteenth-century Spain to various countries of relocation, an approach that guided the early scholars of the Sephardic ballad and still shapes the presentation of these repertories in present-day performance, one would be forced to look only for continuities, for that common stream of Spanish-Jewish tradition. Such a perspective has served until the present to privilege scholarship on songs in the Judeo-Spanish language of the fifteenth-century exiles.[13]

From a late-twentieth-century vantage point, the Sephardic world appears less to have maintained its Spanish heritage intact than to have used it as a foundation upon which to construct new and dynamic musical traditions. As Jews dispersed from Spain and established new lives in quite different geographical and cultural locales, they acquired new local languages and customs. While in

---

[13] Studies of Sephardic song repertories in Hebrew language have been carried out in the last decade. See Seroussi 1989 and Shelemay 1988.

many lands of relocation, Sephardic Jews both perpetuated old songs, including the ballads, and also incorporated new elements into them. This was a process that occurred over time, at different rates of speed in different Sephardic communities, depending upon their accommodation to and acceptance within the new country as well as a variety of other social and economic factors.

Research carried out to date on Sephardic song has been disproportionally weighted toward the ballad. Although they have attracted attention both because of their obvious historical import and their intrinsic beauty, it seems likely that the ballads also provided a convenient unit of analysis because of their consistent adherence to a set literary form. In contrast, the study of two other major categories of Sephardic songs, Judeo-Spanish songs separate from the ballad repertories and paraliturgical hymns in Hebrew, present considerable textual as well as melodic diversity.

Jewish Music Scholarship: Neglected Subjects, Unanswered Questions

Preoccupation with what might be termed the "philological aspects" of the Judeo-Spanish ballad has also left scholars with little time to consider the great promise these materials hold for cultural interpretation. While some ballads sustain images that must have been widely circulated in fifteenth-century Spanish folklore before the Jews' departure, others provide glimpses of the contrasting worlds of Sephardic Jews in the Diaspora. Like the anecdotes or narrations of singular events analyzed by historians to decode the past, Sephardic ballad texts provide a resource on which to base new historical readings (Greenblatt 1990, 3). For example, the texts of many Sephardic ballads contain materials concerning relations between the sexes, often presenting women as either victims or victimizers.[14] These songs hold great promise for expanding our

[14] See Armistead and Silverman (1986, 8–16) for a catalogue of text types found in the author's collection. Henrietta Yurchenco has work in progress on the subject of women and ballad texts.

understanding of gender relations and asymmetries in the communities that sustained them, in different times and different places.

It is also of great importance to acknowledge that, despite their historical relationship to medieval Spanish sources ranging from famous Spanish and French epics, the Sephardic *romances* do not simply replicate their Spanish models. Ballad texts surviving in the twentieth-century Sephardic oral tradition in fact vary widely in content, most existing as hybrids derived from their Spanish precursors, but welded into an aesthetic whole through a "creative incorporation" of postmedieval elements (Greenblatt 1990, 26). In detailed studies of an extensive corpus of Sephardic ballads from the oral tradition, Samuel Armistead and Joseph Silverman have illustrated the problems incurred by ignoring post-Spanish influences, showing, for example, that one Judeo-Spanish ballad perpetuated in Greece, long thought to be of Spanish heritage, was in fact an exact rendering in Judeo-Spanish ballad style, formulas, and motifs, of a widely circulated Greek ballad (Armistead and Silverman 1983–84, 40–41). They cite similar examples from other ballads, as well as from various genres of Sephardic folklore and folk literature, including tales, riddles, proverbs, and poetry (Armistead and Silverman 1983–84, 38–54).

If the *romances* were always distinctive in their textual and musical structure,[15] they were also distinguished by special con-

---

[15] The textual structure of the Sephardic ballad is consistently a sixteen-syllable verse, divided into two eight-syllable hemistiches. Generally, the second hemistich carries assonant rhyme. The musical settings are almost always quatrains, each musical unit carrying two textual verses (that is, thirty-two syllables, divided into four hemistiches). A recent study of Judeo-Spanish songs among Sephardic Jews of Canada indicated that for 65 percent of the 113 *romances* gathered, the most common musical structure was a quatrain composed of four musical phrases, ABCD, corresponding to the four octosyllabic hemistiches of the text. The melody is then repeated, sometimes with subtle variations, for all subsequent strophes (Cohen 1988). To gain an appreciation of the extraordinary historical, linguistic, and musical complexities involved in adequately representing any one ballad, the reader is referred to the presentations in Armistead and Silverman 1986; particularly instructive are the multiple musical transcriptions for each ballad prepared by Israel J. Katz in that volume. Additional examples can be found in Katz 1972 and 1975.

ventions of performance practice that have survived into the twentieth century: they were traditionally sung by a soloist without instrumental accompaniment. Another striking characteristic of Sephardic *romance* transmission is made clear from observation and recording of songs during the last century: the *romances* were primarily sung by women. Ballads were generally performed in mundane domestic settings for entertainment or to pass the time during daily household tasks. Whatever the content of their texts, ballads were often sung to lull children to sleep. A colorful example of this phenomenon is found on a published recording of Sephardic songs from Morocco, where a young Jewish woman in Tetuan sings ballads about biblical prophets and Spanish royalty while rocking her sick child at the kitchen table (Yurchenco 1983).

Twentieth-century recording technology and ethnographic research has therefore opened windows on what otherwise were inaccessible traditions relating to ballad performance and transmission in a variety of countries after relocation. But if scholarship can identify to an impressive degree of specificity the sources of new elements that accrued to ballad texts over the years, there still remain questions about the provenance of many ballad melodies.[16] The problem is twofold. First, we have no direct evidence concerning the original tunes to which the ballads were sung at the time of the expulsion. Second, we cannot ascertain exactly what changes these tunes underwent over the course of centuries in the countries of relocation (Katz 1972, 128).

Change likely occurred in two main ways, foreshadowed in the discussion above. On the broadest and most general level, it is clear that over the years many *romance* tunes were modified, both unconsciously and intentionally, to render them more similar in style and content to music that Sephardic Jews encountered in their new

---

[16] For discussion of possible relationships between notated medieval Spanish secular melodies and those of the Judeo-Spanish ballad, see Avenary 1960. Etzion and Weich-Shahak 1988 propose an analytical method for comparing surviving Sephardic ballad melodies with melodies in early Spanish sources.

homelands. The musical environment of a given place and time served as a catalyst for transformation of the Judeo-Spanish repertories into new hybrids.

If we cannot recapture the past directly, we can point to twentieth-century results of this process of musical syncretism, a fine example of which has been documented among the Jews of Sarajevo, Bosnia. Jews lived in multi-ethnic Sarajevo since at least 1565, when they began to come into close contact with the dominant Moslem culture. Ballads still performed by surviving members of the Sarajevo community closely resemble secular Moslem songs known as *sevdalinke*, the latter sung in Serbo-Croatian language. The *sevdalinke* is clearly the source for several aspects of the Bosnian Sephardic *romance* tradition, including its vocal style with heavy vibrato at the end of phrases, subtle ornamentation, and modal organization.[17]

Beyond the absorption of general musical characteristics from surrounding non-Jewish repertories into Sephardic music, the most common way in which whole melodies penetrated the ballads and other Sephardic songs was through the contrafact process discussed above. A popular song, perhaps one heard in the course of everyday life, would be the likeliest subject for borrowing, its own vernacular text discarded, and its melody re-used to set an existing (or newly composed) Jewish text.

As noted before, the contrafact process may involve borrowing from any source, including melodies already in circulation within the Sephardic tradition. The study of Sephardic song melodies is thus complicated by the presence of contrafacta drawn from both external and internal sources (Seroussi and Weich-Shahak 1990–91). For this reason, too, study of the Sephardic ballad alone without reference to other Sephardic song repertories isolates a genre from repertories with which it in fact shares many salient characteristics as well as specific melodies.

---

[17] See Petrović 1982, 35–48 and 1985, side 1, cuts 3a and 3b.

A Note on the Sephardic Revival

The traditional transmission of Sephardic song diminished during the second half of the twentieth century following the period of forced relocation of many Sephardic communities. However, the performances and circulation of Sephardic song repertories is today more widespread than ever before, exemplifying what must always have been an important characteristic of Sephardic song transmission: an ability to survive extraordinary external changes by absorbing new elements into the old.

Several factors have coincided both to enable and encourage the modern, public performance of Sephardic song, and at the same time, to perpetuate old mythologies. A new sensitivity to the diversity of Jewish tradition, emerging from Israel during the 1960s, aroused, especially in the United States, considerable interest in and potential audiences for Jewish musical traditions outside of the more familiar Central and Eastern European heritage. The existence and relatively easy availability by this period of both scholarly editions of Sephardic songs and field recordings served to bring formerly inaccessible repertories into the hands of singers and, concurrently, into the public eye.

The burgeoning interest in Sephardic song must be contextualized as well within trends affecting the broader musical world. The American folk music revival that began in the 1950s incorporated a cross-cultural repertory. Additionally, around 1960, there began on college campuses an upsurge of intense interest in music of the European Middle Ages and Renaissance. Instrument makers began to reconstruct period instruments and a bumper crop of singers interested in "early music" emerged from music schools and conservatories all over the United States and Europe. Early music ensembles such as the "Waverly Consort" of New York City and the Boston-based "Voice of the Turtle" began to attract a substantial following and soon incorporated Sephardic songs into their concert programs. Hence, just as scholars were beginning to understand better the complexity of its transmission, Sephardic song began to be increasingly associated with its fifteenth-century Spanish roots, both within the Jewish community and to a wider public.

In the late twentieth century, Sephardic songs virtually moribund in private oral transmission have been "revived" in more public, even commercial contexts. In some cases, individuals descended from Sephardic families decided to perform their songs in public. Here the lively career of Flory Jagoda, a Sephardic musician born in Sarajevo, Bosnia, provides an interesting case study: Jagoda both performs the songs she learned from her grandmother as a child in Sarajevo and renews the tradition through composing her own Judeo-Spanish songs in a traditional style.[18] Similarly, the Canadian-based ensemble Gerinaldo, three of whose members are Sephardic Jews of Moroccan descent, combines knowledge derived from longterm personal exposure to Sephardic song traditions with fresh repertory and instrumental skills contributed by a fourth, non-Sephardic singer who is an ethnomusicologist.[19] These new fusions transmit Sephardic song to an increasingly wider public.

Conclusion

The very diversity of Jewish music is in fact the hallmark of a powerful and vital cultural tradition. The preceding discussion has sought to trace the exciting implications, both theoretical and methodological, from acknowledging this reality. Yet while Jewish musical scholarship has moved into the academic mainstream, with recent publications exploring major issues of interest (Mendelsohn 1993), popular perspectives remain largely unchanged. When a scholar suggests in a public lecture that there is no single Jewish music, but that diversity and change have characterized musical expression in Jewish life past and present, she or he is still greeted

[18] In this manner, the relationship between tradition and innovation is fluid and similar to the Hasidic example set forth above. See albums of Sephardic songs published by Jagoda on her own Altarasa Record label (Jagoda n.d. a, b, and c).

[19] Ethnomusicologist Judith Cohen, a member of Gerinaldo, wrote a dissertation on Sephardic musical traditions in Canada (see Cohen 1988).

with ambivalence, characterized as taking a pessimistic or even negative view of the subject.[20] That the myth continues, impervious to scholarly evidence to the contrary, is in fact testimony to its continued strength.

For two millennia, most Jewish communities remained sufficiently connected to a mainstream of Jewish practice to observe what might be characterized as a normative version of liturgy and custom for their respective eras. Yet, if shared sacred texts are seen as being at the heart of the universal Jewish tradition, music must be viewed as its life blood. Music serves to support the text, to prod the memory, and to insure that the word is transmitted to the next generation. However, the precise style of the music is less critical to the maintenance of the tradition than the fact that it be such an integral part of the community's environment that it can sustain the word almost without conscious thought. This is achieved through the emergence of musical traditions that fit each environment, each community. Melodies can only be borrowed when they are already part of the sound world of the singers who would appropriate them.

But music has another role beyond simply sustaining and conveying the sacred—it becomes a symbol of the people who perform and transmit it. Here we approach the genesis, and the continuing power, of the myth of continuity. On a very general level, all Jews understand themselves to have a common ancestry, a shared historical past, and a common belief system. Belief in the existence

---

[20] One of the most striking instances of this situation in my own career (and the incident that encouraged me to draft this essay) occurred when I (and another colleague in Jewish musical studies) spoke at a major university on the Americanization of Jewish music. We gave several presentations over a three-day period, covering aspects of music in the American synagogue and of various communities of Jewish immigrants. After practically every musical example, we were confronted with the same question: "Is this Jewish music?" It became clear that members of our audience, and particularly the donor who was funding the series, were quite frustrated by our answers in an ethnomusicological mode, stressing diversity. We never did succeed in spanning the distance between the donor's dogged allegiance to mythologies of continuity and our scholarly conceptions of the realities of change.

of a shared musical tradition is implicit to this worldview, despite the presence of ubiquitous heterogeneity.

Some years ago, when asked to define Jewish music, the scholar Curt Sachs answered that it was music "by Jews, for Jews, as Jews."[21] In many ways, Sachs's definition remains the best we have, for it captures the essence of tradition as the quintessential social act. In many ways, the longstanding search for the single source of Jewish music is a circular one—one ends where one started, with individuals of every age having contributed to, and in some cases transformed, what must be acknowledged as a vital, and ever-changing, tradition. Like the historian so eloquently described by Yosef Yerushalmi, the music scholar's "task can no longer be limited to finding continuities. . . ." Rather, the "time has come to look more closely at ruptures, breaches, breaks, to identify them more precisely, to see how Jews endured them. . ." (Yerushalmi 1989 [1982], 101). Only through an acknowledgment of both the mythologies and the realities can we come to understand the role of music in Jewish life as well as a central challenge of its study.

[21] See Bayer (1971–73, 555), quoting Curt Sachs at the First International Congress of Jewish Music, Paris 1957.

References

Adler, Israel
    1982   "Problems in the Study of Jewish Music." In *Proceedings of the World Congress on Jewish Music,* Judith Cohen, ed., pp. 15–26. Tel Aviv: The Institute for the Translation of Hebrew Literature Ltd.

Adler, Israel, Bathja Bayer, and Eliyahu Schleifer, eds.
    1986   *The Abraham Zvi Idelsohn Memorial Volume.* Yuval, 5. Jerusalem: The Magnes Press.

Armistead, Samuel G., and Joseph H. Silverman
    1971   *The Judeo-Spanish Ballad Chapbooks of Yacob Abraham Yona.* Berkeley: University of California Press.
    1983–84 "Sephardic Folk Literature and Eastern Mediterranean Oral Tradition." *Musica Judaica* 6:40–41.
    1986   *Folk Literature of the Sephardic Jews.* Vol. 2, *Judeo-Spanish Ballads from Oral Tradition.* Berkeley: University of California Press.

Avenary, Hanoch
    1960   "Études sur le cancionero judéo-espagnol du XVIe et XVIIe siècles." *Sefarad* 20:377–94.

Bayer, Bathja
    1971–73 "Jewish Music." *Encyclopedia Judaica* 12:554–56

Cohen, Judith R.
    1988   "Judeo-Spanish Songs in the Sephardic Communities of Montreal and Toronto: Survival, Function, and Change." Ph.D. Diss., Université de Montréal.

Etzion, Judith, and Susana Weich-Shahak
    1988   "The Spanish and the Sephardic Musical Links." *Ethnomusicology* 32(2):1–27.

Greenblatt, Stephen J.
    1990   *Learning to Curse.* New York and London: Routledge.

Hoffman, Lawrence A.
    1979   *The Canonization of the Synagogue Service.* Notre Dame and London: University of Notre Dame Press.

Idelsohn, Abraham Zvi
    1986   "My Life. A Sketch." In *The Abraham Zvi Idelsohn Memorial Volume.* Yuval, 5. Israel Adler et al., eds., pp. 18–23. Jerusalem: The Magnes Press. Article first published in 1935.

Jagoda, Flory

n.d. a   *Kantikas Di Mi Nona* (Vol. 1, 1001). Falls Church, Virginia: Altarasa Records.

n.d. b   *Memories of Sarajevo* (Vol. 2, 1002). Falls Church, Virginia: Altarasa Records.

n.d. c   *La Nona Kanta* (Vol. 3, 1003). Falls Church, Virginia: Altarasa Records.

Katz, Israel J.

1972   *Judeo-Spanish Traditional Ballads from Jerusalem.* Vol. 1. New York: The Institute of Mediaeval Music Ltd.

1975   *Judeo-Spanish Traditional Ballads from Jerusalem.* Vol. 2. New York: The Institute of Mediaeval Music Ltd.

Koskoff, Ellen

1978   "Contemporary Nigun Composition in an American Hasidic Community." *Selected Reports in Ethnomusicology* 3(1): 153–73.

McNeill, William H.

1986   "Mythistory, or Truth, Myth, History, and Historians." In *Mythistory and Other Essays,* pp. 3–22. Chicago: University of Chicago Press.

Mendelsohn, Ezra, ed.

1993   *Modern Jews and Their Musical Agendas.* Studies in Contemporary Jewry, 9. New York and Oxford: Oxford University Press.

Petrović, Ankica

1982   "Sacred Sephardi Chants in Bosnia." *The World of Music* 3:35–48.

1985   *Traditional Music from the Soil of Bosnia-Hercegovina.* LP 8149, YU 1985.

Schleifer, Eliyahu

1986   "Introduction to Idelsohn's Autobiographical Sketches." In *The Abraham Zvi Idelsohn Memoral Volume.* Yuval, 5. Israel Adler et al., eds., pp. 15–17. Jerusalem: The Magnes Press.

Sendrey, Alfred

1970   *The Music of the Jews in the Diaspora.* New York, South Brunswick, and London: Thomas Yoseloff.

Seroussi, Edwin

1989   *Mizimrat Kedem: The Life and Music of Rabbi Isaac Algazi from Turkey.* Jerusalem: Renanot.

1990   "Rabbi Israel Najara: Moulder of Hebrew Sacred Singing after the Expulsion from Spain" (in Hebrew). *Assuphot* 4:285–310.

1993   "New Directions in the Music of Sephardic Jews. In *Modern Jews and Their Musical Agendas*. Studies in Contemporary Jewry, 9. Ezra Mendelsohn, ed., pp. 61–77. New York and Oxford: Oxford University Press.

Seroussi, Edwin, and Susana Weich-Shahak
1990–91 "Judeo-Spanish Contrafacts and Musical Adaptations: The Oral Tradition." *Orbis Musicae* 10:164–92.

Shelemay, Kay Kaufman
1988   "Together in the Field: Team Research among Syrian Jews in Brooklyn, New York." *Ethnomusicology* 32(3):369–84.

Shelemay, Kay Kaufman, and Sarah Weiss
1985   *Pizmon. Syrian-Jewish Social and Religious Song*. Shanachi Record Corp., Meadowlark ML 105.

Shiloah, Amnon
1992   *Jewish Musical Traditions*. Detroit: Wayne State University Press.

Shiloah, Amnon, and Erik Cohen
1983   "The Dynamics of Change in Jewish Oriental Ethnic Music in Israel." *Ethnomusicology* 27(2):227–52.

Weich-Shahak, Susana
1982–83 "Childbirth Songs among Sephardic Jews of Balkan Origin." *Orbis Musicae* 8:87–103.
1989   *Judeo-Spanish Moroccan Songs for the Life Cycle*. Jerusalem: The Jewish Music Research Centre.

"Wissenschaft"
1972   "Wissenschaft des Judentums." *Encyclopedia Judaica* 16:570–83

Yahalom, Joseph
1982   "R. Israel Najarah and the Revival of Hebrew Poetry in the East after the Expulsion from Spain" (in Hebrew). *Pe'amim* 13:96–122.

Yerushalmi, Yosef Hayim
1989   *Zakhor, Jewish History and Jewish Memory*. New York: Schocken Books. First edition: 1982.

Yurchenco, Henrietta, ed.
1983   *Ballads, Wedding Songs, and Piyyutim of the Sephardic Jews of Tetuan and Tangier, Morocco*. Folkways Records. Album FE 4208.

Notes on Contributors

Judith Becker is a professor of ethnomusicology in the School of Music at the University of Michigan. For seventeen years she was the director of the gamelan ensemble at the University of Michigan. Her publications include books and articles on Javanese music, Burmese music, ritual, and aesthetics.

Philip V. Bohlman teaches ethnomusicology at the University of Chicago, where he is also on the faculties of the Committee on Jewish Studies, the Center for Middle Eastern Studies, and the Committee on Southern Asian Studies. Among other projects, he is currently working on *Jewish Music and Modernity* (Oxford) and *Es geht um die Musik. . .Standort Mitteleuropa* (Bärenreiter).

John Chernoff was educated at Yale University and at the Hartford Seminary Foundation. He studied music in Ghana for seven years. He is currently preparing an ethnography of Dagbon and a study of West African urban youth. His best-known work is *African Rhythm and African Sensibility* (1979).

Michael W. Harris, a visiting professor of African American studies and history at Northwestern University, is the author of *The Rise of Gospel Blues: The Music of Thomas Andrew Dorsey in the Urban Church* (1992) and of a forthcoming history of African American religions.

Jonathan D. Hill is professor of anthropology at Southern Illinois University at Carbondale. He is the author of *Keepers of the Sacred Chants: The Poetics of Ritual Power in an Amazonian Society* (1993) and editor of *Rethinking History and Myth: Indigenous South American Perspectives on the Past* (1988) and *History, Power, and Identity: Ethnogenesis in the Americas, 1492–1992* (1996).

Moshe Idel is professor of Jewish mysticism at the Hebrew University, Jerusalem, and has been a visiting professor at Harvard University and the Jewish Theological Seminary of America. He is the author of numerous publications on Jewish mysticism, including *Kabbalah: New Perspectives* (1988), *The Mystical Experience in Abraham Abulafia* (1988), *Language, Torah and Hermeneutics in Abraham Abulafia* (1989), and *Hasidism: Between Ecstasy and Magic* (1995).

Victoria Lindsay Levine is an associate professor of music at Colorado College, where she teaches ethnomusicology and Southwest Studies. A specialist in Native American musical cultures, she has studied Choctaw and other Southeast Indian musics since 1982.

Seyyed Hossein Nasr is University Professor of Islamic Studies at George Washington University. He has also taught at the American University of Beirut, Tehran University, and Temple University. His publications include: *Islamic Art and Spirituality* (1987); *Traditional Islam in the Modern World* (1987); *Knowledge and the Sacred* (1981); *Man and Nature: The Spiritual Crisis of Modern Man* (1976); and *Sufi Essays* (1972).

Rulan Chao Pian is professor emerita of East Asian languages and civilizations and of music, Harvard University. She is the author of *Sonq Dynasty Musical Sources and Their Interpretation* (1967), which received the Otto Kinkeldey Award in 1968, and is the overseas editor of the English edition of *Musicology in China* (1987–). She has written numerous articles on Chinese dramatic and narrative music.

Regula Burckhardt Qureshi is professor of music and director of the centre for ethnomusicology at the University of Alberta where she also holds appointments in anthropology and religious studies. Her research centers on performance traditions and music as community, with an ethnographic focus on Muslim cultures in India, Pakistan, and Canada. She is the author of *Sufi Music of India and Pakistan: Sound, Context and Meaning in Qawwali* (1986) and co-editor of *The Muslim Community in North America* (1983) and *Muslim Families in North America* (1991).

Kay Kaufman Shelemay is professor of music at Harvard University and chair of the department of music. An ethnomusicologist with specializations in music of Africa, the Middle East, and urban United States, she is the author of *Music, Ritual, and Falasha History* (1986), which won both the ASCAP-Deems Taylor Award in 1987 and the Prize of the International Musicological Society in 1988; *A Song of Longing: An Ethiopian Journey* (1991); and *Let Jasmine Rain Down: Song and Remembrance among Syrian Jews* (forthcoming, University of Chicago Press). She co-authored with Peter Jeffery the three-volume *Ethiopian Christian Chant: An Anthology* (1994–96).

Lawrence E. Sullivan is professor of the history of religions, Harvard Divinity School, and director of the Harvard University Center for the Study of World Religions. He is the author of *Icanchu's Drum: An Orientation to Meaning in South American Religions* (1988), which was the winner of the Award for Best Book in Philosophy and Religion from the Association of American Publishers, and the editor of *Healing and Restoring: Health and Medicine in the World's Religious Traditions* (1989); *Death, Afterlife, and the Soul* (1989); *Hidden Truths: Magic, Alchemy, and the Occult* (1989); and *Native American Religions of North America* (1989).